Inter-State Accountability for Violations of Human Rights

University of Pennsylvania Press
Pennsylvania Studies in Human Rights
Edited by Bert B. Lockwood

A complete list of the books in this series
appears at the back of this volume

Inter-State Accountability for Violations of Human Rights

Menno T. Kamminga

UNIVERSITY OF PENNSYLVANIA PRESS   Philadelphia

Library of Congress Cataloging-in-Publication Data
Kamminga, Menno T.
    Inter-state accountability for violations of human rights / Menno
T. Kamminga.
        p.   cm.—(Pennsylvania studies in human rights)
    Rev. and expanded version of the author's thesis (University of
Leiden).
    Includes bibliographical references and index.
    ISBN 0-8122-3176-7
    I. Title.   II. Series.
K3240.4.K26   1992
341.4'81—dc20   92-12208
                                                    CIP

Contents

Abbreviations

AFDI	*Annuaire français de droit international*
AJIL	*American Journal of International Law*
ArchVR	*Archiv des Völkerrechts*
ASIL	American Society of International Law
Bull. EC	*Bulletin of the European Communities*
BYIL	*British Year Book of International Law*
CMLR	*Common Market Law Review*
CSCE	Conference on Security and Co-operation in Europe
EPC	European Political Cooperation
EuGRZ	*Europäische Grundrechte Zeitschrift*
FCO	Foreign and Commonwealth Office
GAOR	General Assembly Official Records
GYIL	*German Yearbook of International Law*
HRJ	*Human Rights Journal*
HRLJ	*Human Rights Law Journal*
HRQ	*Human Rights Quarterly*
ICJ	International Court of Justice
ICLQ	*International and Comparative Law Quarterly*
ICRC	International Committee of the Red Cross
ILC	International Law Commission
ILM	*International Legal Materials*
NILR	*Netherlands International Law Review*
NYIL	*Netherlands Yearbook of International Law*
OJ EC	*Official Journal of the European Communities*
ÖZöffR	*Österreichische Zeitschrift für öffentliches Recht*
PCIJ	Permanent Court of International Justice
RCADI	*Recueil des cours de l'Académie de droit international*
RGDIP	*Revue générale de droit international public*
RIAA	*Reports of International Arbitral Awards*
UNCIO	Documents of the United Nations Conference on International Organization

UNGA	United Nations General Assembly
YECHR	*Yearbook of the European Convention on Human Rights*
YICJ	*Yearbook of the International Court of Justice*
YILC	*Yearbook of the International Law Commission*
ZaöRV	*Zeitschrift für ausländisches öffentliches Recht und Völkerrecht*

Preface

The topic of this study occurred to me in December 1985. At the time, I was representing Amnesty International at the fortieth session of the UN General Assembly in New York. As these sessions go, it had not been a very productive one. Much time had been taken up with empty speechmaking on the occasion of the UN's fortieth anniversary. Presidents and prime ministers one after another had given speeches expressing their congratulations. For ordinary workers it had been nearly impossible to enter the UN building on certain days, owing to the extensive security arrangements. By the beginning of December, however, the meetings of the Assembly's Third Committee, my main focus of attention, were drawing to a close. Delegates were beginning to talk about their plans for the Christmas break.

On one of those days, the sedate atmosphere suddenly seemed to change. Something dramatic had happened, I was told. Seven delegations had submitted a draft resolution entitled "Inadmissibility of exploitation or distortion of human rights issues for interference in the internal affairs of States." The draft had been worded in time-honored UNspeak. First, and most disturbingly, it reaffirmed "the duty of States to refrain from the exploitation or distortion of human rights issues for interference in the internal affairs of States." Second, it condemned the "defamatory campaign, vilification and hostile propaganda by the *apartheid* regimes of South Africa and Israel for the purpose of . . . interfering in the internal affairs of the neighbouring States." The sponsors were Angola, Czechoslovakia, Ethiopia, the Lao People's Democratic Republic, the Syrian Arab Republic, the Ukrainian Soviet Socialist Republic, and Viet Nam.[1]

Some delegates were convinced that the draft was so cleverly worded that it would be adopted without any difficulty. Who wouldn't support a text that condemned the exploitation or distortion of human rights

1. UN Doc. A/C.3/40/L.83/Rev.1 of 5 December 1985.

issues (or of anything else for that matter)? Moreover, it turned out that this particular paragraph had been taken verbatim from a little-noticed declaration entitled "Inadmissibility of Intervention and Interference in the Internal Affairs of States," which had been adopted by the General Assembly in 1981. Some diplomats—perhaps because they were worn out at the end of a lengthy session—predicted gloomily that adoption of the draft resolution would spell the end of the UN human rights program as we knew it. They searched frantically for an amendment that would remove the sting from the text, but found none.

In the end, the draft was never put to a vote, thanks to a brave speech by the representative of Zimbabwe. In one of the more memorable statements of the session, he explained that he objected to the proposal because it included a perfunctory reference to South Africa "simply to get some votes." *Apartheid* was too serious an affair to be used in such a way, he said. That was the end of the matter. The draft had been discredited, and a decision was postponed until the following year. In fact, the text was never reintroduced. The initiative had failed, but merely because of a tactical error by the sponsors, or so it seemed.

Until then, I had assumed the old rule that a state could not be held internationally accountable for the way it treated its own citizens had long ago become obsolete. Wasn't there extensive UN practice to prove that this was no longer a viable proposition? But why then had experienced delegates been so worried that the rule might be reinstated by the General Assembly? And why had the General Assembly never endorsed the opposite principle, that is, that the expression of concern at violations of human rights in another state does *not* constitute interference in the internal affairs of that state? It seemed that there was an intriguing gap between, on the one hand, the rather restrictive standards the United Nations had laid down for itself with regard to non-interference in the internal affairs of its member states and, on the other hand, its rather liberal practice with regard to the promotion and protection of human rights. I decided that some day I would attempt to write a book on the subject.

The opportunity to realize this intention came in 1987 when I was offered a job as Lecturer in International Law at Erasmus University Rotterdam, the Netherlands. A doctoral dissertation then seemed like an appropriate format for the project. I publicly defended my dissertation, entitled "Inter-State Accountability for Violations of Human Rights," at the University of Leiden on 31 May 1990.

At the UN things tend to occur in cycles. In November 1990, nearly five years after the abortive draft resolution of 1985, the Cuban delegation at the General Assembly introduced a very similar text. The new draft was entitled "Strengthening of United Nations action in the human rights field through the promotion of international co-operation and the strict observance of the principle of non-intervention." One of its operative paragraphs reiterated "that the exploitation and distortion of human rights issues as a means of interfering in the internal affairs of States . . . is as contrary to the basic principles of international law as any other kind of intervention." The ambitious proposal also requested the Commission on Human Rights to elaborate a declaration on the subject.

This time, the opponents of the philosophy underlying the proposal were able to operate more effectively. Australia, supported by the Federal Republic of Germany and the United Kingdom, submitted a series of amendments aimed at neutralizing the Cuban draft. Probably as a result of the changed world political climate, Cuba received little support from other delegations and was forced to accept many of these amendments. General Assembly Resolution 45/163, as finally adopted, carries the innocuous title "Strengthening of United Nations action in the human rights field through the promotion of international co-operation and the importance of non-selectivity, impartiality and objectivity." The resolution bears little resemblance to the original proposal. For one thing, it lacks any reference to non-intervention. I was gratified to learn subsequently that the opponents of the Cuban draft had been able to draw on my dissertation in formulating their reactions. To provide ammunition for such a rebuttal was precisely what I had set out to do five years earlier.

The present book is a revised and expanded version of the dissertation I defended in May 1990.

Erasmus University
Rotterdam, the Netherlands
January 1992

Acknowledgments

The dissertation of which the present volume is an outgrowth was prepared under the supervision of Professor Peter Kooijmans of the University of Leiden and Professor Ko Swan Sik of Erasmus University Rotterdam. The other members of the dissertation committee were Professor E. A. Alkema (University of Leiden), Professor C. Flinterman (University of Limburg), and Professor H. G. Schermers (University of Leiden). The regulations of the University of Leiden do not allow a Ph.D. candidate to render thanks to his thesis supervisors or to the members of his dissertation committee. Presumably, this rule continues to apply even after a dissertation has been publicly defended. However, I am permitted to thank several others who generously agreed to read and comment in detail upon all or parts of the original manuscript, including Christopher Avery, Herman Burgers, Waldo Fortin Cabezas, Ton van Haaften, Nigel Rodley, and my father, Dr. Menno S. Kamminga. I am also indebted to Judge Manfred Lachs and Professor W. Riphagen for having kindly taken the time to discuss a number of questions with me.

I am very grateful to my colleagues at the Department on Constitutional and Administrative Law of Erasmus University's Faculty of Law, in particular Professor Ko Swan Sik and Waldo Fortin Cabezas, not only for their encouragement but also for their willingness to assume all of my teaching and administrative duties during 1989. This enabled me to finish the dissertation within a reasonably short span of time. I received invaluable research assistance from my students Margot Hoppe and Brigitte d'Anjou, who spent many hours patiently searching for obscure documents in the basement of the library of the Peace Palace at The Hague. The staff of this splendid library was invariably friendly and efficient in helping me find my way among its many treasures. Professor David Weissbrodt (University of Minnesota) was instrumental in suggesting that my writing might be suitable for publication in the Pennsylvania Studies in Human Rights series.

Introduction

> Investigation of the shortcomings of a State in regard to human
> rights is a very delicate form of intervention in its internal affairs.
> C. H. M. Waldock, 3 September 1958

Reduced to its barest minimum, this is a study of some aspects of the
tension between a state's right to national sovereignty and political
independence on the one hand, and its duty to respect human dignity
on the other. Both concepts are cornerstones of contemporary international law and have been enshrined inter alia in the Charter of the
United Nations. Of the two, the concept of sovereign equality is
clearly the best established. It represents the basic constitutional doctrine of the law of nations.[1] The duty to respect minimum standards
of human dignity, however, is a relative newcomer that has gained a
firm place under customary international law only during the past
few decades. As this is a zero-sum game, the story of the relationship
between the two concepts is the story of the gradually shifting balance
in favor of the latter.

As Professor J. L. Brierly has put it, before 1945 "no rule was
clearer than that a state's treatment of its own nationals is a matter exclusively within the domestic jurisdiction of that state, is not controlled
or regulated by international law."[2] Even the Armenian massacres in
1915 were, in his opinion, a matter of domestic jurisdiction.[3] Brierly
may have been slightly overstating the rule and in doing so overlooked
some state practice prior to World War II.[4] Nevertheless, his view il-

1. I. Brownlie, *Principles of Public International Law*, 4th ed. (1990), p. 287. See, generally, P. H. Kooijmans, *The Doctrine of the Legal Equality of States* (1964).
2. J. L. Brierly, *The Law of Nations*, 6th ed. (1963), Sir Humphrey Waldock (ed.),
p. 291.
3. J. L. Brierly, "Matters of Domestic Jurisdiction," 6 *BYIL* (1925), pp. 18–19.
4. See *infra* Chapter 1, section 1.

lustrates the dramatic character of the changes that have occurred. Nowadays, diplomatic representations between states in support of the human rights of foreign nationals—often not based on treaty obligations—have become a very common occurrence indeed. The United Nations and other international organizations have adopted countless highly specific resolutions on human rights violations in a large number of named countries.

It should perhaps be emphasized at the outset that this trend toward the internationalization of human rights should not in itself be regarded as a positive development. The history of "intervention" is overwhelmingly the history of powerful states imposing their will on weaker states. Similarly, the history of intercessions on behalf of the human rights of foreign nationals often consists of one-way traffic from stronger toward weaker states. The self-interest of the interceding state is often barely hidden. The United Nations itself exemplifies this sorry state of affairs by its tendency to be much more concerned with human rights abuses in small, politically isolated states than with similar occurrences in more influential states. Accordingly, a healthy skepticism with regard to the motives of the intervening entity is often in order.

From the beginning, it should also be taken into account that the importance of diplomatic action must not be overestimated. The involvement of other states should not be regarded as a panacea for solving serious human rights problems within a country. It seems fair to assume that social change can only be influenced to a limited extent by pressure from the outside. Changes that have no domestic roots but have been imposed by forces outside a country are unlikely to last. In some cases, outside support may even make proposed reforms suspect in the eyes of the local population, and governments may resist reform so as not to appear to be capitulating to outside forces. In the end, it is the people within a country who will need to determine their own destiny.

The underlying purpose of this study, therefore, is not to argue that states and international organizations have or should have an unlimited right to impose their views on other states. Rather, it is to investigate the balance that needs to be struck between the justifiable interest of states that their sovereign rights be respected and the legitimate interest of the international community in its quest for respect for human rights for all. The issue is somewhat more complex than has occasionally been suggested. It is not enough simply to claim that observance of international human rights obligations is no longer a matter of exclusive domestic jurisdiction. This begs the question, not only which "human rights" are referred to, but also how other states are entitled to respond to a breach. Clearly, this is a very sensitive matter. It is one thing to accept *in abstracto* that states are bound by certain international obligations in the field of human rights. It is quite another thing to accept that these obligations can be enforced in one way or another by other states.

The "reserved domain," that is, the area of state activity that is not bound by international law, has long been a favored topic for scholarly research. A considerable amount has also been written on the extent to which the area of human rights now belongs to the international domain. With a few notable exceptions, however, studies have tended to rely on a theoretical analysis of legal instruments and on the works of previous authors rather than on an analysis of actual state practice. While it is often asserted in the literature that the principle of non-intervention in internal affairs does not apply to the international protection of human rights, the evidence needed to back up this assertion has not been systematically collected. Moreover, the large majority of existing studies focus on one international arena only, for example, the UN General Assembly or the Conference on Security and Co-operation in Europe. The present work attempts to examine the issues from a more comprehensive point of view. In doing so, it seeks to follow an inductive approach that is rooted, wherever possible, in state practice.

The central question to which this study seeks an answer is: To what extent can a state be held accountable and responsible under general international law by other states for the way it has treated its own citizens? This central question raises three clusters of subquestions:

1. What are a state's international obligations in the field of human rights? What are its treaty obligations, and what constitutes the customary international law of human rights?
2. How are other states affected by a breach of such obligations? Are they affected merely in a political sense, or are they injured in their legal rights? Does this apply to any breach or merely to "serious" ones?
3. How are other states entitled to respond to such a breach? Can they express concern, lodge a protest, and request information? Can they make an international claim? Can such a claim be considered by an international tribunal?

The emphasis throughout this study will be on the secondary rules addressed in clusters 2 and 3 rather than on the primary rules addressed in cluster 1. This is in keeping with the widely held view that what is needed is not so much more international human rights standards or better interpretations of such standards, but rather better implementation and more effective enforcement of existing norms. The purpose of examining these questions is to indicate as precisely as possible when and how a state—or a group of states—may respond to a breach of an international human rights standard and thereby to provide a helpful frame of reference for both practitioners and scholars.

It is a good practice to define one's key terms from the outset. To do so is especially important here, if only because the terms *interference* and *intervention* are favorite terms of politicians and diplomats and are often used imprecisely. In diplomatic parlance, intervention may range from an innocent remark by a second secretary at a cocktail party to a full-scale military invasion. Most of these types of intervention are beyond the scope of this book. This study is not concerned with humanitarian intervention, that is, forcible intervention by a state on the territory of another state to protect either its own nationals or foreign nationals. This study is also not concerned with sanctions, countermeasures, and similar kinds of coercive action, except insofar as the application of such measures in actual state practice may provide evidence of inter-state accountability. Also excluded from the scope of this study is diplomatic protection in the traditional sense, that is, diplomatic action on behalf of the interceding state's own nationals.

The subject of this study is restricted to peaceful, noncoercive diplomatic action by states attempting to protect the human rights of foreign nationals. A state undertaking such action will be referred to as the *interceding* or *applicant* state. A state that is alleged to have committed human rights violations and is at the receiving end of such actions will be referred to as the *offending* state. The term *interference* will be used in a neutral, nonderogatory sense, roughly comparable to *involvement*. The confusing term *intervention* will be avoided as much as possible.

Although international usage is not always consistent, the terms *accountability* and *responsibility* are not interchangeable. Let us take, as a starting point for the distinction, one of the observations made by the International Court of Justice in the *Corfu Channel* case. According to the Court, "a State on whose territory an act contrary to international law has occurred, may be called upon to give an explanation." This duty to provide an explanation could not be evaded by the offending state with the excuse that it was ignorant of the circumstances of the act and of its authors. But the control exercised by a state over its territory did not give rise to prima facie responsibility for such an act.[5] In other words, a distinction was made between inter-state accountability (which involves a duty to provide an explanation[6] for an act that is apparently contrary to international law) and inter-state responsibility (which involves a duty to provide reparation for an internationally wrongful act). The term *responsibility*, as employed in this study, therefore denotes a limited subcategory of the wider concept of *accountability*.

The subject of inter-state accountability for violations of human rights is complex and may be approached from different angles. In keeping with the inductive method of analysis adopted for this study, it seems most appropriate to distinguish the different international fora in which the subject may arise. In practice, there are three general situations in which an offending state may seek to evade inter-state accountability by raising legal objections of a "preliminary" character:

1. As a bar against diplomatic representations or other direct inter-state measures.
2. As a bar against action contemplated by an intergovernmental organization.
3. As a bar against proceedings instituted at an international tribunal.

These are, therefore, the three general areas of our investigation: diplomatic action (Chapter 1), international organizations (Chapter 2), and international tribunals (Chapter 3). The principal sources relied upon are, for Chapter 1, the various digests of international law, newspaper reports, and parliamentary papers; for Chapter 2, the resolutions, reports, and summary records of international organizations; and for Chapter 3, the case law of international tribunals and the reports of the International Law Commission. In addition, secondary literature, wherever relevant and available, has been utilized for all three chapters. Some recommendations with regard to such literature are included in the bibliography at the end of this book.

5. ICJ Reports 1949, p. 18.
6. "To account" means, according to *Webster's Third New International Dictionary* (1981), inter alia "to furnish substantial reasons or a convincing explanation."

Chapter 1
Diplomatic Action on Behalf of Foreign Nationals

> It is difficult to restrain myself from doing something to stop this
> attempt to exterminate a race, but I realize that I am here as Am-
> bassador and must abide by the principles of non-interference
> with the internal affairs of another country.
> Henry Morgenthau, U.S. Ambassador in Turkey,
> to the U.S. Secretary of State, 11 August 1915

The subject of diplomatic intercessions on behalf of foreign nationals seems an appropriate point to start our investigation. After all, it is through such direct representations that states first began to express concern about violations of human rights in other states, long before the establishment of institutionalized channels consisting of international organizations and international tribunals. It is state practice with regard to such intercessions that can provide us with the first clues as to whether states consider themselves to have a legitimate legal interest—as opposed to a merely humanitarian interest—in the fate of non-nationals.

Formal diplomatic intercessions on behalf of non-nationals may provide significant evidence of the existence of rules of customary international law. This is because they—unlike, for example, speeches in UN bodies—are more likely to be made after careful consideration of all relevant legal factors. Usually there are strong political or economic arguments that militate against making any representations at all. Few ambassadors fancy the prospect of having to see a senior official of the government to which they are accredited with a view to demanding the release of a political prisoner with whom their own country has no link whatsoever. Such a step tends to deteriorate rather than improve relations with the host government. While an ambassador may be fully prepared to issue a protest if his or her own country's material interests have been affected, he or she will need some convincing before taking a similar step on behalf of a foreign national. Consequently, if there are any considerations of a legal nature arguing against a démarche, these are usually fully taken into account. A diplomat's duty not to interfere in the receiving state's internal affairs [1] tends to be foremost among these considerations.

Conversely, the attitude of the authorities of a state that is on the receiving end of a démarche may provide us with evidence as to whether states deem it acceptable that other states take an interest in the human rights of their nationals. The easiest response to an intercession—and the one that comes naturally to most officials—is, "This is none of your business. You are interfering in our internal affairs." The absence of such a reaction is significant. It does not necessarily indicate that the intercession is considered legally acceptable. It may simply be prompted by the fact that the receiving state is politically or economically dependent on the interceding state and cannot afford to be so blatant in its response. Or there is the less likely possibility that the official receiving the démarche is not aware of the fact that he or she can raise the objection of interference in internal affairs. In any case, the explicit or implicit acceptance of an intercession without any protest at least creates the presumption that the offending state does not consider the step inadmissible on legal grounds.

In spite of the obvious importance of diplomatic intercessions on behalf of foreign nationals, little scholarly research has been done on the subject.[2] One reason for this may be that the necessary information is often hard to obtain. Diplomatic representations tend to be made privately, behind closed doors. Detailed published accounts of such events are rare, and even if they are available, the researcher has to be on guard against the reporter's bias. In the large majority of cases the scholar has only one government's version to rely on. The most reliable source consists of diplomatic correspondence: instructions from a minister of foreign affairs to his ambassador, aides-mémoire handed over, and reports from the ambassador to his minister of foreign affairs. Such documentation may give an indication of the *opinio juris* of the interceding state and, if one is lucky, of the offending state

---

1. Art. 41(1), Vienna Convention on Diplomatic Relations.
2. The main exception is E. C. Stowell, *Intervention in International Law* (1921), which contains a stimulating, if not always fully accurate, analysis of some cases pre-World War I. Cf. also M. Ganji, *International Protection of Human Rights* (1962), pp. 9–44.

as well. Unfortunately, such material is generally available only for the period before World War II. For more recent state practice, the researcher is often forced to rely on newspaper reports and other indirect sources. Further evidence of *opinio juris* can sometimes be found in published governmental policy papers and replies to parliamentary questions.

The charge of interference in internal affairs, in connection with attempts to protect the human rights of foreign nationals, may be raised not only in response to acts by representatives of the executive branch of government, but also in response to acts by various other organs of the state, including those exercising legislative or judicial power. Such a response may be triggered, for example, by the adoption of a critical resolution by a national parliament or by the exercise of jurisdiction by a national court over a foreign national accused of having committed human rights violations in his own country. A state may indeed be held responsible for such acts.[3] In this chapter, however, we will be concerned only with conduct by organs belonging to the executive branch.

1. Some Historical Cases

The origins of modern diplomatic action on behalf of foreign nationals can be traced to the history of religious minorities in Europe and the Middle East in the seventeenth, eighteenth, and nineteenth centuries. Because national borders did not always coincide with religious borders, European states took an interest in the fate of members of religious minorities who were, by virtue of their religion, akin to their own citizens, irrespective of nationality. This interest was often expressed through provisions in peace and friendship treaties. International tension resulting from the repression of religious minorities was regarded as one of the causes of war, and such provisions were intended to prevent its recurrence. As early as 1648, the peace treaties of Westphalia[4] established the equality of the Catholic and Protestant faiths in Germany and provided guarantees to religious minorities. In most cases, provisions such as these simply spelled out the religious freedoms that were to be observed. As will be seen below, their non-observance was in itself regarded as sufficient ground for representations and protests by the other states parties.

3. Arts. 5 and 6, part 1, draft articles on state responsibility, *YILC*, 1980, vol. II, Part Two, p. 31.

4. Signed at Osnabruck and Munster, 14 October 1648. Reproduced in C. Parry, *Consolidated Treaty Series*, vol. 1, p. 119.

In some cases, however, treaties contained specific inter-state remedies that entitled states parties to make representations to the offending state and to exercise protection on behalf of foreign members of
religious minorities. Under the 1774 Treaty of Kuçuk-Kainardji, Turkey not only undertook to protect Christianity and its churches, but
also authorized the representatives of the Russian Czar to make representations to the Turkish authorities in case of violation of this
undertaking. Turkey expressly accepted the admissibility of such representations by agreeing to take them into consideration "as if they
had been made by a confidant of a friendly neighbouring Power."[5]
Similarly, the 1878 Treaty of Berlin not only established the principle
of religious freedom and religious equality in the Ottoman Empire. It
also explicitly recognized the right of the states parties to exercise
diplomatic and consular protection on behalf of members of religious
minorities in Turkey.[6]

Diplomatic intercessions on behalf of foreign victims of repression
could therefore often rely on specific treaty obligations undertaken
by the offending state. In the absence of such provisions, intercessions had to be based on customary international law or even on
strictly humanitarian—that is, nonlegally based—grounds. This may
be illustrated by a number of examples of state practice in the eighteenth, nineteenth, and early twentieth centuries. The majority of
these instances concern actions by the United States, which with its
large immigrant population has long shown a special preoccupation
with the fate of the inhabitants of states from which its own citizens originated. Intercessions often were the result of pressures
put on the authorities in Washington by U.S. citizens belonging to
the same religious faith or ethnic group as those being oppressed.
U.S. missionaries abroad also frequently managed to obtain diplomatic assistance for foreign victims of repression.[7] The authorities of
the disintegrating parts of the Ottoman Empire were the most fre-

---

5. "La Sublime Porte promet de protéger constament la religion Chrétienne et ses
églises; et aussi elle permet aux Ministres de la Cour Impériale de Russie de faire dans
toutes les occasions des représentations, tant en faveur de la nouvelle église à Constantinople . . . , que pour ceux qui la desservent, promettant de les prendre en con-
sidération, comme faites par une personne de confiance d'une Puissance voisine et
sincèrement amie." Art. 7, Treaty of Perpetual Peace and Amity between Russia and
Turkey, signed at Kuçuk-Kainardji, 10 July 1774, Parry, *Consolidated Treaty Series*,
vol. 45, p. 373.

6. Art. 62, Treaty between Austria-Hungary, France, Germany, Great Britain, Italy,
Russia and Turkey for the Settlement of Affairs in the East, signed at Berlin, 13 July
1878, Parry, *Consolidated Treaty Series*, vol. 153, p. 171.

7. Cf. O. S. Straus, "Humanitarian Diplomacy of the United States," *Proceedings of
the ASIL*, 1912, p. 48.

quent—but by no means the only—recipients of intercessions in this period.

1.1 Bohemia

One of the earliest recorded diplomatic intercessions on behalf of foreign nationals occurred in Austria in the eighteenth century. On 28 December 1744, the British Envoy in Vienna was instructed to intercede, on humanitarian grounds and in concert with his Dutch colleague, with the Government of Empress Maria Theresia against the forced expulsion of twenty thousand Jews from Prague:

> It is the King's Pleasure, that you should join with Mor. Burmannia in endeavouring to dissuade the Court of Vienna from putting the said Sentence in Execution, hinting to Them in the tenderest and most friendly Manner, the Prejudice that the World might conceive against the Queen's Proceedings in that Affair, if such Numbers of innocent People were made to suffer for the Fault of some few Traytors, and, at the same time, shewing Them, the great Loss that would accrue to her Majesty's Revenue, and to the Wealth and Strength of her Kingdom of Bohemia, by depriving of it at once of so vast Numbers of it's Inhabitants.

The representations were apparently received "in excellent spirits" and the Empress agreed to revoke the decree in question and to permit the Jews to return to their homes.[8]

1.2 Palestine

In Palestine and in particular in Jerusalem, European diplomatic and consular representatives long exercised diplomatic protection on behalf of members of certain religious groups, irrespective of their nationality, even before this right was codified in the Treaty of Berlin.[9] For centuries, for example, France exercised diplomatic protection on behalf of members of the Catholic clergy. This prerogative was jealously guarded. France insisted on exercising it even when members of the Austrian, German, Italian, or Spanish clergy were already under the protection of their own national diplomatic or consular representatives.[10]

British diplomatic representatives were under similar instructions to exercise protection on behalf of Jews in the area. In 1839 the Brit-

---

8. L. Wolf, *Notes on the Diplomatic History of the Jewish Question* (1919), pp. 7–11.
9. Art. 62, *supra* note 6.
10. A. Kiss, *Répertoire de la pratique française en matière de droit international public*, vol. 3, pp. 472–74.

ish Vice-Consul at Jerusalem was instructed by the Foreign Office "that it would be part of his duty, as British Vice-Consul at Jerusalem, to afford protection to the Jews generally." He was subsequently requested to report to the British Embassy at Constantinople "all instances of oppression and injustice suffered by the Jewish population in his district." According to an 1873 Foreign Office memorandum, the British Government had, ever since 1839, afforded consular protection to individual Jews and to the Jewish communities in "the East."[11]

1.3 Holy See

Despite the foregoing examples, it would be wrong to assume that states were generally keen to act on behalf of foreign victims of religious repression. In 1858, the United States Secretary of State declined a request to express condemnation to the Pope about cruelties committed against Jews by the papal authorities in Bologna. The reasons given for declining the request are instructive. They remind the reader of arguments offered by some governments more than a century later:

There are cruelties and outrages of such a revolting nature that it is natural, laudable indeed, that when they occur, they should meet with general condemnation. But this duty to "outraged humanity" should be left to the action of individuals, and to the expression of public opinion, for it is manifest that if one government assumes the power to judge and censure the proceedings of another or the laws it recognizes, in cases which do not affect their own interests, or the rights of their citizens, the intercourse of nations will soon become a system of crimination and recrimination hostile to friendly communication. For, the principle of interference being once admitted, its application may be indefinitely extended, depending for its exercise on the opinion which each country may form of the civil polity of another, and of its practical operation.[12]

1.4 Romania

In 1872, when confronted with reports of the persecution of Jews in the principalities of Moldavia and Wallachia, the then U.S. Secretary of State reached a different conclusion. He instructed his ambassador to make representations, even though these could not rely on relevant

11. Memorandum relative to the grant of British Protection to Foreign Jews in Palestine, Mr. A. S. Green, 16 January 1873, C. Parry, *A British Digest of International Law*, vol. 5, pp. 462–63.

12. Mr. Cass, U.S. Secretary of State, 8 December 1858, J. B. Moore, *A Digest of International Law*, vol. 6, p. 348.

treaty provisions, because he believed American intercessions were justified in view of the extreme seriousness of the violations:

Although we are not a party to that instrument,[13] and, as a rule, scrupulously abstain from interfering, directly or indirectly, in the public affairs of that quarter, the grievance adverted is so enormous, as to impart to it, as it were, a cosmopolitan character, in the redress of which all countries, governments, and creeds are alike interested.[14]

Accordingly, U.S. representations were explicitly made "in the name of humanity."[15] Representations were also made jointly with Austria-Hungary, France, Germany, Great Britain, and Greece. In this case, it cannot be concluded with certainty whether the United States was basing its representations merely on humanitarian grounds or whether it was invoking some standard of general international law. In 1902, however, the United States again protested the treatment of Jews in Romania, and this time it relied on the dual ground of the burden caused to it by the massive immigration of destitute Romanian Jews as well as the principles contained in the Berlin Treaty, though it was not a party to this treaty. On this occasion, the United States appeared to be relying on customary international human rights law *avant la lettre* as codified in the Berlin Treaty:

The United States may not authoritatively appeal to the stipulations of the treaty of Berlin, to which it was not and can not become a signatory, but it does earnestly appeal to the principles consigned therein because they are the principles of international law and eternal justice.[16]

The doctrine presented here did not immediately become a cornerstone of U.S. foreign policy. At a press conference in 1938, on the eve of the outbreak of World War II, the Secretary of State was asked whether he was willing to join the French and British governments in

13. The instrument referred to was the Convention relative to the Organisation of the Principalities of Moldavia and Wallachia, between Austria, France, Great Britain, Prussia, Russia, Sardinia and Turkey, signed at Paris on 19 August 1858, Parry, *Consolidated Treaty Series*, vol. 119, p. 349.

14. Mr. Fish, U.S. Secretary of State, to Mr. Jay, U.S. Ambassador in Austria-Hungary, 22 July 1872, Moore, *A Digest of International Law*, vol. 6, pp. 360–61.

15. Moore, *A Digest of International Law*, vol. 6, pp. 364–65. The French Government expressed its support for the American move. In 1868 France had already made representations on this matter together with Austria and Great Britain. In response, the Romanian Minister of Foreign Affairs had given assurances that compensation would be provided to the victims and that the culprits would be punished. He had not complained of interference in Romania's internal affairs. See Kiss, *supra* note 10, vol. 2, pp. 628–30.

16. Mr. Hay, U.S. Secretary of State, to Mr. Wilson, U.S. Minister to Romania, 17 July 1902. Reproduced in Moore, *A Digest of International Law*, vol. 6, p. 365. Great Britain agreed to join in these representations. See Wolf, *supra* note 8, pp. 44–45.

protests against the treatment of Jews in Romania. The Secretary of State informed the U.S. Legation in Bucharest that he had responded as follows:

[T]hat, notwithstanding the American policy of supporting such doctrines as religious freedom and equal treatment of those of different religions as well as races, the United States Government, standing for the doctrine of non-intervention in the domestic affairs of other nations except where the rights of its nationals were involved, was not in a position to depart from that doctrine in any case but that the United States was not unmindful of developments in every part of the world relating to the treatment of minorities and that it observed with close interest developments in the case under discussion. He instructed the Legation to continue to express general interest in developments which might indicate discriminatory action, because of the interest of public opinion in the United States, without taking any action which might be construed as intervention in the domestic affairs of Rumania not involving rights of American citizens.[17]

1.5 Russia

In 1891, the U.S. Government expressed its concern at the repression of Jews in Russia, but carefully avoided the suggestion that Russia's repressive activities were in themselves incompatible with international law. Instead, it referred to the harmful consequences of the repression for the United States. Thus it could be said that it justified its legal interest by relying on the principle of *sic utere tuo ut alterem non laedas*:

The Government of the United States does not assume to dictate the internal policy of other nations, or to make suggestions as to what their municipal laws should be or as to the manner in which they should be administered. Nevertheless, the mutual duties of nations require that each should use its power with a due regard for the results which its exercise produces on the rest of the world. It is in this respect that the condition of Jews in Russia is now brought to the attention of the United States, upon whose shores are cast daily evidences of the suffering and destitution wrought by the enforcement of the edicts against this unhappy people. I am persuaded that His Imperial Majesty the Emperor of Russia and his councilors can feel no sympathy with measures which are forced upon other nations by such deplorable consequences.[18]

On other occasions, the United States was willing to intercede more forcefully. In a speech in 1904, President Theodore Roosevelt justi-

17. Mr. Hull, U.S. Secretary of State, to the U.S. Legation in Romania, 2 January 1938, G. H. Hackworth, *Digest of International Law*, vol. 2, pp. 152–53.
18. Mr. Blaine, U.S. Secretary of State, to Mr. Smith, U.S. Ambassador in St. Petersburg, 18 February 1891, *Papers Relating to the Foreign Relations of the United States* (1891), p. 739.

fied in the following terms the representations which had been made by the U.S. Government in response to the pogroms in a large number of Russian cities:

Nevertheless there are occasional crimes committed on so vast a scale and of such peculiar horror as to make us doubt whether it is not our manifest duty to endeavour at least to show our disapproval of the deed and our sympathy with those who have suffered by it. The case must be extreme in which such a course is justifiable.[19]

1.6 Congo

It should not be assumed that representations were exclusively directed at governments outside Western Europe and the United States. From time to time, the governments of Western Europe and the United States also expressed concern among themselves. In the early twentieth century, the United States and Great Britain made repeated and occasionally combined representations to the Government of Belgium to express concern about King Leopold II's slaverylike practices in the Congo. These representations relied on the General Act for the Repression of the African Slave Trade to which all three states were parties.[20] For example, in a memorandum handed to the Belgian Government on 7 April 1908, the United States called for a number of reforms in the Congo, including the exemption of the native population from excessive taxation, the prohibition of forced labor, and the establishment of an independent judiciary.[21] Shortly afterward, as a result of the foreign pressure, the King agreed to transfer sovereignty over the Congo from himself to Belgium. These intercessions do not appear to have been inspired by other considerations than genuine concern at the conditions of the native population in the Congo.[22] Belgium apparently did not maintain that these representations constituted interference in its internal affairs.

1.7 Morocco

Morocco provides another case, not only in which the interceding states lacked any religious or ethnic ties with the victims, but in which they could not rely on any treaty provisions to justify their interest.

19. President Theodore Roosevelt, 4 December 1904, quoted in Straus, *supra* note 7, p. 52.
20. General Act for the Repression of the African Slave Trade, signed at Brussels, 2 July 1890, Parry, *Consolidated Treaty Series*, vol. 173, p. 293.
21. *Papers Relating to the Foreign relations of the United States* (1908), pp. 560–61.
22. See, generally, Stowell, *supra* note 2, pp. 162–79.

Moulay Hafid, Sultan of Morocco from 1908 to 1912 (when Morocco became a French protectorate), was known for the extreme cruelty with which he maintained his power. According to a contemporary British journalist, his "palace was a constant scene of barbarity and torture."[23]

On 10 August 1909, the right hands of a dozen captured rebels and the right hands and left feet of some twenty others were amputated by way of punishment.[24] In response, on 30 August 1909, the collective consular corps in Fez (consisting of the consuls of France, Great Britain, and Spain) headed by its doyen, the French consul, presented a letter of protest to the Sultan. In it they demanded in the name of "the laws of humanity" (a rather ambiguous expression) the abolition of all forms of torture and corporal punishment causing mutilation or slow death. The Sultan replied that the people of Morocco were not yet sufficiently civilized and that in order to prevent insurgencies it was sometimes necessary to employ methods no longer customary in Europe. Nevertheless, he gave a solemn undertaking that he would in future respect the laws of humanity and that such methods would no longer be used.

Professor Antoine Rougier, who analyzed this case in 1910, has pointed out that in order to justify their interference in Morocco's administration of justice, the consuls could not invoke any firm standard of international law by which Morocco was bound.[25] Morocco was a sovereign state and it could have been argued that it was free to treat its own citizens as it pleased. Even with due allowance being made for the dependent position in which Morocco found itself, the reliance by the interceding governments on the laws of humanity and the admittedly reluctant acceptance by the Sultan of this concept appear significant.

The case was not an isolated incident. A year later, the French and British consuls went a step further by exercising protection on behalf of a specific individual of Moroccan nationality who had been tortured in prison. In June 1910, the two consuls received reports that Lalla Batoul, the wife of the former pasha of Fez, had been arrested and subjected to torture to make her reveal the place where her husband had hidden his money. The consuls, acting in concert, made repeated representations to the Sultan and arranged a medical examination in prison. According to the doctor's report, the woman had been crucified, as a result of which her left arm had been broken and

23. W. Harris, *Morocco That Was* (1921, reissued 1983), p. 297.
24. Kiss, *supra* note 10, vol. 2, pp. 632–33.
25. A. Rougier, "Maroc: la question de l'abolition des supplices et l'intervention européenne," 17 *RGDIP* (1910), pp. 98–102.

her shoulder had been heavily sprained. The consuls subsequently managed to obtain her release.[26]

1.8 Armenia

Under Article 61 of the Treaty of Berlin, the Turkish Government had undertaken to guarantee the security of the Armenian people and to report periodically to the other states parties on the measures taken to this end. Nevertheless, between 1890 and 1930, hundreds of thousands of Christian Armenians were massacred by Muslim Turks and Kurds.[27] The other states parties to the treaty repeatedly put pressure on Turkey to comply with its obligations under Article 61. In 1880, for example, two years after the treaty was signed, they submitted a collective note in which they demanded the "complete and immediate execution" of the treaty and called on the Turkish Government "to state explicitly what the steps are which they have taken in order to fulfill the provisions of this Article."[28]

Again, because the United States was not a party to the Treaty of Berlin, it could not invoke its provisions. In spite of this, the U.S. Government repeatedly expressed its concern to the Turkish authorities. In 1915, at the height of the massacres, the U.S. Ambassador in Turkey, Henry Morgenthau, played a key role. His telegrams to the State Department graphically demonstrated his worries and his awareness of what was taking place. He was kept well informed by U.S. consular officials and missionaries in the field. Although the State Department apparently backed the ambassador in his efforts, he himself clearly felt restricted in how far he could go: "It is difficult for me to restrain myself from doing something to stop this attempt to exterminate a race, but I realize that I am here as Ambassador and must abide by the principles of non-interference with the internal affairs of another country."[29]

The Turkish Government, in response to his intercessions, repeatedly warned Morgenthau that he should not interfere in the country's internal affairs.[30] At one point, however, the Turkish authorities declared themselves willing to exempt Protestant and Catholic Armeni-

---

26. Kiss, *supra* note 10, vol. 2, pp. 634–36.
27. See, generally, L. B. Sohn and Th. Buergenthal, *International Protection of Human Rights* (1973), pp. 181–92. This work also reproduces much of the diplomatic correspondence referred to in this section.
28. C. A. Macartney, *National States and National Minorities* (1934), p. 169.
29. The U.S. Ambassador in Turkey (Henry Morgenthau) to the Secretary of State, 11 August 1915, *Papers Relating to the Foreign Relations of the United States*, 1915, Supplement, p. 986.
30. *Ibid.*, pp. 982–84.

ans from deportation to the interior (this would have amounted to some 10 percent of the total population; the other 90 percent were Gregorian[31]). This was in obvious deference to prevailing religions in the United States and may perhaps be regarded as an indication that the exercise of diplomatic protection based on the link of religion was considered acceptable by Turkey. Morgenthau clearly found it easier to intercede on behalf of Armenians who were in some way connected with the United States through American missions, schools, or hospitals in Turkey.[32] Morgenthau's encounters with Turkey's cold-blooded rulers, who did not hide their plan to physically eliminate the Armenians, are vividly described in his memoirs.[33] No sophisticated arguments of international law appear to have been raised in these meetings.

The German Ambassador in Turkey also repeatedly expressed concern to the Turkish authorities about the deportations, although in much less forceful terms than Morgenthau. The authorities curtly responded that the measures taken with regard to the Armenian population belonged to the area of internal administration. Since the measures did not affect foreign interests, they could not be the subject of diplomatic intercession.[34]

2. Some Contemporary Cases

It would have been possible to continue this review of diplomatic intercessions on behalf of foreign nationals with some examples from the period between World War I and World War II. Such examples will be discussed in Chapter 3, in the section dealing with protection of minority rights under the League of Nations. It would also have been possible to analyze, for example, the efforts made by the Allied governments to prevent the extermination of the Jews in Europe during World War II. Such an analysis would have shown that the Allies did consider themselves fully entitled to intercede with the German authorities to try and prevent the Holocaust. This was most clearly demonstrated when on 17 December 1942 the governments of Belgium, Czechoslovakia, Greece, Luxembourg, the Netherlands, Norway, Poland, the United States, the United Kingdom, the Soviet Union, and Yugoslavia and the French National Committee issued a

31. So called after Gregorius Illuminator, who founded the Armenian Church in the third century.

32. *Supra* note 29, p. 987.

33. H. Morgenthau, *Ambassador Morgenthau's Story* (1918), pp. 326–63.

34. Ambassador Metternich to Reichskanzler von Bethman Hollweg, 23 December 1915, in J. Lepsius (ed.), *Deutschland und Armenien 1914–1918: Sammlung Diplomatischer Aktenstücke* (1919), p. 210.

declaration on the German policy of extermination of the Jewish race. The declaration not only condemned "in the strongest possible terms [the] bestial policy of coldblooded extermination" of Jews by the German authorities. It also threatened that "those responsible for these crimes shall not escape retribution."[35]

Clearly, the sentiments expressed in this declaration went well beyond mere diplomatic expressions of concern and reflected the *opinio juris* that the German Government could be held responsible for the atrocities. It is true that this declaration was followed by disappointingly little actual effort to rescue Jews from the occupied countries. This was not because the Allied governments did not consider themselves entitled to act on behalf of foreign Jews, however, but because of various policy considerations. Among other reasons, it was felt that absolute priority should be given to winning the war.[36]

Instead of pursuing this historical path, we will jump to the present to consider some contemporary instances of diplomatic intercessions on behalf of foreign nationals. At the same time, our focus will become more specific and change from situations to individual cases. The examination of contemporary state practice, unlike that of the historical period analyzed above, is made difficult by the fact that relevant diplomatic correspondence is often inaccessible. The best information available tends to derive from various newspaper reports and is therefore less authoritative than in the instances discussed above. The contemporary cases examined below are therefore not fully comparable to the historical ones discussed above. Nevertheless, a careful analysis of some recent cases in which states made diplomatic representations on behalf of foreign nationals may provide some evidence of the current status of customary international law in this area.

The better known a case, the more information on the exchanges between the interceding state and the offending state tends to be available. An examination will therefore be made of the representations that were made on behalf of the following well-known political prisoners from different parts of the world: Ali Bhutto (Pakistan), Kim Dae-jung (Republic of Korea), Orton and Vera Chirwa (Malawi), and Andrei Sakharov (Union of Soviet Socialist Republics). It is of course realized that any findings regarding these relatively well publicized cases will not necessarily apply to intercessions on behalf of non-nationals generally. Nevertheless, they should at least provide a starting point of our inquiry and help to identify elements that need to be pursued further.

35. 7 *Department of State Bulletin* (1942), p. 1009.
36. See, generally, M. N. Penkower, *The Jews Were Expendable: Free World Diplomacy and the Holocaust* (1983).

2.1 Pakistan: Ali Bhutto

On 18 March 1978, Pakistan's former prime minister, Zulfikar Ali Bhutto, was sentenced to death by the Lahore High Court for alleged complicity in the murder of a political opponent. His appeal was dismissed by the Supreme Court on 6 February 1979. The case had strong political undertones. There were particularly good reasons not to execute Mr. Bhutto in view of the fact that the conviction was based almost entirely on the evidence of accomplices who had been granted pardon in return for giving evidence for the prosecution. Moreover, three of the seven Supreme Court judges had taken the view that there was insufficient evidence to establish Mr. Bhutto's guilt.[37]

The reactions by other states to the death sentence imposed on Mr. Bhutto highlighted an apparently widely held conviction that in such cases it is legitimate for other states to appeal for commutation of the sentence, without having to demonstrate a direct material interest. The sentence provoked an unprecedented number of high-level appeals from other governments. Among those who appealed publicly for clemency were President Carter of the United States, President Brezhnev of the Union of Soviet Socialist Republics, President Giscard d'Estaing of France, President Tito of Yugoslavia, King Khaled of Saudi Arabia, King Juan Carlos of Spain, Pope John Paul II, and the prime ministers of the People's Republic of China, Denmark, the Federal Republic of Germany, Norway, Sweden, the United Kingdom, and Viet Nam. Appeals were also made by most of the Arab states, including Algeria, Egypt, Iraq, Jordan, Kuwait, Libya, Morocco, Oman, Qatar, Somalia, Sudan, Syria, and the United Arab Emirates.[38]

Remarkable in this case was not only the high governmental level but also the wide political spectrum from which the appeals originated. Both President Brezhnev[39] and Chairman Hua Kuo-feng[40] prefaced their appeals by the customary assurance that the case was entirely Pakistan's internal affair. They both made it quite clear, however, that they did not wish to see Mr. Bhutto executed, Mr. Brezhnev out of "purely humane motives" and Mr. Hua out of a nonspecified "concern about this matter." The content of King Khaled's appeal was not made public, but no doubt his intercession put heavy pressure on President Zia-ul-Haq in view of Saudi Arabia's influential position in the Islamic world.

---

37. *Amnesty International Report 1979*, pp. 106–7.
38. *Keesing's Contemporary Archives*, 1979, p. 29697.
39. *New York Times*, 10 February 1979, pp. 1 and 5.
40. *New York Times*, 12 February 1979, p. A3.

President Zia reacted to the representations with apparent irritation, and he delayed receiving the various ambassadors who had requested meetings with him to present their government's appeals.[41] He also denounced the "club of foreign politicians" by which the appeals were made.[42] He does not appear to have claimed that the matter was entirely Pakistan's internal affair, however.

The intercessions were not successful. Mr. Bhutto was hanged in Rawalpindi Prison on 4 April 1979, after President Zia had rejected all appeals for clemency. The execution was publicly deplored or condemned by inter alia the governments of Belgium, the People's Republic of China, Egypt, France, the Netherlands, Turkey, the United Kingdom, and the United States.[43]

2.2 Republic of Korea: Kim Dae-jung

Kim Dae-jung, the South Korean opposition leader, was sentenced to death by a military tribunal in Seoul on 17 September 1980, on charges of rebellion and having funded student disturbances for this purpose.[44] The trial failed to meet internationally recognized standards.[45] The death sentence was nevertheless confirmed by a military appeals court on 4 November 1980.[46]

The sentence provoked expressions of concern and appeals for clemency from inter alia the governments of Australia, Japan, Norway, Sweden, the United States, and Yugoslavia.[47] Most governments interceded privately. The United States, the most influential power in the Republic of Korea because of its forty thousand troops stationed there, interceded strongly and repeatedly at the highest governmental levels.[48] The nine member states of the European Community on three occasions made private representations to the South Korean authorities.[49] Japan, on the other hand, repeatedly interceded publicly and threatened to cut off economic aid. The Federal Republic of

41. *Le Monde*, 15 February 1979, p. 5.

42. *Le Monde*, 25–26 March 1979, p. 5.

43. *Keesing's Contemporary Archives*, 1979, p. 29698.

44. *Keesing's Contemporary Archives*, 1980, p. 30609.

45. *Amnesty International Report 1981*, p. 232.

46. *New York Times*, 4 November 1980, p. 4.

47. *Keesing's Contemporary Archives*, 1980, p. 30609.

48. The U.S. Ambassador in Seoul later reported with apparent annoyance that for six months—apparently starting before the beginning of the trial—Kim's fate consumed more of his time than any other matter. See W. H. Gleysteen, Jr., "Korea: A Special Target of American Concern," in *The Diplomacy of Human Rights* (1986), D. D. Newsom (ed.), p. 97.

49. Revealed by the French Foreign Minister to the French National Assembly, *Le Monde*, 7 November 1980, p. 10.

Germany also threatened such retaliatory measures if Mr. Kim were executed.[50]

The South Korean authorities reacted to this foreign pressure in different ways. Expressions of concern by the United States and Japan prior to the beginning of the first trial were rejected as "premature" and "tantamount to an attempt to manipulate the judicial process of a friendly country." This may be translated as reliance on the requirement of exhaustion of domestic remedies. A spokesperson of the U.S. State Department had rather undiplomatically called the charges against Mr. Kim "pretty farfetched."[51] Japan's intercessions after the appeal hearing were also criticized by the South Korean authorities as attempts to meddle in South Korea's internal affairs.[52] This reaction may have been prompted by annoyance at the amount of pressure exerted by Japan. Nevertheless, when at a later stage President Chun Doo-hwan announced that the death sentence would be commuted, he cited requests from "friendly nations and persons" as one of the reasons for taking this step.[53] He thereby provided a rare example of a government openly acknowledging that it was bowing to foreign appeals on behalf of a political prisoner.

Kim Dae-jung's sentence was commuted to life imprisonment in January 1981. He was released on 24 December 1982[54] and stood as a presidential candidate in 1987.

2.3 Malawi: Orton and Vera Chirwa

On 5 May 1983, a traditional court in Soche, Malawi, sentenced to death on charges of treason the country's opposition leader and former minister of justice, Orton Chirwa, and his wife Vera. There were strong indications that the Chirwas had been arrested on account of their nonviolent opposition to the government, and that the proceedings in their trial had been unfair. Not only were the defendants denied legal representation and refused permission to call certain witnesses, but it was doubtful whether the judges were truly independent from the executive authorities.[55]

This case—like the Kim Dae-jung case—is instructive in that it demonstrates the apparent view of some states that victims of human rights violations must have exhausted all legal remedies before in-

50. *New York Times*, 26 December 1980, p. A9.
51. *Keesing's Contemporary Archives*, 1980, p. 30609.
52. *New York Times*, 27 November 1980, p. A4.
53. *New York Times*, 24 January 1981, p. 3.
54. *Amnesty International Report 1983*, p. 210.
55. *Amnesty International Report 1984*, p. 65, and *Amnesty International Report 1985*, pp. 61–62.

tercessions may be made on their behalf. Initially it was not clear whether the Chirwas would be able to lodge an appeal against their conviction. Fearing that their execution might be imminent, President Daniel arap Moi of Kenya (in his capacity as chairman of the Organization of African Unity) and President Shehu Shagari of Nigeria immediately appealed for clemency to Malawi's Life-President Kamuzu Banda.[56] Other governments hesitated before taking this step. A spokesperson of the British Foreign Office put the reason as follows: "Until all the existing legal channels have been exhausted it would be inappropriate for any plea to be entered by her Majesty's Government."[57]

In the end, the Chirwas were permitted to lodge an appeal before the National Traditional Court of Appeal. On 7 February 1984, this court rejected the appeals and confirmed the death sentences.[58] On 17 February 1984, the French Ambassador in Malawi, accompanied by the British High Commissioner and the German Ambassador, presented an appeal for clemency on behalf of the member states of the European Community.[59]

On 30 June 1984, the Government of Malawi announced that Life-President Banda had commuted the two death sentences to life imprisonment.[60]

2.4 USSR: Andrei Sakharov

On 22 January 1980, the Soviet scientist and human rights campaigner Andrei Sakharov was arrested in Moscow, stripped of his decorations, and banished to the city of Gorky.[61] No charges were brought against him and he was not tried, but it seemed clear that the measure had been taken because of Dr. Sakharov's human rights activities.

The banishment—and subsequent hunger strikes by Dr. Sakharov

56. *The Times* (London), 2 June 1983, p. 6, and 8 June 1983, p. 7.
57. *The Times* (London), 2 June 1983, p. 6.
58. *Amnesty International Report 1985*, p. 61.
59. Earlier, on 14 February 1984, the UN Commission on Human Rights had decided without a vote to send the following telegram to the President of Malawi: "The Commission on Human Rights has learned that the Malawi National Traditional Court of Appeal has turned down the appeal of Orton Chirwa and his wife Vera against the death sentence passed on them. Being seized by a purely humanitarian concern deriving from its recognition of the singular importance of the right to life, the Commission appeals most respectfully and strongly that clemency be granted to Mr. Chirwa and his wife." UN Commission on Human Rights, decision 1984/102. See also *infra* Chapter 2, note 174.
60. *Amnesty International Report 1985*, p. 62.
61. *Amnesty International Report 1980*, p. 307.

and his wife—provoked strong reactions, almost exclusively from Western governments. Among those who expressed their concern to the Soviet Union were the governments of Belgium, Denmark, the Federal Republic of Germany, France, Italy, Norway, Portugal, Sweden, the United Kingdom, and Pope John-Paul II.[62] The member states of the European Community also interceded collectively.[63]

The legal grounds relied on by the interceding governments deserve some scrutiny. In the three death penalty cases discussed above representations were, as far as can be gathered, all made on strictly humanitarian grounds, that is, without invoking any international standards. In the Sakharov case, at least three governments—France, the United Kingdom, and the United States—relied specifically on the Helsinki Final Act[64] when making their initial representations. The United States claimed that the banishment of Dr. Sakharov constituted "a direct violation of the Helsinki accords."[65] The British Government, somewhat ambiguously, informed the Soviet Ambassador in London that it deeply deplored any action against Dr. Sakharov that contravened the Helsinki Final Act.[66] The French Government, more carefully, expressed the view that the measure was "contrary to the spirit of the Helsinki Final Act."[67]

This enthusiastic use of the Helsinki Final Act is slightly puzzling. First of all, the Final Act is not a binding legal instrument. Second, it is not immediately obvious which provisions of the Final Act the interceding governments may have had in mind. The human rights provisions of the Final Act are vague and add little or nothing to more specific provisions contained in legal instruments that were binding on the USSR, such as the International Covenants on Human Rights. The United States, not being a party to the majority of these instruments, was not in a position to invoke them. But why did France and the United Kingdom not choose to rely on stronger legal grounds? Did they perhaps consider that citing the Final Act rather than the International Covenant on Civil and Political Rights would cause more political embarrassment to the USSR? These questions will be addressed below in a more general context.[68]

62. *Le Monde*, 24 January 1980, p. 3; 9 December 1981, p. 3; and 19 May 1984, pp. 1 and 4.

63. *Le Monde*, 22 May 1984, p. 2.

64. Final Act of the Conference on Security and Co-operation in Europe, adopted at Helsinki on 1 August 1975, reproduced in 14 *ILM* (1975), pp. 1293–325, and 70 *AJIL* (1976), pp. 417–21 (Declaration of Principles only).

65. *Le Monde*, 25 January 1980, p. 3.

66. *The Times* (London), 23 January 1980, p. 1.

67. *Le Monde*, 25 January 1980, p. 3.

68. *Infra* section 3.1.

If the forcefulness of official protests made by states is an indication of *opinio juris* on their part, the Sakharov case presents considerable evidence that a number of states considered themselves fully entitled to object to his treatment. The Swedish Foreign Minister said he deplored the "scandalous measure" taken against Dr. Sakharov.[69] The British Foreign Office issued a statement according to which the treatment of Dr. Sakharov demonstrated "the callous disregard of the Soviet Government for the commitments which they undertook in signing the Helsinki Final Act."[70] The U.S. State Department condemned the Soviet Union's "inhuman and incomprehensible" treatment of Dr. Sakharov and his wife.[71]

The Soviet Union, on the other hand, maintained with equal vigor that the measures taken against Dr. Sakharov constituted a strictly internal matter. No assurances were given in response to the protests. On the contrary, on two occasions reported in the press, the Soviet Union clearly indicated that this was not a matter that could be discussed with other states. During a visit to Moscow on 29 May 1984, Australia's Foreign Minister Bill Hayden expressed to his counterpart Andrei Gromyko concern about the health of Dr. Sakharov and his wife. He said he would appreciate information about their condition. Mr. Gromyko responded that this was an internal affair and that the Soviet Union "will not be told how to deal with the Sakharovs by other countries." According to Mr. Hayden, Mr. Gromyko then said: "The conversation on this subject ends here" and terminated the dialogue.[72]

A public confrontation at the highest governmental level occurred during the official visit of France's President Mitterand to Moscow in June 1984. In a dinner speech, Mr. Mitterand raised Western Europe's concern at the fate of "Professor Sakharov and many unknown people in all countries of the world [*sic*] who invoke the Helsinki accords."[73] According to Mr. Mitterand, by naming Dr. Sakharov he had sent a shiver through the Russians present at the banquet.[74] President Chernenko had already delivered his prepared speech and he did not respond. However, the displeasure of the Soviet authorities may be inferred from the following passage, which was added to Mr. Chernenko's speech as it appeared in *Pravda* the next day: "And those who try to give us advice in the area of human rights evoke only an

69. *Le Monde*, 24 January 1980, p. 3.
70. *The Times* (London), 8 December 1981, p. 6.
71. *New York Times*, 9 May 1984, p. 7.
72. *New York Times*, 30 May 1984, p. 8.
73. *Le Monde*, 23 June 1984, p. 3.
74. *The Times* (London), 23 June 1984, p. 6.

ironic smile from us. . . . we will allow no one to interfere in our affairs." [75]

Dr. Sakharov was released from exile in December 1986.[76] In 1989, shortly before his death, he was elected to the Congress of People's Deputies.

3. Policies and Practices of Some States

In order to be able to arrive at firm conclusions on the status of international law with regard to the exercise of diplomatic protection on behalf of foreign nationals, more information is needed, not only on the extent of the practice but especially on the *opinio juris* on which it is based. We will therefore examine in more detail the policies and practices of two groups of states that, at least until recently, tended to maintain opposing views on the matter: the West European and Other States on the one hand, and the East European States on the other. This subdivision follows a long-standing UN classification. To find out whether any common ground can be established between them, the east-west confrontation of views will then be examined in the context of the Conference on Security and Co-operation in Europe. Finally, the north-south confrontation of views between the member states of the European Community and a major part of the Non-Aligned Movement will be examined in the context of the so-called Lomé Conventions.

3.1 West European and Other States

In 1985, the Ministerial Conference on Human Rights of the Council of Europe adopted a "Declaration on Human Rights in the World at Large" which contains the following preambulary paragraph:

Reaffirming the conviction that the protection of human rights and fundamental freedoms is a legitimate and urgent concern of the international community and its members and that *expressions of concern that such rights are not observed in a certain State cannot be considered as interference in the domestic affairs of that State*.[77] (emphasis added)

In 1986, the ministers of foreign affairs of the twelve member states of the European Community adopted a "Declaration on Human Rights," which contains very much the same notion:

75. *Le Monde*, 23 June 1984, p. 3. *Pravda*, 22 June 1984, p. 2, as translated in *Current Digest of the Soviet Press*, vol. 38, no. 25, p. 10.
76. *New York Times*, 20 December 1986, p. 8.
77. Declaration on Human Rights in the World at Large, Council of Europe, Ministerial Conference on Human Rights, Vienna, 20 March 1985, in *Activities of the Council of Europe in the Field of Human Rights in 1985*, Doc. H (86) 2, p. 80.

The Twelve seek universal observance of human rights. The protection of human rights is the legitimate and continuous duty of the world community and of nations individually. *Expressions of concern at violations of such rights cannot be considered interference in the domestic affairs of a State.*[78] (emphasis added)

At first sight, these statements may seem clear and satisfactory. There is nothing here with which any of the non-European members of the Western Group are likely to disagree. President Jimmy Carter, for example, had already declared on 23 February 1977 that the United States had "a responsibility and a legal right to express [its] disapproval of violations of human rights."[79] On reflection, however, it will be seen that these pronouncements are less than clear-cut. First, the term *expressions of concern*, which is employed in both texts, has a political rather than legal connotation. Does this mean that the drafters wished to imply that interceding states merely have a limited right to protest against violations rather than a full legal right to insist on compliance with international standards? Second, does the term *violations of human rights* refer not only to civil and political rights, but also to economic, social, and cultural ones? Third, do the statements intend to cover all violations, whether large or small, massive or individual?

In the absence of *travaux préparatoires* of these two declarations, it is necessary to examine the individual practice of Western states to be able to answer these questions. A number of Western governments (including Denmark,[80] the Netherlands[81] and Switzerland[82]) have produced policy papers on human rights and foreign policy which include sections on the question of interference in internal affairs. Other gov-

78. Declaration on Human Rights, adopted by the Foreign Ministers of the European Community, 21 July 1986, 19 *Bull. EC* (1986), no. 7/8, para. 2.4.4.

79. *Department of State Bulletin*, vol. 76, no. 1969, p. 252. The policies of the Carter administration in this regard are said to have constituted a watershed in comparison to previous administrations. See O. Schachter, "Les aspects juridiques de la politique américaine en matière de droits de l'homme," 23 *AFDI* (1977), pp. 55–59. Following the 1967 military coup d'état in Greece, for example, the United States still refused to raise alleged human rights violations with the Greek Government, on the grounds that these were matters within Greece's domestic jurisdiction. See J. J. Shestack and R. Cohen, "International Human Rights: A Role for the United States," 14 *Virginia Journal of International Law* (1973), pp. 677–78. See also P. C. Szasz, "The International Legal Aspects of the Human Rights Program of the United States," 12 *Cornell International Law Journal* (1979), pp. 161–74.

80. Danish Ministry of Foreign Affairs, *Denmark and Human Rights in International Relations*, November 1977, p. 21.

81. Netherlands Ministry of Foreign Affairs, *Human Rights and Foreign Policy*, 3 May 1979, pp. 88–90. Also reproduced in 11 *NYIL* (1980), pp. 193–95.

82. Département fédéral des affaires étrangères, *Rapport sur la politique de la Suisse en faveur des droits de l'homme*, 2 June 1982, p. 10.

ernments (including France, the Federal Republic of Germany,[83] and the United Kingdom[84]) have explained their points of view in response to parliamentary questions. Some simply claim that the objection of interference in internal affairs can no longer be raised in human rights cases.[85] Others have a more nuanced approach and draw the line at consistent patterns of gross violations of human rights. According to this latter view, outside interference is appropriate "particularly" if the violations are sufficiently grave and if those violations appear to be the result of a systematic governmental policy.[86] But this does not mean, apparently, that in the view of these states intercessions in less serious cases would not be legally permitted.

There is, however, a perhaps more fundamental difference in approach among the Western states. Some states appear to draw a basic distinction between the exercise of diplomatic protection on behalf of their own nationals and the exercise of protection on behalf of foreign nationals; other states treat both categories in one breath. When in 1976 the U.S. State Department reported to the Committee on International Relations of the House of Representatives on human rights initiatives it had taken vis-à-vis Argentina and Peru, it did not make a fundamental distinction between representations on behalf of U.S. citizens and those made on behalf of foreign citizens.[87] The Government of the Federal Republic of Germany, when reporting in 1986 on its efforts on behalf of "disappeared" persons, political detainees, people sentenced to death, and people attempting to leave their own country, referred to nationals and non-nationals in one breath, without making a fundamental distinction.[88] The United Kingdom and to a more limited extent also France,[89] however, have made much of the distinction between these two categories.

In the British view, "[i]ntervention in the sense of exercising diplomatic or consular protection has to be confined to British nationals in accordance with rules of international law."[90] The British Govern-

83. Federal Republic of Germany Minister of Foreign Affairs, 23 January 1986, Deutscher Bundestag, Doc. 10/4716.

84. The Parliamentary Under-Secretary of State, FCO, 16 June 1986, 57 *BYIL* (1986), p. 542.

85. Denmark, *supra* note 80. Switzerland, *supra* note 82.

86. The Netherlands, *supra* note 81. The Federal Republic of Germany, 30 January 1978, UN Doc. E/CN.4/1273/Add.2, p. 5.

87. *Digest of United States Practice in International Law*, 1976, pp. 174 and 176.

88. Federal Republic of Germany Minister of Foreign Affairs, reply to parliamentary question, 23 January 1986, Deutscher Bundestag, Doc. 10/4715, para. II.4.

89. *Pratique française du droit international*, 25 *AFDI* (1979), p. 958.

90. The Parliamentary Under-Secretary of State, FCO, reply to parliamentary question, 16 June 1986, 57 *BYIL* (1986), pp. 506–7.

ment has frequently employed this justification as a convenient pretext for declining to undertake diplomatic steps on behalf of foreign victims of human rights violations. For example, in 1981 it replied to a parliamentary question: "We have no formal locus standi to intercede with the Salvadorean Government on matters concerning its citizens";[91] in 1982 it stated: "Her Majesty's Government have no locus standi to make a démarche to the Cuban Government about the imprisonment in Cuba of one of their nationals";[92] and in 1986 it said: "Nepal is a sovereign country, and we have no locus standi to intervene on behalf of Nepalese citizens."[93]

These statements are inconsistent with the diplomatic and consular protection exercised by British representatives on behalf of Jews in Palestine in the nineteenth century.[94] They are also difficult to reconcile with the representations the British Government has made in recent years in response to violations of human rights of non-nationals in a wide range of countries, without apparently being troubled by a lack of legal standing. These statements should therefore not be interpreted as blank refusals to act on behalf of foreign nationals. Instead, they should perhaps be regarded as attempts to emphasize that no formal international claims can be made on behalf of such persons. All these individuals can hope for are informal, less emphatic intercessions by the British authorities.[95] Clearly, alleged lack of legal standing is a convenient device that can be invoked by governments not wishing, for political reasons, to intercede in a given case.[96]

What, then, is the true legal value that Western states attach to their intercessions on behalf of foreign nationals? Does their practice reflect the opinion that intercessions on behalf of non-nationals can be made as a matter of right? Or is it their view that such intercessions can only be made on humanitarian grounds? Are they demanding compliance with international law, or are they merely appealing to general humanitarian values? The answer to these questions is complicated by the remarkable fact that in their intercessions Western governments only rarely invoke specific international human rights

91. The Minister of State, FCO, reply to parliamentary question, 23 June 1981, 52 *BYIL* (1981), p. 375.

92. The Parliamentary Under-Secretary of State, FCO, reply to parliamentary question, 2 February 1982, 53 *BYIL* (1983), p. 350.

93. The Parliamentary Under-Secretary of State, FCO, reply to parliamentary question, 11 June 1986, 57 *BYIL* (1986), p. 506.

94. *Supra* section 1.2.

95. Cf. the Parliamentary Under-Secretary of State, FCO, reply to parliamentary question, 7 December 1983. 54 *BYIL* (1983), p. 382. See also *Pratique française du droit international*, 25 *AFDI* (1979), p. 958.

96. See also *Pratique française du droit international*, 34 *AFDI* (1988), pp. 951–54.

standards, even if this could easily be done.[97] Curiously enough, the only international instrument referred to with any frequency in intercessions has long been the Helsinki Final Act, which is not in itself binding and which does not contain very specific human rights provisions.[98]

Several explanations may be given for this phenomenon. First, the extent to which the death penalty is or is not permitted under international law is controversial. It is understandable, therefore, that governments tend not to cite international standards when appealing for the commutation of death sentences, since this might provoke a discussion on the legality of the penalty rather than help to save a human life. Second, in cases involving extreme violations—torture, "disappearances," or summary executions, for example—citing standards of international law will often be unnecessary. Such a course might detract from rather than reinforce the strength of the concern expressed. Third, and perhaps most important, quoting international standards may be perceived as pedantry by the receiving state and therefore be counterproductive. An appeal to strictly humanitarian considerations—as well as the Helsinki Final Act—may often be considered more effective. In other words, the infrequent reliance on binding standards of international law should not in itself be regarded as evidence of the nonlegal character of intercessions on behalf of foreign nationals.

Not only is it unusual to find citations of international standards in Western intercessions on behalf of non-nationals. In fact, in deciding whether or not to intercede, little thought seems to be given to the consideration whether the offending state is a party to any relevant binding human rights instrument together with the interceding state. Démarches are frequently made to states that are not parties to such instruments.[99] This can be explained in two ways: either the intercessions are made on humanitarian grounds only or the abuses interceded against are regarded by the intercessors as violations of customary international law or of the Charter of the United Nations. Support for the latter view can be found in the policy statements of some Western governments.[100] In the final analysis, however, the sheer scale and

97. *Pratique française du droit international*, 29 *AFDI* (1983), p. 883.

98. *Pratique française du droit international*, 31 *AFDI* (1985), p. 992. Cf. also the Sakharov case discussed in section 2.4.

99. See, for example, *Völkerrechtliche Praxis der Bundesrepublik Deutschland im Jahre 1980*, 42 *ZaöRV* (1982), p. 531.

100. "In accordance with current international law States cannot oppose a *demand for compliance* [Forderung nach Einhaltung] with human rights by invoking the prohibition of interference in internal affairs (UN Charter, Universal Declaration of Human Rights, covenants on human rights, CSCE Final Act)" [emphasis added], Federal Re-

intensity of intercessions by Western states must alone be the determining factors. It is difficult to imagine that these states would be willing so frequently to put their relations with other states in jeopardy if they did not consider themselves on firm legal grounds. In other words, ultimately the *opinio juris* can be inferred implicitly from the extent of the practice itself.

Western states tend to intercede especially in cases of grave or gross violations of human rights, particularly when these abuses appear to result from a systematic governmental policy. No common Western or West European definition has been produced of this concept.[101] Nevertheless, from the practice of some key countries it may be deduced that it involves violations of the right to life, the right to liberty and integrity of the person, the right to freedom of religion, and the right to leave one's country. Accordingly, Western governments have tended to intercede in cases of summary or arbitrary executions, death sentences, "disappearances," torture, political imprisonment, persecution of religious minorities, and persistent refusals to grant exit visas.[102] Intercessions responding to violations of economic, social, and cultural rights are much more exceptional, although they do occur occasionally.[103]

The United States takes a unique position among members of the Western Group in that its human rights policy has been laid down in specific legislation, as a result of congressional dissatisfaction with the policies pursued by the executive branch. Section 502B of the 1961 Foreign Assistance Act (as amended), for example, provides that "a principal goal of the foreign policy of the United States shall be to promote the increased observance of internationally recognized human rights by all countries." According to the same provision, in the absence of extraordinary circumstances "no security assistance may be provided to any country the government of which engages in a consistent pattern of gross violations of internationally recognized human rights."[104] Similar provisions prohibit economic assistance to

---

public of Germany Minister of Foreign Affairs, reply to parliamentary question, 23 January 1986, Deutscher Bundestag, Doc. 10/4716, para. I.1.

101. According to Section 502B of the U.S. Foreign Assistance Act 1961, "a consistent pattern of gross violations of internationally recognized human rights" includes torture or cruel, inhuman, or degrading treatment or punishment; prolonged detention without charges and trial; and other flagrant denial of the right to life, liberty, or the security of person. For the Netherlands view of this concept, see 16 *NYIL* (1985), p. 422.

102. Federal Republic of Germany: *supra* note 88, para. 4. France: 32 *AFDI* (1986), pp. 994–95. Netherlands: *supra* note 81.

103. For example, in June 1988, the Netherlands Foreign Ministry protested to the Romanian Ambassador in The Hague at the destruction of historic buildings in Bucharest. See *NRC Handelsblad*, 23 June 1988, p. 7.

104. For an analysis of the actual implementation of this policy, see S. B. Cohen,

gross violators of human rights. Little specific information is available, however, on the cases in which the United States has, in recent years, made diplomatic representations on behalf of foreign victims of human rights violations.[105]

Démarches may relate to general aspects of the human rights situation in a particular country, or they may relate to the fate of specific, named individuals. Both interceding governments and target governments tend to regard the latter category as more sensitive, perhaps because cases of this type resemble more closely the classic exercise of diplomatic protection on behalf of the interceding state's own nationals. It must therefore be regarded as significant that at least one Western state (France) is reported to have interceded more and more frequently on behalf of named individuals.[106]

Governments tend to be reluctant to provide precise information on the instances in which they have or have not interceded on behalf of foreign nationals. The reason often given is that this might undermine the effectiveness of the intercessions. In truth, this attitude also provides a convenient excuse to avoid outside scrutiny. Occasionally there has been more openness in the context of the so-called European Political Cooperation (EPC).[107] In 1986, the governments of the member states of the European Community presented to the Political Affairs Committee of the European Parliament at its request a "Memorandum on Action Taken in the Framework of European Cooperation in the Field of Human Rights."[108]

"Conditioning U.S. Security Assistance on Human Rights Practices," 76 *AJIL* (1982), pp. 246–79. See also D. Weissbrodt, "Human Rights Legislation and United States Foreign Policy," 7 *Georgia Journal of International and Comparative Law* (1977), pp. 231–87, and E. Zoller, *Enforcing International Law through U.S. Legislation* (1985). A useful compilation of relevant legislation is R. B. Lillich (ed.), *U.S. Legislation Relating Human Rights to U.S. Foreign Policy*, (3d ed. 1982).

105. Excerpts from a series of rare reports by the U.S. State Department on diplomatic representations made to the governments of Argentina, Haiti, Indonesia, Peru and the Philippines during the early 1970s may be found in *Digest of United States Practice in International Law*, 1976, pp. 173–77.

106. 30 *AFDI* (1984), p. 987.

107. "European Political Cooperation" (EPC) refers to the process of foreign policy coordination between the member states of the European Community. The purpose of the process is to arrive at common views and to promote common action in the area of foreign policy. EPC consultations are chaired by representatives of the member state that has the presidency of the European Community's Council of Ministers. This position changes biannually. The Presidency acts as the Community's spokesperson on foreign policy matters. The obvious idea behind EPC is that common views carry more weight than the views of individual member states. See Article 30 of the Single European Act of 17 February 1986, reproduced in 25 *ILM* (1986), pp. 517–18.

108. 7 May 1986, 2 *European Political Cooperation Documentation Bulletin* (1986), no. 1, 86/137. This report was prepared under the Dutch Presidency of the European Community. Unfortunately, reports prepared under subsequent presidencies have been much less informative.

The memorandum demonstrated that there had been considerable EPC activity in the field of human rights during the preceding five years. From 1981 to 1986, between ninety and a hundred démarches were made on behalf of the member states of the European Community. Of these intercessions, twenty-six were directed at countries in Latin America, fifteen at countries in Europe, forty-eight at countries in Africa and the Middle East, including thirteen at South Africa, and seven at countries in Asia. Approximately forty démarches concerned "purely humanitarian cases, for example requests for clemency for people sentenced to death."[109] The precise contents of these intercessions were occasionally made public. For example, in July 1986 the Presidency of the European Community conveyed to the authorities of Guinea-Bissau the regret of the Twelve that six opposition leaders had been executed in spite of appeals for clemency from governments and international organizations.[110] In December of the same year, the Twelve expressed their "sadness and concern" at the death in prison of the Soviet dissident Anatoly Marchenko and called upon the Soviet Government to honor its commitments under the Helsinki Final Act.[111] By 1991, the number of human rights démarches made in the context of the EPC had increased to one hundred and fifty per year. This is especially significant if one realizes that each démarche requires the consent of all twelve European Community member states.

Intercessions by individual Western states reveal a similarly wide-ranging pattern. During 1986, France interceded on behalf of non-nationals with the authorities of at least the following eighteen countries: Chile, Cuba, Ethiopia, GDR, Haiti, Indonesia, Israel, Laos, Morocco, Nicaragua, Paraguay, Poland, Romania, South Africa, Turkey, Viet Nam, Yugoslavia, and the USSR.[112] France's intercessions in previous years were comparable in number and in geographical and political spread.[113] During 1989, the British Government informed Parliament that it had made representations on humanitarian issues to the authorities of Bahrain, Bangladesh, Brunei, Bulgaria, Burundi, Chile, China, Colombia, Czechoslovakia, Ethiopia, the GDR, Indonesia, Iraq, Israel, Kenya, Peru, Romania, South Africa, Turkey, and the

109. From the context it appears that "humanitarian cases" should be understood as "individual cases." No details were made public on representations made in 1987. In 1988, approximately fifty démarches were made by the Twelve, but only those directed at Israel and South Africa were made public. See Annual Report on Action Taken by the Twelve in the Field of Human Rights, 8 May 1989, 5 *European Political Cooperation Documentation Bulletin* (1989), no. 1, p. 155.
    110. 19 *Bull. EC* (1986), no. 7/8, para. 2.4.3.
    111. 19 *Bull. EC* (1986), no. 12, para. 2.4.3.
    112. 32 *AFDI* (1986), p. 992.
    113. 30 *AFDI* (1984), p. 984, and 31 *AFDI* (1985), p. 992.

USSR.[114] In May 1989, the Australian Foreign Minister reported that during the past twelve months Australia had raised over four hundred human rights cases with sixty-eight different countries. These representations concerned both individual cases and situations of widespread and systematic abuse. Responses had been received in 25 percent of these cases, and some form of positive result had been achieved in at least 14 percent of the cases. The minister stated that although some representations had met with resistance or even hostility on the part of individual officials, there had been no identifiable instance where a country had retaliated in economic or other unrelated areas to human rights criticisms.[115]

In sum, the declared policies and actual practices of Western states constitute ample proof of their collective conviction that if the human rights of foreign nationals have been violated, diplomatic expressions of disapproval are permitted under customary international law.[116] This applies particularly, but not exclusively, if the violations suffered are both gross and the result of a consistent governmental policy. However, Western states have generally been reluctant to go a step further by presenting their intercessions as international legal claims. Their intercessions tend to express concern and request information rather than to formally insist on compliance with specific human rights obligations binding on the offending state. This may partly explain the striking preference of Western states to base their representations to East European states on the Helsinki Final Act rather than on legally binding human rights instruments. The United States is perhaps the most typical exponent of this approach. It clearly considers itself entitled to make representations to other states on behalf of non-nationals, and it does not contest the right of other states to make such representations to the United States. But it is most reluctant to subject itself to representations that may be presented as formal claims under international law.

This limited use of the available arsenal tends to be justified by Western policymakers on grounds of effectiveness. They argue that the presentation of formal legal claims on behalf of foreign victims of

---

114. 60 *BYIL* (1989), pp. 612–24.

115. Keynote address by Senator Gareth Evans, Minister for Foreign Affairs and Trade, to the National Annual General Meeting of Amnesty International Australia, Sydney, 19 May 1989 (not published).

116. A 1983 Chatham House colloquium convened by the American Association for the International Commission of Jurists and attended by senior foreign ministry officials responsible for human rights in eleven Western states concluded that "intervention in the sense of governments expressing disapproval of improper behaviour is broadly accepted as an appropriate form of response." See American Association for the International Commission of Jurists, *Human Rights & Foreign Policy: The Role of Government* (1985), p. 13.

human rights violations risks being regarded as a highly unfriendly act by offending states.[117] The suggestion is that pressing such claims is often not the most effective strategy to achieve the desired result. The problem with this "political" approach, however, is that it risks being regarded by the offending state as an exercise in imperialist power diplomacy rather than as a legitimate exercise of international law. It is one thing for the International Committee of the Red Cross in its work on behalf of political prisoners to choose not to rely on an offending state's formal obligations under international law.[118] It is quite another for a major Western power to follow the same course. The offending state may thus be led to perceive intercessions as part of a political bargaining process rather than as an effort to make it comply with its international obligations. Under the so-called *Freikauf* policy, for example, thousands of political prisoners in the German Democratic Republic were until recently permitted to emigrate to the Federal Republic of Germany each year in return for payment by the FRG Government.[119] Cases have also been reported in which the authorities of an offending state, in return for the requested release of a political prisoner, expected personal favors from the interceding consular official, such as special assistance in obtaining visas.[120]

There is little or no evidence in the practice of West European states, however, to support the thesis that they would consider such legal claims as impermissible under customary international law. The choice to avoid such claims is based on tactical considerations rather than legal constraints.

3.2 East European States

It seems fair to assume that, as a result of the profound political changes in Eastern Europe during the late 1980s, the attitude of East

117. Cf., for example, the testimony by George H. Aldrich, Acting Legal Adviser, U.S. Department of State, before the Subcommittee on International Organizations and Movements of the House Foreign Affairs Committee, on 20 September 1973: "While there is no question, from a legal point of view, that the protection of human rights is a matter of legitimate international concern, most countries still regard statements directed to them about their activities involving the human rights of their own citizens as interference in their own internal affairs and as politically unfriendly. This is true of both democratic and autocratic governments, and it is a reality that profoundly affects our dealings with foreign governments on human rights issues." See *Digest of United States Practice in International Law*, 1973, pp. 122–23.

118. Cf. J. Moreillon, *Le comité international de la Croix-Rouge et la protection des détenus politiques* (1973), p. 190.

119. See, for example, *Amnesty International Report 1987*, p. 294.

120. D. C. McGaffey, "Policy and Practice: Human Rights in the Shah's Iran," in *The Diplomacy of Human Rights*, (1986), D. D. Newsom (ed.), p. 73.

European states toward the concept of inter-state accountability for violations of human rights will now change correspondingly. Important East European states, such as the Soviet Union, the German Democratic Republic and Yugoslavia, no longer exist and new states are being created at breakneck speed. Nevertheless, for two reasons it remains instructive to examine the attitude of East European states during the 1970s and early 1980s. First, because the East European views put forward in this period represent the most sophisticated doctrine formulated so far to oppose the idea of inter-state accountability for violations of human rights. And, second, because Eastern Europe is no longer the standard-bearer of this philosophy, other states— such as China or Cuba—may well feel compelled to take over the banner.

The policies and practices of the states belonging to the East European Group of States until recently exhibited such a degree of similarity that they can be conveniently discussed together. Unfortunately, for these states the type of information that is available on Western Europe cannot be obtained. There are no governmental policy papers and no governmental replies to questions posed by members of parliament. There are, of course, statements made by East European government representatives in multilateral fora, such as the United Nations and the Conference on Security and Co-operation in Europe. But such statements tend to address the circumstances under which the particular forum is competent to deal with human rights abuses in a given country. They usually shed little light on the question to be examined in this chapter, that is, the extent to which a state can be held directly accountable by other states for the way it has observed international human rights standards.

Nevertheless, this question has been explored by a number of Soviet scholars,[121] and their views represent a reasonably coherent doctrine. The writings of these publicists cannot have the same authority

121. A. P. Movchan, "The Human Rights Problem in Present-Day International Law," in *Contemporary International Law* (1969), G. Tunkin (ed.), pp. 233–50. G. I. Tunkin, *Theory of International Law* (1974), pp. 81–83. V. Kartashkin, "Human Rights and Peaceful Coexistence," 9 *HRJ* (1976), pp. 5–20. *Id.*, "International Relations and Human Rights," *International Affairs* (Moscow), 1977, no. 8, pp. 29–38. V. Chkhikvadze, "Human Rights and Non-Interference in the Internal Affairs of States," *International Affairs* (Moscow), 1978, no. 12, pp. 22–30. Y. Rechetov, "International Responsibility for Violations of Human Rights," in *UN Law/Fundamental Rights* (1979), A. Cassese (ed.), pp. 237–48. G. Ostroumov and S. Belenkov, "Socialist Foreign Policy and Human Rights," *International Affairs* (Moscow), 1982, no. 5, pp. 30–38. V. Chkhikvadze, "Inter-state Cooperation on Human Rights," *International Affairs* (Moscow), 1985, no. 11, pp. 29–36. V. A. Tumanov, "International Protection of Human Rights: Soviet Report," in *International Enforcement of Human Rights* (1987), R. Bernhardt and J. A. Jolowicz (eds.), pp. 21–24.

as the official pronouncements of government representatives. But all of these authors were either Soviet officials or members of academic institutions closely linked to the former Soviet Government. Some were also members of UN human rights bodies.[122] It must be assumed that they would not have reached and maintained these positions if the Soviet Government had not approved of their ideas on this sensitive matter. Their collective views may therefore be regarded as a reliable substitute for Soviet *opinio juris*. An additional source of information on the attitude of the Soviet Union toward the international protection of human rights consists of a number of studies by Western authors and Soviet scholars who have emigrated to the West.[123]

The overriding impression that strikes the student of Soviet writings published on this question until a few years ago is their defensive character. Their main purpose appears to have been to reduce to a bare minimum a state's international accountability for any breaches of human rights obligations. Unlike many of their Western counterparts, Soviet scholars tended to exhibit little or no sense of international solidarity in their essays on this subject. Although these writers liked to portray the Soviet Union as the main *auctor intellectualis* of UN human rights instruments,[124] the emphasis in their publications was on the sovereign equality of states rather than on human rights. Much importance was attached to a state's right to determine its own political system without outside interference. Attention was drawn to Article 2(7) of the UN Charter, Article 1(1) of the International Covenant on Civil and Political Rights and Principle I of the Helsinki Final Act rather than to the human rights provisions in these same instru-

---

122. Anatoly Movchan was a member of the Human Rights Committee set up under the International Covenant on Civil and Political Rights from its inception in 1977 until 1988. Viktor Chkhikvadze has been an alternate member of the UN Sub-Commission on Prevention of Discrimination and Protection of Minorities.

123. E.g., G. Hafner, "Die Souveränität in Beziehung zur Einzelperson gemäss der sowjetischen Völkerrechtsdoktrin," 4 *EuGRZ* (1977), pp. 220–28; R. N. Dean, "Beyond Helsinki: The Soviet View of Human Rights in International Law," 21 *Virginia Journal of International Law* (1981), pp. 55–95; F. Jhabvala, "The Soviet Bloc's View of the Implementation of Human Rights Accords," 7 *HRQ* (1985), pp. 461–91; A. Bloed and F. van Hoof, "Some Aspects of the Socialist View of Human Rights," in *Essays on Human Rights in the Helsinki Process* (1985), A. Bloed and P. van Dijk (eds.), pp. 29–55; O. S. Ioffe, "Soviet Attitudes toward International Human Rights Law," 2 *Connecticut Journal of International Law* (1987), pp. 361–65.

124. With regard to the Universal Declaration of Human Rights, this is a rather dubious assertion. On 10 December 1948, the USSR abstained on the adoption of this instrument. Its representative in the General Assembly, Mr. Vyshinsky, stated on that occasion that "[t]he USSR delegation had pointed out that a number of articles completely ignored the sovereign rights of democratic Governments, moreover, that the draft contained provisions directly contradicting those of the Charter, which prohibited interference in the internal affairs of States." See GAOR, 183d plenary meeting, p. 923.

ments. In support of their interpretations, Soviet scholars tended to rely on the *travaux préparatoires* rather than on the way these instruments had actually been applied through state practice.

The underlying reason for this defensiveness was the apparent conviction of the authors that the Soviet Union had more to lose than to gain from international disputes over the implementation of international human rights standards. As Viktor Chkhikvadze disarmingly put it: "It should be emphasized that the human rights issue is being employed most frequently as a pretext for imperialist interference in the internal affairs of other countries. It is generally known that the main thrust of this activity has been directed at the socialist countries."[125] Another argument put forward by Soviet publicists was that if states were permitted to complain to each other of violations of human rights, this would lead to increased international tensions. According to Vladimir Kartashkin: "If states were given the right to arbitrarily interfere in each other's domestic affairs to correct imaginary or real breaches of the rights of individuals, the world would be plunged into chaos, anarchy and endless conflicts."[126]

This view was in apparent contradiction with the doctrine expressed on other occasions that human rights violations may reach such a level that they threaten international peace and security and thereby become a matter of international concern. Professor Grigory Tunkin emphasized "that a close link exists between a state's ensuring basic human rights and freedoms and the maintenance of international peace and security," although he failed to explain the consequences of this statement.[127] In reality, Soviet scholars appear to have regarded international expressions of concern at human rights abuses as a cause of international tensions when these were directed at themselves or their allies, but as a useful tool to reduce such tensions when protests were directed at their ideological enemies.

The Soviet Union's restrictive attitude applied particularly to the rights of individuals. Soviet doctrine held that individuals are not subjects of international law. Accordingly, it comes as no surprise that in the view of Soviet authors, individual victims of human rights violations were not in a position to avail themselves of international remedies.[128] Chkhikvadze was again frank with his explanations: "The idea to grant international organs the right to examine complaints by individuals against their governments is fraught with grave danger to

125. Chkhikvadze, "Human Rights and Non-Interference in the Internal Affairs of States," *supra* note 121, p. 27.
126. Kartashkin, "International Relations and Human Rights," *supra* note 121, p. 36.
127. Tunkin, *supra* note 121, p. 81.
128. Movchan, *supra* note 121, pp. 239–40.

national sovereignty. Under the guise of concern for human rights and freedoms, it was really devised to give imperialist circles a free hand in interfering in the internal affairs of other countries."[129]

In his eagerness to argue that human rights treaties do not grant rights directly to individuals, Tunkin conceded that such instruments do establish "mutual obligations of states to grant such rights to individuals." Other Soviet authors would not go even that far. They maintained that since the obligations contained in human rights treaties are usually not sufficiently clearly defined, compliance cannot be insisted upon by the other states parties.[130] A second line of defense held that the only permissible international supervisory activity was that which had been specifically included in the treaty in question, even if it was merely optional. If such a treaty-based supervisory machinery had been established, states were thereby prevented from exercising any other remedies to obtain compliance by the other states parties.[131]

Soviet doctrine did not claim that states were not bound by the human rights obligations they had undertaken. It held simply that the implementation of those obligations through municipal law was entirely an internal affair of the state concerned. As Tunkin put it, human rights are not "directly regulated" by international law.[132] Kartashkin went to great lengths to demonstrate that the terms *international protection* and *international implementation* of human rights were misguided.[133] In fact, his argument was semantic rather than substantive. International law allows states to follow either a monistic or a dualistic path to ensure compliance with international obligations. No one has claimed, moreover, that the actual task of transforming and ensuring the observance of international human rights standards at the domestic level is the responsibility of anyone else but the national authorities. A related theory, adhered to also by some Western authors, maintained that states themselves have retained the right to make authoritative interpretations of their international obligations.[134]

Whatever may be the merits of these theories, the fact remains that

129. Chkhikvadze, "Human Rights and Non-Interference in the Internal Affairs of States," *supra* note 121, p. 28.

130. Rechetov, *supra* note 121, p. 240.

131. See, for example, the statement by Mr. Lopatka (Poland) in the UN Commission on Human Rights, 5 March 1982, UN Doc. E/CN.4/1982/SR.51/Add.1, pp. 18–21. For a discussion of this argument, see *infra*, Chapter 3, section 2.6.

132. Tunkin, *supra* note 121, pp. 82–83.

133. Kartashkin, "Human Rights and Peaceful Coexistence," *supra* note 121, pp. 7–11.

134. See *infra* Chapter 2, notes 31 and 247.

the official Soviet view was for many years that, in spite of international obligations in the field of human rights, states cannot in principle be held accountable by other states unless they have specifically given their consent.[135] This is the heart of the matter.

But what is the current attitude of East European states? First of all, it must be noted that although other East European scholars have tended to follow the lead of their Soviet counterparts on this issue, there has never been absolute unanimity. As early as 1976, the Polish scholar Anna Michalska wrote provocatively, "Under present realities, the thesis that the leaving of human rights to the exclusive competence of the state is the only progressive and democratic solution is unacceptable." She added that in contrast to other fields of international law where states must establish a direct legal interest before they can bring a claim, "in the field of the international protection of human rights, States are slowly agreeing to a different principle. A State may start an international action in order that another State fulfill its international obligations concerning human rights; this is so because human rights have been recognized as values in respect of which each State has an interest."[136]

Even in the Cold War period, East European states in the context of international human rights conventions agreed to a number of quasi-judicial procedures, thereby demonstrating that in practice the lines were not always drawn as tightly as they were in theory.[137] They accepted the inclusion of the right of inter-state complaint as an integral part of the Convention on the Elimination of All Forms of Racial Discrimination,[138] and they subsequently became parties to this treaty. They accepted the inclusion of an inquiry procedure in the UN Convention against Torture and Other Cruel, Inhuman or Degrading Treatment or Punishment,[139] although they initially made a reservation to this provision when becoming parties. They accepted the adoption of an Optional Protocol to the International Covenant on Civil and Political Rights that enables individual victims of violations of the Covenant to submit complaints to the Human Rights Commit-

135. Jhabvala, *supra* note 123, p. 491.
136. A. Michalska, *Podstawowe prawa czowieka w prawie wewnatrznym a pakty pruw cztowieka* [The Basic Human Rights in Internal Law and the Covenants on Human Rights] (1976), pp. 167–69, quoted in R. Szawlowski, "The International Protection of Human Rights—a Soviet and Polish View," 28 *ICLQ* (1979), pp. 779–80.
137. See M. Nowak, "The Attitude of Socialist States Towards the Implementation of UN Human Rights Conventions," 6 *SIM Newsletter* (1988), no. 1, pp. 85–89.
138. Art. 11. Convention adopted by UNGA Resolution 2106 A (XX) of 21 December 1965.
139. Art. 20. Convention adopted by UNGA Resolution 39/46 of 10 December 1984.

tee. Although they did not initially become parties to the Optional Protocol, the East European members of the Human Rights Committee actively participated in its implementation.

In the second half of the 1980s, the attitude of East European states relaxed even further, and this trend was reflected in their acceptance of new treaty obligations. In 1988, Hungary acceded to the Optional Protocol to the International Covenant on Civil and Political Rights. In 1989, the Soviet Union withdrew the reservations it had maintained against the compulsory jurisdiction of the International Court of Justice to consider disputes on the interpretation and application of six major UN human rights treaties.[140] The Soviet Union also announced that it would in due course become a party to the Optional Protocol to the International Covenant on Civil and Political Rights.[141]

There is not much evidence yet that East European governments themselves have begun to intercede more actively on behalf of victims of human rights violations in other countries with which they have no ethnic connections. But it is clear that when these states are on the receiving side of such representations these days, they seldom claim that such intercessions constitute impermissible interference in their internal affairs. Where this used to be a standard response, it now occurs less and less frequently.[142] Official reactions such as were given in response to expressions of concern about the fate of Andrei Sakharov are now unlikely to happen. A similar change of policy may be observed in multilateral fora, such as the United Nations and the Conference on Security and Co-operation in Europe (to be discussed below).

East European scholars have as yet produced little writing that clearly reflects new thinking on the issue of inter-state accountability for violations of human rights. One exception, however, is Chkhikvadze, author of some of the hard-line views cited above and until 1987 an alternate member of the UN Sub-Commission on Prevention of Discrimination and Protection of Minorities. In 1988 he adopted a totally new approach when he wrote that "[t]here are no reasons why

140. Convention on the Prevention and Punishment of the Crime of Genocide; Convention for the Suppression of the Traffic in Persons and of the Exploitation of the Prostitution of Others; Convention on the Political Rights of Women; International Convention on the Elimination of All Forms of Racial Discrimination; Convention on the Elimination of All Forms of Discrimination against Women; and Convention against Torture and Other Cruel, Inhuman or Degrading Treatment or Punishment. Letter reproduced in 83 *AJIL* (1989), p. 457.

141. Mr. Adamishin (USSR), 8 March 1989, UN Doc. E/CN.4/1989/SR.55, para. 15.

142. Netherlands Minister of Foreign Affairs, "Het beleid ten aanzien van Oost-Europa, Joegoslavië en Albanië" [Memorandum on Netherlands policy towards Eastern Europe, Yugoslavia and Albania], 25 May 1988, Tweede Kamer, vergaderjaar 1987–1988, 20564, nr. 2, p. 25.

we should exhibit extreme sensitivity in discussing in international agencies and conferences the issue of rights and freedoms of citizens in the USSR." He also observed that sovereignty should not be used as a "brake" on cooperation between states on human rights.[143] Y. A. Rechetov, another scholar who formerly held restrictive views, has also adopted quite a different approach in his new capacity as his country's representative in the Third Committee of the UN General Assembly:

[E]ach country could legitimately take a position in regard to another country which flouted individual freedoms. His country believed that international monitoring did not constitute interference in the internal affairs of States if it was free of bias, ideological connotations or ulterior political motives. On the contrary, the more States participated in the system of international monitoring, the more likely the community's stated objectives were to be fulfilled.[144]

An authority not tainted by association with Cold War schools of thought is R. A. Mullerson, Director of the International Law Section of the Institute of State and Law of the Academy of Sciences of the USSR and a current member of the (UN) Human Rights Committee, who has written:

It is not, of course, appropriate to regard as interference in internal affairs any statements, even by official persons, on the state of human rights in another state, especially if these statements are in line with reality. Equally, it is hardly possible to regard as interference in internal affairs questions and approaches by leaders of one state to the leadership of another state in connection with the fate of specific individuals. This is particularly so where such approaches are of a confidential nature and are not undertaken for propaganda purposes.
    However, one of the necessary conditions for the legality of interference by other states, . . . in questions of the safeguarding of human rights in another state, is the presence of actual and systematic breaches of human rights.[145]

If these pronouncements are indeed representative of the current East European view of the matter, this is of course a giant step forward, compared to the official opinion held by the USSR until the mid-1980s. Instead of the basically negative undertone that has dominated Soviet officialese for so long, here we have an essentially posi-

143. Quoted in J. Quigley, "Human Rights Study in Soviet Academia," 11 *HRQ* (1989), p. 457.
    144. Mr. Y. A. Rechetov (USSR), 27 November 1990, UN Doc. A/C.3/45/SR.53, para. 88.
    145. R. A. Mullerson, "Human Rights and the Individual as Subject of International Law: A Soviet View," 1 *European Journal of International Law* (1990), pp. 42–43.

tive attitude toward inter-state accountability for violations of human rights. It is important to recognize, however, that the doctrine outlined here contains one proviso never cited by Western governments: for an intercession to be acceptable, the motives of the interceding state must be pure and genuine. There are still echoes here of the attempts by some socialist states to promote adoption by the UN General Assembly of a resolution that would have condemned "the exploitation or distortion of human rights issues for interference in the internal affairs of States."[146] The persistent supporters of this idea seem to overlook the unfortunate fact that it is very rare indeed for an offending state to accept that an interceding state may be motivated by genuine concern for human rights, irrespective of the nationality of the victims.

3.3 The Conference on Security and Co-operation in Europe

The confrontation between East European and Western schools of thought on the question of international accountability for human rights violations appeared most clearly in the context of the Conference on Security and Co-operation in Europe (CSCE). The Declaration of Principles of the 1975 Helsinki Final Act[147] is an obvious example of a package deal containing elements favored by each camp.[148] The East European signatories long tended to emphasize Principle I (sover-

146. See the Preface of this study.
147. Final Act of the Conference on Security and Co-operation in Europe, adopted at Helsinki, 1 August 1975, reproduced in 14 *ILM* (1975), pp. 1292–325 and 70 *AJIL* (1976), pp. 417–21 (Declaration of Principles only).
148. There is a vast literature on the Final Act and its implications. Useful general reviews include H. S. Russell, "The Helsinki Declaration: Brobdingnag or Lilliput?" 70 *AJIL* (1976), pp. 242–72; and P. van Dijk, "The Final Act of Helsinki—Basis for a Pan-European System?" 11 *NYIL* (1980), pp. 97–124. Of the literature focusing specifically on the Final Act's human rights aspects, three collections of essays are particularly helpful: Th. Buergenthal (ed.), *Human Rights, International Law and the Helsinki Accord* (1977); A. Bloed and P. van Dijk (eds.), *Essays on Human Rights in the Helsinki Process* (1985); and A. Bloed and P. van Dijk (eds.), *The Human Dimension of the Helsinki Process* (1991). See also G. Arangio-Ruiz, "Human Rights and Non-Intervention in the Helsinki Final Act," 157 *RCADI* (1977), pp. 199–331; O. Kimminich, "Konferenz über Sicherheit und Zusammenarbeit in Europa und Menschenrechte," 17 *ArchVR* (1977/78), pp. 274–94; L. Hannikainen, "Human Rights and Non-Intervention in the Final Act of the CSCE," 48 *Nordisk Tidsskrift for International Ret* (1979), pp. 27–37; U. Beyerlin, "Menschenrechte und Intervention," in *Zwischen Intervention und Zusammenarbeit* (1979), B. Simma and E. Blenk-Knocke (eds.), pp. 157–99; V. Dimitrijevic, "The Place of Helsinki on the Long Road to Human Rights," 13 *Vanderbilt Journal of Transnational Law* (1980), pp. 253–73 (see also the other articles on the Final Act in this issue of the *Vanderbilt Journal*); A. Manin, "The Helsinki Final Act and Human Rights," 4 *Chinese Yearbook of International Law and Affairs* (1984), pp. 175–83; M. J. Bossuyt, "Human Rights and Non-Intervention in Domestic Matters," *Review of the International Commission of Jurists* (1985), no. 35, pp. 45–52.

eign equality, respect for the rights inherent in sovereignty) and Principle VI (non-intervention in internal affairs), while the Western signatories tended to draw near-exclusive attention to Principle VII (respect for human rights and fundamental freedoms, including the freedom of thought, conscience, religion or belief). Some of the Western media even fell into the habit of referring to the "Helsinki accords on human rights." In the heat of the propaganda battle, little attention was paid to Principle X, which provides unambiguously that each of the principles must be interpreted taking into account the others.

From a legal point of view, the reasons for the initial excitement about the human rights provisions of the Final Act are not immediately obvious. The Final Act is a political rather than a legal document,[149] and it does not in itself create binding legal obligations.[150] Nevertheless, given the effort that went into it and the level at which it was adopted, it may be regarded as a potential source of customary international law.[151] Moreover, while a breach by a participating state cannot in itself serve as a basis for invoking that state's formal international responsibility, the Final Act and its follow-up documents offer a basis for inter-state accountability (that is, diplomatic representations) regarding their implementation.[152]

As far as its contents are concerned, the Final Act is not a very innovative instrument. It closely follows existing international law, particularly as codified in the UN Declaration on Friendly Relations.[153] Unlike the Declaration on Friendly Relations, however, it combines provisions on non-interference with provisions on human rights. It thus more clearly resembles the system of the UN Charter,[154] which may help to explain what the common ground was—if any—between East European and Western states on the question of international accountability for violations of human rights.

Although Principle VI is obviously inspired by its equivalent in the Friendly Relations Declaration, there are some subtle differences between the two. The Western objective was to restrict the prohibition of intervention by explicitly limiting it to coercive intervention. This

149. Editorial comment by N. MacDermot, *The Review of the International Commission of Jurists*, 1977, no. 18, p. 15.

150. Buergenthal, *supra* note 148, p. 6.

151. Russell, *supra* note 148, pp. 247–48.

152. O. Schachter, "The Twilight Existence of Nonbinding International Agreements," 71 *AJIL* (1977), pp. 296–304.

153. Declaration on Principles of International Law concerning Friendly Relations and Co-operation among States in accordance with the Charter of the United Nations, UNGA Resolution 2625 (XXV) of 24 October 1970.

154. See *infra*, Chapter 2, section 2.

would have left peaceful diplomatic intercessions between the participating states unequivocally outside the scope of Principle VI. This strategy did not entirely succeed, however. "Coercion" appears in the third paragraph of Principle VI as a subcategory or an example of intervention. It is not an integral element of the definition of intervention as provided in the first paragraph of Principle VI.[155] Nevertheless, because Principle VII does not in so many words prohibit noncoercive methods of intervention, such methods must be deemed to be permitted. This interpretation is supported by the fact that, unlike the Friendly Relations Declaration, Principle VI lacks the obscure prohibition of "all other forms of interference." Furthermore, Principle VI states explicitly that the prohibition of intervention applies only to matters within domestic jurisdiction. In the Friendly Relations Declaration this has to be deduced from the title of the relevant provision rather than from the provision itself.

The East European states, for their part, were not successful in their halfhearted attempt to broaden the prohibition contained in Principle VI from "intervention" to the wider concept of "interference."[156] They did manage, however, to obtain new language in Principle I according to which the participating states would respect each state's "right to determine its laws and regulations."

The fact that the Final Act, unlike the Declaration on Friendly Relations, contains a provision on human rights may be regarded as a significant upgrading of this aspect of international law. However, the seasoned observer of intergovernmental cooperation in the field of human rights is unlikely to be impressed by the contents of Principle VII. The Principle does not establish a new pan-European catalogue of human rights. Instead, it reminds the reader of the generalities contained in the human rights provisions of the Charter of the United Nations. Surely not a compliment for an instrument drafted thirty years later!

"Basket" Three of the Final Act, entitled "Co-operation in Humanitarian and Other Fields," contains, it is true, some more specific elements. But here again the provisions often appear to remain below the level of binding undertakings already accepted by the large majority of the participating states.[157] For example, the Basket's vague statements of intent with regard to "human contacts" do not compare

155. Russell, *supra* note 148, p. 267.
156. The Russian term *vmeshatel'stvo* can mean both *interference* and *intervention*. See Bloed and van Dijk, "Human Rights and Non-Intervention," in Bloed and van Dijk, *supra* note 148, pp. 66–67.
157. For a critical assessment, see V. Chalidze, "The Humanitarian Provisions of the Helsinki Accord: A Critique of their Significance," 13 *Vanderbilt Journal of International Law* (1980), pp. 429–50.

very favorably with the obligation to permit everyone to leave any country, including his or her own, contained in Article 12(2) of the International Covenant on Civil and Political Rights. Moreover, the legal status of Basket Three is even more modest than that of the Declaration of Principles. In the former the participating states for the most part simply "declare their readiness" to take "measures which they consider appropriate" and "express their intention" to "favourably consider" certain applications. The concluding documents of the first two follow-up meetings added little substance.[158] Only at the third follow-up meeting, held in Vienna from 1986 to 1989, were some substantial new undertakings agreed upon in the areas "human contacts" and "information."[159] A meeting on the "human dimension" held in Copenhagen in 1990 finally added some significant commitments, particularly on the rule of law and free and fair elections.[160]

It is not surprising, therefore, that the drafters of the Final Act attempted to strengthen their text by inserting references to existing international human rights instruments. Principle VII provides that the participating states will fulfill their human rights obligations as set forth in the international declarations and agreements by which they may be bound, including the International Covenants on Human Rights. This does not appear very significant; an agreement does not become more binding than it is already through such a statement. More significant is the proviso that the participating states will act in conformity with the Universal Declaration of Human Rights. This particularly affects those participating states that have not so far become parties to any of the major international human rights agreements (currently Albania, Estonia, the Holy See, Latvia, Lithuania, Monaco, and the United States). It is perhaps the closest the United States has yet come to formally accepting the main UN human rights standards.

To what extent, then, is each of the participating states entitled to insist on compliance with Principle VII (in conjunction with Basket

158. The Concluding Document of the Belgrade meeting, adopted at Belgrade on 8 March 1978, does not mention human rights at all. See 17 *ILM* (1978), pp. 414–16. The Concluding Document of the Madrid meeting, adopted at Madrid on 9 September 1983, contains some minor new elements and employs somewhat stronger language ("The participating States . . . Agree now to implement the following"). Reproduced in 22 *ILM* (1983), pp. 1398–1405.

159. Concluding Document of the Vienna Meeting, reproduced in 28 *ILM* (1989), pp. 543–46.

160. Document of the Copenhagen Meeting of the Conference on the Human Dimension of the CSCE, reproduced in 29 *ILM* (1990), pp. 1306–22. See also the Charter of Paris for a New Europe, that confirms the Copenhagen results, reproduced in 30 *ILM* (1991), pp. 193–208.

Three) by each of the others? Principle X provides that all principles contained in the Declaration of Principles are of primary significance and that each shall be interpreted taking into account the others. Accordingly, neither the old East European school of thought, which relied primarily on Principles I and VI, nor the Western school of thought which relied primarily on Principle VII, can be accepted. An attempt must be made to reconcile these provisions with each other. Two types of action may be distinguished: demands for compliance made in the context of the follow-up conferences and demands made directly between the participating states. In the final clauses of the Final Act, the participating states "declare their resolve" to proceed to a "thorough exchange of views" on the implementation of its provisions.

In order to exclude the human rights provisions of the Final Act from the scope of this review process, it would have to be necessary to argue that such a review would constitute intervention in matters falling within domestic jurisdiction as prescribed in Principle VI. This assertion fails on two grounds. First, as explained above, Principle VI does not prohibit noncoercive intercessions. Second, no support can be found in the Final Act for the view that the participating states intended to leave the supervision of the implementation of the human rights provisions to each other's exclusive domestic jurisdiction. Arie Bloed and Pieter van Dijk have concluded on the basis of a study of the *travaux préparatoires* that Soviet attempts to incorporate this view into the Final Act were unsuccessful.[161]

Subsequent practice increasingly bears out this interpretation. Although the first follow-up meeting in Belgrade was still fairly antagonistic, instances of businesslike discussions on human rights issues were reported from the second follow-up meeting in Madrid.[162] A significant breakthrough with regard to inter-state accountability for violations of human rights occurred at the third follow-up meeting in Vienna, which ended in January 1989. According to the concluding document of the Vienna meeting, the participating states recognized the need to improve the implementation of their CSCE commitments and their cooperation in the area referred to as the "human dimension" of the CSCE (this includes human rights, human contacts, and other humanitarian issues). They therefore decided:

161. Bloed and van Dijk, "Human Rights and Non-intervention," in Bloed and van Dijk, *supra* note 148, pp. 70–71. Hannikainen also concludes that violations of human rights may be raised at the follow-up conferences but adds that participating states should do this in a non-accusatory way "unless they have a valid reason for it." Hannikainen, *supra* note 148, pp. 30–35.
162. Bloed and van Dijk, *supra* note 161, p. 71.

1. to exchange information and respond to requests for information and to representations made to them by the other participating States on questions relating to the human dimension of the CSCE. Such communications may be forwarded through diplomatic channels or be addressed to any agency designated for these purposes;

2. to hold bilateral meetings with other participating States that so request, in order to examine questions relating to the human dimension of the CSCE, including situations and specific cases with a view to resolving them. The date and place of such meetings will be arranged by mutual agreement through diplomatic channels;

3. that any participating State which deems it necessary may bring situations and cases in the human dimensions of the CSCE, including those which have been raised at the bilateral meetings described in paragraph 2, to the attention of other participating States through diplomatic channels;

4. that any participating State which deems it necessary may provide information on the exchange of information and the responses to its requests for information and to representations (paragraph 1) and on the results of the bilateral meetings (paragraph 2), including information concerning situations and specific cases, at the meetings of the Conference of the Human Dimension as well as the main CSCE Follow-up Meetings.[163]

This new "mechanism" thus contains four components: (1) a duty of offending states to respond to representations and to provide relevant information; (2) a duty of offending states to consult on specific cases and situations with a view to resolving them; (3) a right of interceding states to inform other participating states; (4) a right of interceding states to raise cases and situations at CSCE meetings. The mechanism's most advanced aspect is the duty to consult on cases and situations "with a view to resolving them," as set out in component 2. This goes considerably beyond a mere duty to exchange information and suggests that participating states have an actual say in the way other states ought to treat their own citizens in specific circumstances. It is also noteworthy that the scope of the mechanism is not limited to situations or patterns of serious violations. Individual cases are also covered.

Unlike the formal inter-state complaints procedures established under most of the main human rights treaties, the Vienna mechanism has not remained a dead letter. By the end of October 1990, it had already been used more than a hundred times, mostly by Western states against East European states, but also in some cases by East European states against Western states.[164] The degree of cooperation offered by offending states appears to have been high.

163. 28 *ILM* (1989), p. 547.
164. See A. Bloed and P. van Dijk, "Supervisory Mechanism for the Human Dimension of the CSCE: Its Setting-up in Vienna, its Present Functioning and its Possible Development towards a General Procedure for the Peaceful Settlement of CSCE Dis-

Further significant steps were taken at the Moscow meeting on the human dimension that ended in October 1991. The concluding document of this meeting[165] contains, first of all, an emphatic statement of principle that rivals similar statements made in the context of the European Community and the Council of Europe. The participating states "categorically and irrevocably declare that the commitments undertaken in the field of the human dimension of the CSCE are matters of direct and legitimate concern to all participating States and do not belong exclusively to the internal affairs of the State concerned." This certainly represents a far cry from the tiresome CSCE discussions on this subject during the 1970s and 1980s.

The Moscow document also provides for a procedure whereby independent experts or rapporteurs may be appointed to investigate human rights violations on the territory of an offending state. If ten participating states (about a quarter of the states participating in the CSCE) consider that a particularly serious threat to the fulfilment of the provisions of the CSCE human dimension has arisen, rapporteurs may even visit an offending state without its specific consent. The offending state is obliged to let the mission enter its territory and to grant it all the access necessary for the exercise of its functions. It remains to be seen, of course, how effective this procedure will turn out to be in practice. It is difficult to imagine that such missions will be undertaken without at least the tacit approval of the offending state, if only because the physical security of the rapporteurs will need to be guaranteed. But on paper at least, the Moscow procedure represents an interesting deviation from the principle so far generally accepted in international human rights monitoring that the sending of a fact-finding mission into the territory of a state without its specific permission constitutes unacceptable interference in its internal affairs.

As a result of the work done within the CSCE, a significant amount of common ground between two initially highly antagonistic schools of thought has therefore been established on the question of interstate accountability for violations of human rights. It has been established, both through the text of the Final Act itself and through subsequent state practice, that participating states are entitled to insist on the compliance of the others with the Final Act's human rights provisions and through it with the provisions of international agreements by which they may be bound. The provisional culmination of

---

putes," in *The Human Dimension of the Helsinki Process* (1991), A. Bloed and P. van Dijk (eds.), p. 79; and F. Coomans and L. Lijnzaad, "Initiating the CSCE Supervisory Procedure: The Case of the Netherlands and Czechoslovakia," *ibid.*, pp. 109–27.

165. Document of the Moscow Meeting of the Conference on the Human Dimension of the CSCE, 3 October 1991, reproduced in 30 *ILM* (1991), pp. 1670–91.

the consensus-building process on this question has been the mechanism adopted at the Vienna meeting, followed by the procedure for appointing rapporteurs adopted at the Moscow meeting. The Vienna mechanism—which provides for an implicit right to intercede and an explicit duty to provide information and to consult—constitutes the most comprehensive and authoritative definition so far of the concept of inter-state accountability for violations of human rights. Like the Final Act, the Vienna meeting's concluding document is not in itself a binding legal instrument and the mechanism therefore does not in itself have binding force. As a carefully negotiated compromise between East and West, however, it represents strong evidence of the existence of a duty of inter-state accountability under general international law.

3.4 The Lomé Conventions

An analysis has so far been made of the general attitude of the Western Group of States, the East European Group of States, and the common ground established between their two schools of thought in the context of the Conference on Security and Co-operation in Europe. A logical next step would now be to consider the attitude of the remaining group of states, the Group of 77 or the Non-Aligned Movement. A study could be made, for example, of the resolutions adopted at conferences of the Non-Aligned Movement. Such a study would no doubt reveal a shared suspicion that intercessions by Western states under the guise of concern about human rights are in fact inspired by neo-colonialist or imperialist motives. Beyond this general sentiment, however, few elements of the debate that have not been considered so far are likely to be identified.[166]

As a more promising exercise, an examination will be made of the confrontation between a large part of the Western Group (the member states of the European Community) and a significant part of the Non-Aligned Movement (the so-called ACP states: currently sixty-nine states in Africa, the Caribbean, and the Pacific) in the context of the Lomé Conventions.[167] The views of the ACP states may be considered broadly representative of those held by members of the Non-Aligned Movement generally. An examination of the confrontation

166. R. J. Vincent attempts to identify a "Southern doctrine on human rights" in his *Human Rights and International Relations* (1986), pp. 79–83. See also A. Cassese, *International Law in a Divided World* (1986), pp. 307–309.

167. This section draws on an article by the author that has already appeared under the title "Human Rights and the Lomé Conventions," in 7 *Netherlands Quarterly of Human Rights* (1989), pp. 28–35. For a very thorough examination of the subject, see G. Oestreich, *Menschenrechte als Elemente der dritten AKP-EWG-Konvention von Lomé* (1990).

may shed light not only on the precise differences of opinion between two opposing schools of thought, but also on any common ground that may have been established between them.

It is notoriously difficult to pursue human rights objectives in the context of international trade and aid policies.[168] The results of the attempts to introduce a human rights element into the so-called Lomé Conventions represent a pioneering effort in this respect. They offer a telling illustration of the pitfalls that need to be avoided and the solutions that may be envisaged. The four Lomé Conventions provide a general framework for trade and aid relations between the member states of the European Community and the ACP states. The Lomé I Convention[169] covered the period 1975–1980; the Lomé II Convention[170] covered the period 1980–1985; the Lomé III Convention[171] covered the period 1985–1990; and the current Lomé IV Convention covers the period 1990–2000.[172] The conventions inter alia provide for financial and technical assistance as well as for preferential trade between the Community and the ACP states. One important element of the conventions is a system to stabilize the export earnings of some basic products from the ACP countries (Stabex). Under the conventions, a joint institutional framework has been set up consisting of a Council of Ministers, a Committee of Ambassadors, and a Joint Assembly.

The problem of human rights in the context of the Lomé Conventions clearly presented itself for the first time in 1977. At that time, extreme atrocities were simultaneously occurring in the Central African Empire under Emperor Jean Bedel Bokassa, in Equatorial Guinea under President Macias Nguema, and in Uganda under President Idi Amin. As parties to the Lomé I Convention, all three states were entitled to certain trade preferences and financial and technical aid from the European Community. Politically, the Community came under pressure to respond to the charge that through its assistance it was in fact helping to perpetuate the repression in these countries. In legal terms, the Community was forced to consider whether to continue to comply with its treaty obligations. The Lomé I Convention

168. On this issue see, generally, Ph. Alston, "Linking Trade and Human Rights," 23 *GYIL* (1980), pp. 126–58; and *idem*, "International Trade as an Instrument of Positive Human Rights Policy," 4 *HRQ* (1982), pp. 155–83.

169. Signed at Lomé, Togo, 28 February 1975. Reproduced in 14 *ILM* (1975), p. 595.

170. Signed at Lomé, Togo, 31 October 1979. Reproduced in 19 *ILM* (1980), p. 327.

171. Signed at Lomé, Togo, 8 December 1984. Reproduced in 24 *ILM* (1985), p. 571.

172. Signed at Lomé, Togo, 15 December 1989. Reproduced in 29 *ILM* (1990), p. 783.

did not specifically provide for the possibility of terminating or suspending the agreement in case of serious human rights violations.
Neither did it define its objectives in terms of promoting respect for
human rights. Under Article 92, however, the convention could be
denounced by the Community in respect of each ACP state upon six
months notice.

As it turned out, the Community was unwilling to apply this radical
sanction. It was also unwilling to invoke the *clausula rebus sic stantibus*
to terminate the Lomé I Convention with regard to Uganda.[173] Instead, in a public statement, the Community's Council of Ministers
declared that steps would be taken to ensure that Community aid to
Uganda would "not in any way have as its effect a reinforcement or
prolongation of the denial of basic human rights to its people."[174] In
other words, aid was not to be halted but henceforth to be channeled
in such a way that it would directly benefit the people. No more projects that might serve to strengthen the regime would be approved.
Similar policies were later adopted with regard to the Central African Empire and Equatorial Guinea. The new policy toward Uganda
caused a considerable reduction in expenditure on financial and technical assistance. Its impact on trade relations was apparently minimal,
however. Payments under the Stabex scheme, for example, were not
suspended.[175] The United States, on the other hand, was willing to
go much further in its response to the atrocities. In sharp contrast to
the Community, it imposed both a trade and an aid embargo on
Uganda.[176]

The Community's failure to come to grips with these situations convinced some EC governments (particularly the United Kingdom and
the Netherlands) of the need to include appropriate references to
human rights in the Lomé II Convention. In the negotiations on this
issue with the ACP countries, however, the EC member states were
divided, and the European Commission proved unable to produce
convincing proposals.[177] The ACP countries for their part strongly

173. Reply from the Commission to parliamentary question 115/78, *OJ EC* C 199
of 21 August 1978, p. 27. The *clausula rebus sic stantibus* has been codified in Article 62
of the Vienna Convention on the Law of Treaties.
174. Statement of 21 June 1977, *Bull. EC* (1977), no. 6, para. 2.2.59.
175. Ph. Alston, "International Trade as an Instrument of Positive Human Rights
Policy," 4 *HRQ* (1982), p. 164.
176. See S. C. Andrews, "The Legitimacy of the United States Embargo of Uganda,"
13 *Journal of International Law and Politics* (1979), pp. 651–73.
177. For a critical account of these negotiations, see A. Young-Anawaty, "Human
Rights and the ACP-EEC Lomé II Convention: Business as Usual at the EEC," 13 *New
York University Journal of International Law and Politics* (1980), pp. 63–98. See also R. J.
H. Smits, "The Second Lomé Convention: An Assessment with Special Reference to
Human Rights," *Legal Issues of European Integration* (1980/2), pp. 47–74.

resisted the inclusion of a human rights provision on the grounds that this would provide an excuse for interference in their internal affairs. As a result, no agreement could be reached on any human rights clause, and no such provision was included in the Lomé II Convention.

Shortly after the adoption of Lomé II, however, the Community's Council of Ministers took a nonpublished internal decision according to which, in connection with the Lomé Conventions, it would take "appropriate" action to ensure that continued aid would benefit only the neediest if flagrant violations of human rights should occur in one of the ACP states.[178] The policy adopted toward Uganda had thereby become generalized. Nevertheless, the cautious wording of the decision indicated that the Community would only in exceptional cases be prepared to interrupt its assistance to the ACP countries. This was clearly demonstrated when in December 1982 the military authorities of Suriname summarily executed fifteen critics of the regime. The Netherlands, an EC member state and one of the parties to the Lomé II Convention, quickly responded by suspending its own treaty on development cooperation with Suriname while invoking the *clausula rebus sic stantibus*.[179] The European Commission, on the other hand, stated that it was unable to suspend aid to Suriname, because this would have been incompatible with the Lomé system.[180]

In view of this unsatisfactory record, it is not surprising that the question of human rights was raised again during the negotiations for the Lomé III Convention.[181] This time, the climate turned out to be

178. Young-Anawaty, *supra* note 177, p. 94.

179. See, generally, H. H. Lindemann, "Die Auswirkungen der Menschenrechtsverletzungen in Surinam auf die Vertragsbeziehungen zwischen den Niederlanden und Surinam," 44 *ZaöRV* (1984), pp. 64–91; M. Kohnstamm and C. Sanders, "Kan Suriname Nederlandse Ontwikkelingshulp Afdwingen?" [Can Suriname Enforce Dutch Development Aid?], 63 *NJB* (1988), pp. 54–55; E. W. Vierdag, "Spanning tussen Recht en Praktijk in het Verdragenrecht" [Tensions between Law and Practice in the Law of Treaties], *Mededelingen van de Nederlandse Vereniging voor Internationaal Recht* (1989), no. 99, pp. 75–87. Vierdag points out that the treaty on development cooperation between the Netherlands and Suriname had not yet entered into force so that, instead of invoking the *clausula rebus sic stantibus*, the Netherlands could have simply notified Suriname of its intention to suspend the provisional operation of the treaty.

180. Mr. Pisani, 16 December 1982, Proceedings of the European Parliament, *OJ EC*, no. 1–292.

181. On the attempts to introduce a human rights element in Lomé III, see P. Buiratte-Maurau, "Les difficultés de l'internationalisation des droits de l'homme à propos de la Convention de Lomé," 21 *Revue Trimestrielle de Droit Européen* (1985), pp. 463–86. For general reviews of Lomé III, see K. Simmonds, "The Third Lomé Convention," 22 *CMLR* (1985), pp. 389–419; D. Frisch, "Lomé III—Das neue Abkommen zwischen der Europäischen Gemeinschaft und den AKP-Staaten," 40 *Europa Archiv* (1985), pp. 57–68; J. P. VerLoren van Themaat, "Lomé III: oplossingen van de jaren '70 voor de problemen van de jaren '80" [Solutions of the Seventies for the Problems of the Eighties], 39 *Internationale Spectator* (1985), pp. 121–27.

more favorable for an agreement. The ACP states had by then become more interested in the concept of human rights and fundamental freedoms, and they no longer regarded it as a mere ploy for neo-colonialist interference in their internal affairs. Their own views on human rights had been reflected inter alia in the African Charter on Human and Peoples' Rights[182] and in the concept of the right to development then being discussed at the United Nations. By drawing on these initiatives, the ACP states were able to formulate their own proposals and to develop a less defensive attitude in the negotiations.

The human rights package of the Lomé III Convention consisted of three main elements: a preambulary paragraph, which reaffirmed the parties' adherence to the principles of the UN Charter; Article 4, which introduced respect for human dignity as one of the objectives of the cooperation; and a joint declaration on Article 4, which elaborated the concept of human dignity. The package for the most part studiously avoided the term *human rights* and it did not refer to existing international human rights instruments beyond the UN Charter. Perhaps the convention's authors had tried to introduce some ideas sui generis, based on the concept of *human dignity*.[183]

The joint declaration also added an important and welcome element of reciprocity by clarifying that an individual is entitled to respect for his dignity "in his own country or in a host country." This was an apparent reference to the rights of migrant workers and students from ACP countries in the Community.[184] As a further concession to the ACP countries, the declaration contained specific references to economic, social, and cultural rights, peoples' rights, and the eradication of *apartheid*. Perhaps understandably in the context of a treaty that is primarily concerned with economic development, civil and political rights did not receive similar emphasis. It had to be assumed, however, that the objective of human dignity could only be achieved if both categories of rights were respected. To assume otherwise would have run counter to the philosophy frequently endorsed by the United Nations that all human rights and fundamental freedoms are indivisible and interdependent and that equal attention should be given to the implementation of both civil and political rights and social, economic, and cultural rights.[185]

A final major step forward was taken as a result of the human rights

---

182. Adopted at Nairobi, 27 June 1981. Reproduced in 21 *ILM* (1982), pp. 59–68.

183. See O. Schachter, "Human Dignity as a Normative Concept," 77 *AJIL* (1983), pp. 848–54.

184. Cf. Annex IX to the Final Act of Lomé III: Joint declaration on ACP migrant workers and ACP students in the Community.

185. E.g., UN General Assembly Resolution 32/130 of 16 December 1977.

provisions incorporated in the Lomé IV Convention, adopted in December 1989.[186] These provisions seem to indicate that the parties have finally lost their cold feet with regard to the term human rights. This concept now appears repeatedly in Article 5, in the body of the text, in the chapter dealing with the objectives and principles of the cooperation. Human rights are unambiguously defined here as including both civil and political rights and economic, social, and cultural rights. These rights are said to be indivisible and interrelated. The preamble of Lomé IV refers not only to the UN Charter but also to the Universal Declaration of Human Rights, the International Covenants on Human Rights, and the African, American, and European Conventions on Human Rights. Article 5, moreover, clearly defines development, the main objective of the convention, in terms of progress in the enjoyment of human rights. It states that "respect for human rights is recognized as a basic factor of real development."

These provisions leave little to be desired. Many of the points made by human rights groups during the past fifteen years have finally been taken on board by the Lomé partners. If some skepticism remains, it is about the manner in which Article 5 is likely to be implemented. This is uncharted territory, and the "positive approach" outlined here will require considerable creativity and skill in avoiding sensitivities. It is a pity, therefore, that the new convention does not provide for a specific implementation mechanism, such as a coordinating committee, to supervise the implementation of Article 5. Perhaps the greatest problem with this provision is that it risks remaining a dead letter.

What, then, are the implications of these new provisions for interstate accountability for violations of human rights? Is there still a risk that the Community might become an accomplice to serious violations of human rights because of its Lomé commitments? Which countermeasures might now be taken by the Community when faced with a consistent pattern of serious assaults upon human dignity in one of the ACP countries?[187] Although the new convention does not specifically provide for such countermeasures, different options are nevertheless available.

First, as under the previous Lomé Conventions, the convention

186. See, generally, H. D. Kuschel, "Das neue Lomé-Abkommen zwischen den EG und den AKP-Ländern," 45 *Europa Archiv* (1990), pp. 333–40; F. Nicora, "Lomé IV: processus, phases et structures de la négotiation," *Revue du Marché Commun*, 1990, no. 337, pp. 395–403.

187. On this question see J. A. Winter, "De Europese Gemeenschap, Ontwikkelings-samenwerking en de Rechten van de Mens" [The European Community, Development Cooperation, and Human Rights], inaugural lecture, Free University of Amsterdam, 20 September 1985, p. 14.

could be *denounced* by the Community, upon six months' notice, in respect of each ACP state.[188] No grounds need to be put forward for such a step. Where this is considered too blunt a weapon, Lomé IV permits the adoption of a more restrictive measure, based on the introduction of a major human rights provision in the chapter on the objectives and principles of the cooperation. Since, through Article 5, ensuring respect for human rights has become one of the key objectives of Lomé IV, a consistent pattern of gross breaches of this objective would amount to a violation of a provision essential to the accomplishment of the purpose of the treaty, as defined in Article 60(3)(b) of the Vienna Convention on the Law of Treaties. This would apply particularly if the breaches reached such a scale that an orderly development policy could no longer be pursued. The operation of the convention could in such a case be *suspended* in whole or in part on the grounds that a material breach of a provision essential to the accomplishment of the purpose of the treaty had occurred, pursuant to Article 60(2)(b) of the same Vienna Convention.

The Community could also—as in the past—express its concerns in other, more subtle ways. For instance, following the example of the policy adopted toward Uganda under Idi Amin, it could begin to approve only projects that would be likely to support the basic needs of the population. This could now clearly be justified with reference to Article 5. The Uganda experience has shown that such a policy may cause significant reductions in financial and technical assistance within a short time, in spite of existing Lomé commitments toward the country in question. The Community could also signal its displeasure with human rights abuses by simply delaying the approval of proposed projects. And finally, of course, it could use the numerous Lomé channels to express its views, formally or informally, to the government in question. In view of the Community's past record, however, not too much should be expected. It is likely that significant steps will be taken only in extreme cases, that is, if abuses reach such a level that they jeopardize the orderly conduct of the economic development process.[189]

The obsessive preoccupation with sanctions as an instrument for promoting respect for human rights has been rightly criticized by some authors.[190] Sanctions have not often been effective, and they can easily be abused for political reasons. The Lomé Conventions have

---

188. Art. 367, Lomé IV.

189. J. Kranz, "Lomé, le dialogue et l'homme," 24 *Revue Trimestrielle de Droit Euro-péen* (1988), pp. 471–72 and 478.

190. Ph. Alston, "International Trade as an Instrument of Positive Human Rights Policy," 4 *HRQ* (1982), p. 155.

never been denounced, and in future this weapon will no doubt be resorted to rarely. In this spirit, the Lomé IV Convention reflects a clear preference for the *approche positive*, that is, for the carrot rather than the stick. The essential importance of the new provisions is therefore not so much that they permit the Community to impose sanctions, but that they provide a framework for dialogue between the parties on the promotion of respect for human rights as part of the development process. Raising human rights issues within this context can no longer be labeled as interference in internal affairs. If necessary, demands to respect human rights, within the terms of Lomé IV, could also be presented as formal legal claims. It is important that this has now been agreed between the eighty-odd parties, instead of being imposed unilaterally by the Community.

4. Conclusions

Contemporary state practice with regard to diplomatic action on behalf of foreign nationals has its roots in nineteenth- and early twentieth-century practice. Then too, states were primarily concerned with the fate of their own citizens, and they could most easily be persuaded to intercede with another state if one of their own nationals had suffered injustice. At that time, however, there was already considerable elasticity in the size of the group of people on behalf of which they were prepared to act diplomatically. This may be visualized as an infinite number of concentric circles. While the preferred link—which defines the inner circle—was clearly that of nationality, more tenuous links, such as religion or ethnic kinship or even education or medical treatment in institutions of the interceding state, could occasionally justify an intercession as well. In a pinch, mere concern expressed by citizens of the interceding state could provide sufficient justification for an intercession. This sliding scale also tended to be accepted by offending states. The closer the link between the individual and the interceding state, the more they were inclined to consider an intercession admissible. But there was no absolute limit beyond which interceding states were not considered to have a legitimate interest.

Today, states are still primarily interested in the fate of persons belonging to their inner circle, but their willingness to stand up for individuals belonging to the outer circles has steadily increased. The practice of making diplomatic representations on behalf of foreign victims of human rights violations has become very widespread indeed. No precise figures can be given, but there are likely to be thousands of instances every year. Such intercessions are made by states belonging to all regional and political groupings, although, as in the nineteenth century, they are still made most frequently by states belonging to the Western Group. Intercessions can be very numerous in some individual cases, as when more than thirty states—from all parts of the world except Latin America—interceded at the highest governmental level in an attempt to prevent the execution of former Prime Minister Ali Bhutto in 1979.

Although intercessions are occasionally made in response to violations of economic, social, and cultural rights, the overwhelming majority concern violations of civil and political rights. Even states that tend to emphasize the importance of economic, social, and cultural rights—such as in the past the countries of Eastern Europe—are rarely inclined to intercede directly with other states if those rights have been violated, except for obvious propaganda purposes.

It is inevitable that political considerations play an important role in a state's decision whether or not to intercede in a particular case. It is a well-established rule of international law that a state is under no obligation to exercise diplomatic protection on behalf of its own nationals. It follows *a fortiori* that a state is, in principle, not obliged to exercise any kind of protection on behalf of foreign nationals.[191] A refusal by a state to intercede on the formal grounds that the victim is not a national should therefore be interpreted with some caution. This should not necessarily be regarded as evidence of *opinio juris* on the part of that state that it does not consider itself entitled to intercede on behalf of non-nationals. More likely, the refusal was motivated by political opportunism, which may be apparent if intercessions are readily made in similar cases in other offending states.

In the nineteenth and early twentieth centuries, interceding states often found it necessary to stress the legal basis for their intercessions. The preferred legal basis was of course the breach of a treaty provision by which the offending state had committed itself vis-à-vis the interceding state. In the absence of such treaty provisions, interceding states occasionally saw fit to justify their *locus standi* with reference to rules of general international law. For example, in 1891 the United States apparently relied on the principle of *sic utere tuo ut alterem non laedas* when it expressed concern at the repression of Jews in Russia by drawing the czar's attention to the injury it was suffering as a result of the arrival on its territory of large numbers of Jewish refugees who were attempting to escape persecution.

Even in those times, states also occasionally interceded on behalf of foreign citizens with whom they had no ethnic or religious ties when such action could be justified neither with reference to relevant treaty

191. But see *infra* Chapter 3, section 2.7.

provisions nor with reference to any other material interest of the interceding state. Such intercessions tended to be made only in extreme cases, when the character and the scale of the violations were exceptionally atrocious. Examples are the British and French intercessions against corporal punishments in Morocco in 1909. The grounds relied on in such cases tended to be "the laws of humanity." It is not apparent whether this refers to humanitarian—nonlegal—grounds or to customary international human rights law *avant la lettre*. Nowadays, such strictly "disinterested" intercessions are much more common.

Today, interceding states appear only rarely to make a point of invoking the applicable international standards, in spite of the fact that such standards are more abundantly available. Instead, they prefer to rely on humanitarian grounds, whatever the case. No difference can be perceived in the character of intercessions addressed to states bound by relevant treaty provisions and intercessions addressed to states not formally bound by such obligations. The only international instrument invoked with any frequency has been the Helsinki Final Act, which has often been referred to by Western states in their intercessions with East European states. This is remarkable because the Final Act is not in itself a binding legal instrument, and there are numerous, more specific, binding instruments that could have been invoked, at least by Western states other than the United States. It should not be concluded from this preference for a strategy based on "accountability" rather than "responsibility," however, that interceding states generally consider that they cannot couch their intercessions as legal claims. More probably, it is an indication of their belief that representations based on humanitarian grounds are likely to be more effective—because they cause less irritation—than formal démarches based on international law.

Many intercessions are prefixed by the soothing formula "without wishing to interfere in your internal affairs" or words to that effect. This is a device whereby the interceding state signals that it has considered whether its action might be contrary to the prohibition of interference in internal affairs and that it has arrived at a negative conclusion. Accordingly, it may be regarded as an indication of *opinio juris* on the part of the interceding state that its action is legally justified from that point of view.

The attitude of offending states is more difficult to assess than that of interceding states. It is impossible to establish with any precision how frequently offending states today continue to respond to intercessions on behalf of foreign nationals by raising preliminary objections. It is even more difficult to judge whether any such responses reflect genuine *opinio juris* or whether they are mere political expediency on their part. In the five contemporary cases studied, a full-blown claim of domestic jurisdiction, barring any expressions of concern by other states, appears to have been made only in the case of Andrei Sakharov. The ancient view that a state's treatment of its own citizens belongs to the area of domestic jurisdiction and is not bound by international law has been thoroughly discredited and is rarely invoked these days. A more sophisticated version, however, was articulated by Soviet scholars in the 1970s. It accepted that a state is bound to respect certain human rights of its citizens, to the extent that it has formally agreed to do so, for example, by becoming a party to a treaty. But it maintained that the *implementation* of these obligations was the exclusive responsibility of the state concerned. According to this doctrine, other states were not entitled to partake in the supervision of the implementation process, unless the offending state had specifically consented to such international supervision.

At present, East European states themselves no longer appear to subscribe to this questionable philosophy. Through the Helsinki Final Act they have accepted the principle of international accountability for violations of human rights toward the other participating states. More importantly, the principle has been borne out by their subsequent practice. The new consensus between East and West on this issue has been reflected in the mechanism agreed upon at the Vienna follow-up meeting in 1989. According to this mechanism, offending states have a duty to provide information and to consult on situations and specific cases "with a view to resolving them," at the request of one of the participating states. East European states now rarely respond to Western intercessions on human rights issues by raising preliminary objections.

More information on the attitude of developing countries will be presented in the next chapter on international organizations. It has already been noted, however, that through the Lomé IV Convention, sixty-nine countries of Africa, the Caribbean, and the Pacific formally accepted the principle of international accountability for violations of human rights in their trade and aid relations with the member states of the European Community. The fact that this was done through a treaty compounds its significance.

In view of these developments, the question must be asked whether the point has now been reached at which diplomatic action on behalf of foreign victims of human rights violations may be fully equated with the exercise of diplomatic protection on behalf of the interceding state's own nationals. As we have seen, there are indications that when certain states make diplomatic representations on behalf of victims of human rights violations, they no longer make a fundamental distinction between nationals and non-nationals.[192] If this is indeed the case, it represents a radical departure from the classic doctrine of international law as expressed, for example, by the Permanent Court of International Justice in the *Panevezys-Saldutiskis Railway* case:

[I]n taking up the case of one of its nationals, by resorting to diplomatic action or international judicial proceedings on his behalf, a State is in reality asserting its own right, the right to ensure in the person of its nationals respect for the rules of international law. This right is necessarily limited to intervention on behalf of its own nationals because, in the absence of a special agreement, it is the bond of nationality between the State and the individual which alone confers upon the State the right of diplomatic protection, and it is as a part of the function of diplomatic protection that the right to take up a claim and to ensure respect for the rules of international law must be envisaged. Where the injury was done to the national of some other State, no claim to which such injury may give rise falls within the scope of diplomatic protection which a State is entitled to afford nor can it give rise to a claim which that State is entitled to espouse.[193]

State practice examined in the present chapter indicates that, in the field of human rights, this rigid distinction between diplomatic action on behalf of nationals of the interceding state on the one hand and on behalf of foreign nationals on the other has increasingly become untenable. State practice is indeed beginning to catch up with the views so forcefully expressed by F. V. García Amador in his 1956 report to the International Law Commission on state responsibility.[194] He suggested that by "internationalizing" human rights and fundamental freedoms, human beings would be placed under the direct protection of international law, irrespective of their nationality. Whether the person in question was a citizen or an alien would then be irrelevant.[195]

The blurring of the distinction may be perceived, for example, with regard to the requirement of prior exhaustion of local remedies. It is a well-established rule that informal diplomatic action to express concern about the treatment of nationals of the interceding state may be taken *before* the individuals concerned have exhausted local remedies. The purpose here is to bring the matter to the attention of the authorities of the offending state and to prevent the occurrence of an

192. *Supra* notes 87 and 88.
193. PCIJ, 1939, Series A/B, No. 76, p. 16. Quoted with approval in the *Nottebohm* case, ICJ Reports 1955, p. 24. For the classic scholarly view that "citizenship is an essential condition of diplomatic protection," see E. M. Borchard, *The Diplomatic Protection of Citizens Abroad* (1927), p. 462.
194. *YILC*, 1956, vol. II, p. 203.
195. See also, F. V. García Amador, "State Responsibility: Some New Problems," 94 *RCADI* (1958), pp. 435–39.

internationally wrongful act.[196] The requirement of prior exhaustion of local remedies is a precondition only for the presentation of a formal international claim. State practice examined in the present chapter shows that the same applies to diplomatic action taken on behalf of foreign victims of human rights violations. In such cases too, concern may be expressed, information may be requested, and protests may be lodged before the individuals concerned have exhausted local remedies.[197] Thus, when the Republic of Korea in the Kim Dae-jung case[198] and the United Kingdom in the case of the Chirwas[199] maintained that intercessions could not be made until local remedies had been exhausted, this was correct only insofar as the presentation of formal international claims was concerned. Informal diplomatic intercessions to prevent these executions could have been made—and were in fact made by many states—without contravening the local remedies rule.

Considerable support can in fact be found in state practice for the proposition that states have a right to express concern about and to protest against violations of the human rights of foreign nationals on the same basis as if they were their own nationals. While in practice this may not always be done with the same enthusiasm and vigor as when action is taken on behalf of nationals of the interceding state, the reasons for this appear to be political rather than legal. The international standards relied upon—either implicitly or explicitly—are the same in both cases.

The rapid development of the modern international law of human rights and its increasing absorption of large parts of the traditional international law of state responsibility for injury to aliens[200] therefore increasingly call into question the restrictive doctrine expressed

196. *YILC*, 1977, vol. II, Part Two, p. 50. See also W. Riphagen, "State Responsibility: New Theories of Obligation in Interstate Relations," in *The Structure and Process of International Law* (1983), R. St. J. Macdonald and D. M. Johnston (eds.), p. 611, notes 8 and 9.

197. As the American Law Institute's *Restatement (Third) of the Foreign Relations Law of the United States* (1987) puts it in § 703, Comment d: "The individual's failure to exhaust domestic remedies is not an obstacle to informal intercession by a state on behalf of an individual."

198. *Supra* section 2.2.

199. *Supra* section 2.3.

200. On this subject, see, e.g., R. B. Lillich and S. C. Neff, "The Treatment of Aliens and International Human Rights Norms: Overlooked Developments at the UN," 21 *GYIL* (1978), pp. 97–118; R. B. Lillich, "The Current Status of the Law of State Responsibility for Injuries to Aliens," in *International Law of State Responsibility for Injuries to Aliens* (1983), R. B. Lillich (ed.), pp. 26–29; and Th. E. Carbonneau, "The Convergence of the Law of State Responsibility for Injury to Aliens and International Human Rights Norms in the Revised Restatement," 24 *Virginia Journal of International Law* (1985), pp. 99–123.

in the *Panevezys-Saldutiskis Railway* case. Extensive state practice of diplomatic action on behalf of foreign victims of human rights violations points to the conclusion that, by taking diplomatic steps on behalf of such persons, a state is similarly asserting its own right, that is, its right to ensure respect for the international law of human rights. In view of the reluctance of states to invoke formally another state's international responsibility, however, no comprehensive conclusion can be reached on the basis of a review of state practice alone. Whether states may indeed make formal international claims on behalf of foreign victims of human rights violations and exercise diplomatic protection on their behalf will be considered further in Chapter 3, in the light of international case law and legal opinion.

Chapter 2
Accountability Toward International Organizations

> We would be less than honest if we did not say openly and clearly that the people of Uganda were deeply disappointed by the silence of this Organization at the time of their greatest need. . . . For how long will the United Nations remain silent while Governments represented within this Organization continue to perpetrate atrocities against their own people?
>
> Godfrey Lukongwa Binaisa, President of Uganda, at the UN General Assembly, New York, 28 September 1979

As has become apparent in the preceding chapter, exclusive reliance on the remedy of diplomatic intercessions to supervise compliance with international human rights standards has some obvious drawbacks. Most states cannot easily be persuaded to make representations on behalf of foreign nationals because they derive no direct, material benefits from such actions. If they do intercede they can easily be suspected—rightly or wrongly—of having political motives. Intercessions on behalf of foreign nationals may cause international tensions and jeopardize relations with the offending state. It is not surprising, therefore, that interceding states often prefer to operate in concert with others. This enables them to hide behind each other and at the same time to intercede more forcefully. The collective intercessions by the parties to the Treaty of Berlin[1] are an example of this practice. Such intercessions require unanimous agreement between the intercessors on each occasion, however, and such agreement will often not be possible. The uncertainty and ineffectiveness of the system of ad

---

1. *Supra* Chapter 1, note 6.

hoc intercessions, combined with the wish to avoid bilateral disputes between states, inspired the establishment of the permanent and collective system of supervision of minority rights under the League of Nations.[2]

1. The League of Nations

One of the most striking aspects of the system for the protection of minority rights set up under the League of Nations was its limited scope. The obligation to protect minority rights was not incorporated in the Covenant of the League of Nations, and accordingly it was not a duty incumbent on all members of the League. The obligation was merely imposed on certain states, most of which were smaller and East European: Albania, Austria, Bulgaria, Czechoslovakia, Estonia, Finland (regarding the Aaland Islands), Germany (regarding Upper Silesia), Greece, Hungary, Iraq, Latvia, Lithuania, Poland, Romania, Turkey, and Yugoslavia. Acceptance of the obligation to respect certain minority rights and supervision of this obligation by the League of Nations was the price to be paid by these "new" states in return for their international recognition in the wake of World War I and their admission to the League of Nations.[3] Other states with substantial minority populations, such as Italy, were not incorporated into the system, ostensibly because the existence of minorities in these countries was not considered a potential threat to international peace and security.

The minority provisions were contained in special minority treaties, peace treaties, and unilateral declarations made upon admission to the League of Nations.[4] The substantive stipulations in these instruments were all similar in character. They guaranteed to minorities both the right not to be discriminated against (including equality before the law, freedom of religion, and equal access to public employment and commerce) and the right to be different (including the right to use the minority language and the right to maintain the minority's own educational institutions).

More importantly from the point of view of the present study, the minority instruments also established a remarkable system of ac-

---

2. J. Stone, *International Guarantees of Minority Rights* (1932), pp. 3–4. See the letter from Georges Clémenceau to Ignacy Paderewski of 24 June 1919. Reproduced in *Documents Concerning the Protection of Minorities*, League of Nations, Official Journal, Special Supplement No. 73 (1929).

3. I. L. Claude, Jr., *National Minorities: An International Problem* (1955), pp. 14–15.

4. For a list of these instruments, see Stone, *supra* note 2, Appendix II.

countability toward the League of Nations. For the purpose of analyzing this system, reference is usually made to Article 12 of the first of these instruments, the Minorities Treaty between the Principal Allied and Associated Powers (the British Empire, France, Italy, Japan, and the United States) and Poland.[5] Subsequent minority instruments all contained similar arrangements. Under the first paragraph of Article 12, Poland agreed that the minority provisions constituted "obligations of international concern," which were to be placed "under the guarantee of the League of Nations." This had the important effect of removing the protection of minority rights from the area of exclusive domestic jurisdiction and putting it firmly within the jurisdiction of the League of Nations.

This principle was further elaborated in paragraphs 2 and 3 of Article 12. Under previous treaties containing minority provisions, the right to intercede to obtain compliance had been restricted to the states parties to the treaty in question. But under paragraph 2 of Article 12, any member of the Council of the League (most of which were not parties to the Polish treaty)[6] became entitled to bring "any infraction, or any danger of infraction" of its minority provisions to the attention of the Council. The Council could thereupon "take such action and give such direction as it may deem proper and effective in the circumstances." Accordingly, when action was taken under this provision, the plea of domestic jurisdiction could not be made, either against the member of the Council that had raised the matter or against the Council itself. Even more significantly, pursuant to paragraph 3 of Article 12, *any member of the Council of the League* became entitled to refer a dispute concerning the implementation of the minority provisions to the Permanent Court of International Justice for a binding ruling. In other words, in these circumstances the interceding state derived its *jus standi* not from being a party to the Polish treaty, but from the sole fact of being a member of the Council of the League of Nations.

It should be stressed again, however, that the scope of the system remained limited to the sixteen states that had specifically accepted it. Moreover, although formally the minority obligations had been placed "under the guarantee of the League of Nations," in fact the

5. Signed at Versailles on 28 June 1919, C. Parry, *Consolidated Treaty Series*, vol. 225, p. 413.

6. The permanent members of the Council of the League of Nations were the British Empire, France, Italy (until 1937), Japan (until 1933), Germany (1926–1935), and the Soviet Union (1934–1939). There were four non-permanent members. See Art. 4(1), Covenant of the League of Nations. Of these members of the Council, only the British Empire, France, Italy, and Japan were parties to the Polish Treaty.

guarantee could only be exercised by the members of the Council. Nonmembers of the Council were not entitled to put infractions of the minority provisions before the Council unless they could demonstrate that the infractions had caused a threat to peace.[7] In all other cases, nonmembers were merely entitled to submit "information" under the so-called petitions procedure.[8] Such petitions were considered by a committee of members of the Council in order to determine whether an infraction of a minority instrument had occurred that should be drawn to the attention of the Council as a whole.[9] Nonmembers were also not entitled to refer disputes to the Court. But in spite of these limitations, the supervisory role given to the Council and the Court constituted a clear first step toward the establishment of a system of state accountability vis-à-vis international organizations for violations of human rights.

Article 15(8) of the Covenant of the League of Nations provided that the Council could take no action on a dispute arising out of a matter which by international law was solely within the domestic jurisdiction of the state concerned.[10] It is therefore worth noting that in no case did the states bound by the minority instruments formally raise the plea of domestic jurisdiction in response to alleged infractions brought before the Council.[11] The minority states were certainly not happy with the fact that they could no longer be shielded behind this defense. But they appear to have accepted that the minority instruments had effectively removed minority affairs from the sphere of their exclusive domestic jurisdiction. Instead, their criticism of the supervisory system tended to be that it invited abuse and especially that it was discriminatory because it did not cover all states with minorities.[12] In 1934, Poland withdrew from the system on these latter grounds. This signaled the beginning of the system's gradual collapse, which coincided with the breakdown of the League of Nations itself.[13]

7. The matter could then be brought to the attention of the Council under Article 11 of the Covenant of the League of Nations.

8. Stone, *supra* note 2, pp. 150–51.

9. *Ibid.*, pp. 87ff.

10. The full text of Article 15(8) is: "If the dispute between the parties is claimed by one of them, and is found by the Council, to arise out of a matter which by international law is solely within the domestic jurisdiction of that party, the Council shall so report, and shall make no recommendation as to its settlement."

11. In the Aaland Islands dispute between Sweden and Finland, Finland did make the plea of domestic jurisdiction under Article 15(8). The dispute was about self-determination of the Aalanders, however, rather than about the implementation of the minority instrument accepted by Finland with regard to the Aaland Islands. See League of Nations, Official Journal, Special Supplement No. 3 (1920).

12. C. A. Macartney, *National States and National Minorities* (1934), pp. 371–72.

13. Claude, *supra* note 3, p. 30.

2. The United Nations

Unlike the Covenant of the League of Nations, the Charter of the United Nations contains numerous human rights provisions with a universal scope.[14] The price to be paid for this novelty, however, was that the Charter's articles on human rights are considerably less specific than both the substantive and the procedural provisions contained in the League's minority instruments. Because of the resulting uncertainty, the plea of domestic jurisdiction has played a much more important role at the United Nations, with regard to human rights, than at the League of Nations, with regard to minority rights.

Especially in the early years of the United Nations, offending states frequently relied on Charter Article 2(7) when attempting to avoid UN scrutiny based on the Charter's human rights provisions. One of these provisions, Article 55, provides in part that "the United Nations shall promote . . . universal respect for, and observance of, human rights and fundamental freedoms for all." Moreover, under Charter Article 56, "[a]ll Members pledge themselves to take joint and separate action in co-operation with the Organization for the achievement of the purposes set forth in Article 55." Article 2(7), on the other hand, provides in part that "[n]othing in the present Charter shall authorize the United Nations to intervene in matters which are essentially within the domestic jurisdiction of any state."

Some of the key questions that need to be addressed in this chapter, therefore, are: In the field of human rights, which matters—if any—are "essentially within the domestic jurisdiction of any state"? Which types of UN action in this area do and which do not amount to "intervention"? and, Who can authoritatively decide these questions in specific instances?

The general rule for the interpretation of treaties is contained in Article 31(1) of the Vienna Convention on the Law of Treaties.[15] It provides that first of all a treaty must be interpreted "in accordance with the ordinary meaning to be given to the terms of the treaty in their context and in the light of its object and purpose." Examination of the terms of the three Charter provisions, then, on the basis of their wording alone, yields two important conclusions:

1. Article 2(7) cannot act as a bar against the application of enforcement measures under Chapter VII of the Charter.

14. Including Articles 1(3), 13, 55, 56, 62(2), 68, and 76.
15. The principles of treaty interpretation contained in Articles 31–33 of the Vienna Convention on the Law of Treaties reflect customary international law. See Sir Ian Sinclair, *The Vienna Convention on the Law of Treaties*, 2d ed. (1984), p. 153.

2. Article 2(7) merely prohibits intervention in matters that are essentially within domestic jurisdiction; in other words, if the matter acted upon by the UN is not essentially within domestic jurisdiction the injunction against intervention does not apply.

Beyond these two findings, however, few significant conclusions can be drawn from the text of the Charter itself. The Charter offers no firm clues as to the meaning of the terms *intervene* and *domestic jurisdiction*. Moreover, unlike the Covenant of the League of Nations, the Charter does not indicate which organ is to decide on controversial cases. Taking into account the object and purpose of the Charter does not add to the understanding of these provisions. On the one hand, it could be argued that since the prime object of the Charter is the prevention of war, the prohibition of interference in internal affairs should be broadly interpreted in order to prevent the creation of international tensions. On the other hand, it could be argued with equal justification that the prohibition should be restrictively interpreted, since human rights violations themselves are a cause of international tensions.

East European scholars of the Cold War school of thought have often shown a preference for basing their interpretations of the above three Charter provisions on the Charter's *travaux préparatoires*. Such a means of interpretation is permitted under Article 32 of the Vienna Convention on the Law of Treaties, but only as a supplementary method. According to Article 32, recourse may be had to the *travaux préparatoires* only if the meaning of a provision remains ambiguous or obscure after application of the general rule of interpretation referred to in Article 31 of the same instrument.

It is submitted that the meaning of the Charter's provisions on human rights and non-interference can most reliably be gathered by relying on the principle contained in Article 31(3)(b) of the Vienna Convention: "any subsequent practice in the application of the treaty which establishes the agreement of the parties regarding its interpretation." As has been demonstrated by the International Court of Justice in several advisory opinions, subsequent practice by member states is one of the most dependable tools for the interpretation of a treaty that is the constituent instrument of an international organization.[16] A provision of a constitution of an international organization may even be interpreted in the light of practice running counter to its wording.[17] Much of the present chapter will therefore consist of an

16. *Competence of the General Assembly for the Admission of a State to the United Nations*, ICJ Reports 1950, p. 9. *Certain Expenses* case, ICJ Reports 1962, p. 157 and *passim*.
17. *Namibia* case, ICJ Reports 1971, para. 22.

analysis of the way these Charter provisions have actually been applied by the United Nations during the past forty-five years.

Before embarking upon this analysis of state practice, however, some attention will be devoted to the genesis of Article 2(7) of the Charter on the one hand and Articles 1(3), 55, and 56 on the other. This review will be summary in scope, first, because of its limited importance in clarifying contemporary issues, more than forty years after the adoption of the Charter, and second, because such a review has already been thoroughly undertaken by previous authors, especially with regard to Article 2(7).[18]

2.1 Defining the UN's Role

2.1.1 The Duty of Non-Interference

The authors of what was later to become Article 2(7) of the Charter of the United Nations took their initial inspiration from Article 15(8) of the Covenant of the League of Nations, which, it may be recalled, ran as follows:

If the dispute between the parties is claimed by one of them, and is found by the Council, to arise out of a matter which by international law is solely within the domestic jurisdiction of that party, the Council shall so report, and shall make no recommendation as to its settlement.

The 1944 Dumbarton Oaks Conference produced a text that closely followed this provision of the Covenant. It proposed that the Charter's provisions on peaceful settlement of disputes by the Security Council would "not apply to situations or disputes arising out of matters which by international law are solely within the domestic jurisdiction of the state concerned."[19] At the 1945 San Francisco Conference, however, the Sponsoring Governments replaced this text with a substantially revised proposal that grosso modo later found its place among the principles of the new organization:

Nothing contained in this Charter shall authorize the Organization to intervene in matters which are essentially within the domestic jurisdiction of

18. See, in particular, L. Preuss, "Article 2, Paragraph 7 of the Charter of the United Nations and Matters of Domestic Jurisdiction," 74 *RCADI* (1949), pp. 553–650. See also P. Berthoud, "La compétence nationale des Etats et L'Organisation des Nations Unies," 4 *Annuaire Suisse de Droit International* (1947), pp. 17–104; M. S. Rajan, *United Nations and Domestic Jurisdiction*, 2d ed. (1961), pp. 32–109; D. R. Gilmour, "The Meaning of 'Intervene' within Article 2(7) of the United Nations Charter—an Historical Perspective," 16 *ICLQ* (1967), pp. 330–51; G. Guillaume, "Article 2: Paragraphe 7," in *La Charte des Nations Unies* (1985), J.-P. Cot and A. Pellet (eds.), pp. 141–60.

19. UNCIO, vol. 3, p. 14.

the State concerned or shall require the members to submit such matters to settlement under this Charter; but this principle shall not prejudice the application of Chapter VIII, Section B.[20]

The proposal was introduced at the San Francisco Conference by the United States delegation.[21] It was adopted with only minor modifications. The main differences between the provision on domestic jurisdiction contained in the Covenant of the League of Nations and the corresponding provision in the Charter of the United Nations deserve some scrutiny because they help to explain the apparent intentions of the framers of the Charter. These differences are

1. The widening of the field of application.
2. The omission of the reference to international law.
3. The replacement of "solely" by "essentially."
4. The introduction of the term "to intervene."
5. The omission of a proviso on *Kompetenz Kompetenz*.

1. The Covenant provision applied only to the procedure for the pacific settlement of disputes by the Council. Other organs of the League of Nations were not bound by it. The Charter provision, on the other hand, applies to all organs and activities of the United Nations, with the exception of enforcement measures under Chapter VII. This follows not only from the text itself, but also from its place in Article 2 as one of the principles of the United Nations. The framers of the Charter felt that since the new organization had been endowed with considerable new powers in the economic and social field, its members had to be protected against interference in their internal affairs in this area.[22] The potential significance of the Charter provision is therefore much wider than that of its equivalent in the Covenant.

2. According to the Covenant provision, the determination whether or not a matter was within domestic jurisdiction had to be made on the basis of international law. The Charter provision omits this yardstick. The argument used in support of the deletion was that the body of international law on the subject was indefinite and inadequate and should not be "frozen into the new Organization."[23] This was a curious argument because surely any international tribunal called upon

20. UNCIO, vol. 3, p. 623.
21. See the introductory statement by the U.S. delegate, John Foster Dulles, on 14 June 1945, UNCIO, vol. 6, p. 508.
22. U.S. Department of State, *Report to the President on the Results of the San Francisco Conference*, 26 June 1945, Department of State Publication No. 2349, p. 42.
23. *Ibid*, p. 45.

to interpret the international law criterion would have applied international law as it had in the meantime developed, and not as it stood at the time of the drafting of the Charter. The authors of the provision do not seem to have had an alternative yardstick in mind. They merely wished to ensure that no outdated standards of international law would be used to determine whether or not a matter was domestic. It must be concluded that this result would have been achieved even if the international law criterion had been maintained.

3. While according to the Covenant a matter could not be dealt with by the Council if it was "solely" within a state's domestic jurisdiction, under the Charter there is a lower threshold: the prohibition applies if a matter is "essentially" within its domestic jurisdiction. In support of this amendment, the United States argued that "[i]t seemed ineffectual to use 'solely' as a test in view of the fact that under modern conditions what one nation does domestically almost always has at least some external repercussions. It seemed more appropriate to look at what was the essence, the heart, of the matter."[24] H. V. Evatt, the influential Australian delegate, who supported the proposal, gave as an example the concept of full employment, which in his view was "essentially" but not "exclusively" within domestic jurisdiction.[25] Joseph Nissot has even suggested that a matter such as nationality could, through the conclusion of a treaty, cease to be "solely" within the domestic jurisdiction of a state but remain "essentially" within it.[26] Be that as it may, the manifest intention of the framers of the Charter was to provide for a wider area of domestic jurisdiction than that prevailing under the Covenant of the League of Nations.

4. The records of Committee I/1, which drafted the Principles of the Charter, do not contain clear clues as to the meaning of the term *intervene*. The word has therefore been the subject of much controversy among scholars. Some, such as Hersch Lauterpacht, favored a restrictive interpretation based on the term's established meaning under international law. In this view, *intervention* meant "dictatorial, mandatory interference intended to exercise direct pressure upon the State concerned. It does not rule out action by way of discussion, study, enquiry and recommendation falling short of intervention." Since the General Assembly and the Economic and Social Council cannot, in general, take legally binding decisions, they are by defini-

---

24. *Ibid.*
25. UNCIO, vol. 6, p. 512.
26. J. Nissot, "Art. 2, Par. 7, of the United Nations Charter as Compared with Art. 15, Par. 8, of the League of Nations Covenant," 43 *AJIL* (1949), pp. 776–79. This view was later quoted with approval by Judge S. B. Krylov in his dissenting opinion in the *Peace Treaties* case. See ICJ Reports 1950, p. 112.

tion not in a position to "intervene." According to the Lauterpacht school of thought, the prohibition of intervention contained in Article 2(7) thus has a very limited scope indeed.[27]

Others favored a much broader interpretation of the term and therefore of the prohibition of intervention. According to Hans Kelsen, the term *intervene* covers any activity of the organization. In his view, the only activity permitted under Article 2(7) is discussion and investigation with a view to reaching a decision whether or not a matter is within domestic jurisdiction. Once a positive determination has been made, no further action by the organ in question is allowed.[28] Lawrence Preuss and D. R. Gilmour have demonstrated convincingly that it was indeed the intention of the delegations most intimately involved in the drafting of Article 2(7)—the four Sponsoring Powers plus Australia—to give a broad interpretation to the term. They did not intend to restrict its meaning to "dictatorial intervention" but meant it to cover all action by the United Nations, including discussion and recommendation.[29]

It is true that the *travaux préparatoires* of the committee that prepared Article 2(7) may seem somewhat ambiguous on this point. The conservative intentions of the Sponsoring Powers appear more clearly, however, from the consideration of Charter Article 10, which governs the powers of discussion of the General Assembly. Andrei Gromyko, the Soviet delegate, objected to an initial formula that would have given the General Assembly the power to "discuss any matter within the sphere of international relations." He feared that this might permit the organization to interfere in the internal affairs of member states, in spite of Article 2(7). Dr. Evatt, the Australian delegate, replied that he agreed with Gromyko's objective, but felt that the text did not permit such interference. Nevertheless, in order to satisfy Gromyko the wording was amended so that this implication was clearly excluded.[30] Article 10 therefore now restricts the Assembly's powers of discussion to "any matters within the scope of the present Charter."

---

27. Lauterpacht argued, "It is probable that the only legally relevant—and efficacious—purpose of that provision is to prevent intervention by way of legislative action of the United Nations in such matters as regulation of tariffs and admission of aliens." See Oppenheim/Lauterpacht, *International Law*, 8th ed. (1955), vol. 1, pp. 415–419. See also H. Lauterpacht, "The International Protection of Human Rights," 70 *RCADI* (1947), pp. 19–22.

28. H. Kelsen, *The Law of the United Nations* (1950), p. 772.

29. *Supra* note 18: Preuss, p. 583; Gilmour, pp. 330–51, *passim*; and, similarly, Berthoud, pp. 69–70.

30. UNCIO, vol. 5, pp. 522–37; vol. 9, pp. 233–35.

5. While Article 15(8) of the Covenant of the League of Nations provided unambiguously that the Council was to decide on its interpretation, Article 2(7) of the UN Charter is silent on the issue of *Kompetenz Kompetenz*. The question therefore arises to which authority the authors of the Charter intended to assign this role: to the member state concerned, to the UN organ confronted with the claim, or to the International Court of Justice. Leo Gross has taken the view that since the United Nations is based on the principle of sovereign equality, each member has retained the right to decide on its obligations under the Charter as long as this right has not been explicitly surrendered.[31] Similarly, Bernhard Graefrath has suggested that since Article 2(7) is silent on *Kompetenz Kompetenz* and since inclusion of a provision on this was specifically rejected at San Francisco,[32] member states themselves have retained the right to determine whether a certain matter is within their domestic jurisdiction.[33]

Hersch Lauterpacht, on the other hand, has qualified this proposition as a manifest absurdity. He has pointed out that most Charter provisions do not indicate which authority is to decide upon disputed questions and that this power belongs, in principle, to the organ charged with the provision's application.[34] At San Francisco, Committee IV/2 similarly took the view that it was inevitable that each organ would interpret such parts of the Charter as were applicable to its particular functions.[35] Preuss has moreover demonstrated convincingly on the basis of the discussions held in Committee I/1, that the Sponsoring Governments assumed throughout that the political organs of the UN themselves would be competent to decide on the applicability of Article 2(7). A Greek amendment to the effect that such questions should be referred to the International Court of Justice at the request of the party concerned received majority support but failed to obtain the required two-thirds majority.[36]

It can therefore be concluded that the intentions of the principal framers of Article 2(7) were generally clear and unambiguous: they intended to give a broad meaning to the concepts of "intervention"

31. L. Gross, "The Charter of the United Nations and the Lodge Reservations," 41 *AJIL* (1947), pp. 541–42.

32. Neither a Greek amendment, which would have left the decision to the International Court of Justice, nor a Belgian amendment, which would have left the decision explicitly to the Organization, were adopted. See UNCIO, vol. 6, pp. 509–12.

33. B. Graefrath, *Die Vereinte Nationen und die Menschenrechte* (1956), pp. 45–46.

34. H. Lauterpacht, "The International Protection of Human Rights," 70 *RCADI* (1947), pp. 31–32.

35. See Report of the Rapporteur of Committee IV/2, as approved by the Committee, UNCIO, vol. 13, p. 709.

36. Preuss, *supra* note 18, pp. 594–97.

and "domestic jurisdiction," but they wished to leave the actual interpretation of the provision to the political organs concerned. These findings now need to be applied to the Charter's substantive provisions on human rights.

2.1.2 The Duty to Promote Respect for Human Rights

Article 1(3) of the Charter mentions the following as one of the purposes of the United Nations:

> To achieve international co-operation in solving international problems of an economic, social, cultural, or humanitarian character, and in promoting and encouraging respect for human rights and for fundamental freedoms for all without distinction as to race, sex, language, or religion.

It should be noted, first of all, that this provision refers to "promoting and encouraging" respect for human rights rather than simply to "the international protection" of human rights. As has been emphasized by some (East European) authors, this was intentional.[37] At San Francisco, Committee I/1/A rejected proposals along the latter lines on the grounds that "assuring" or "protecting" human rights is primarily the concern of each state. The committee felt that fundamental rights and freedoms only cease to be the sole concern of each state if they are grievously outraged so as to create conditions that threaten the peace or to obstruct the application of provisions of the Charter.[38]

Charter Article 55 similarly provides that the United Nations shall "promote" universal respect for, and observance of, human rights, thus creating for the organization an indirect rather than direct role in the protection of human rights. The question nevertheless arises to what extent the framers of the Charter intended to make the observance of human rights a matter of concern for the United Nations. In Hersch Lauterpacht's view, since "intervention" means "dictatorial intervention," the competent organs of the United Nations may respond to alleged violations of human rights by having a discussion, by initiating a study, or by adopting a general recommendation or a specific recommendation addressed at the member state concerned. Only an inquiry on the territory of a state against its will or "direct legislative interference" by the United Nations—defined as "an attempt to impose upon States rules of conduct as a matter of right"—would amount to impermissible "intervention."[39]

37. E.g., V. Kartashkin, "The Socialist Countries and Human Rights," in *The International Dimensions of Human Rights* (1982), K. Vasak (ed.), p. 637.
38. UNCIO, vol. 6, p. 705.
39. H. Lauterpacht, *International Law and Human Rights* (1950), pp. 167–71.

Graefrath has criticized the Lauterpacht approach inter alia on the grounds that it would give the United Nations the power to investigate and make recommendations even if, for example, in a particular country women were not paid the same salaries as men.[40] The question facing us here can thus be divided into two subquestions: First, what exactly did the framers of the Charter mean by "human rights and fundamental freedoms for all without distinction as to sex, language or religion?" Second, what powers did they wish to convey on the United Nations to respond to violations of these rights and freedoms?

The notion of human rights and fundamental freedoms has not been further defined in the Charter. Although at San Francisco some delegations favored the inclusion in the Charter of specific human rights obligations, the large majority of delegations did not wish to give the organization the powers that might have been implied by such provisions. The issue was put off on the understanding that more specific obligations would in future be included in the international bill of rights.[41]

It must be considered, therefore, whether the human rights provisions of the Charter are sufficiently clear and precise to be able to give rise to specific obligations for member states. While this question initially caused some controversy among commentators, the International Court of Justice later responded to it in the affirmative, based on subsequent UN practice. In its advisory opinion in the *Namibia* case, the Court observed: "To establish . . . , and to enforce, distinctions, exclusions, restrictions and limitations exclusively based on grounds of race, colour, descent or national or ethnic origin which constitute a denial of fundamental human rights is a flagrant violation of the purposes and principles of the Charter."[42]

It could be argued that this finding was not yet very significant, in view of the fact that Charter Articles 1(3) and 55 contain an explicit prohibition of discrimination. In the case concerning *US Diplomatic and Consular Staff in Tehran*, however, the Court went a step further by interpreting the human rights provisions of the Charter on the basis of the Universal Declaration of Human Rights: "Wrongfully to deprive human beings of their freedom and to subject them to physical constraint in conditions of hardship is in itself manifestly incompatible with the principles of the Charter of the United Nations, as well as with the fundamental principles enunciated in the Universal

---

40. Graefrath, *supra* note 33, pp. 40–41.
41. J. P. Humphrey, "The UN Charter and the Universal Declaration of Human Rights," in *The International Protection of Human Rights* (1968), E. Luard (ed.), pp. 40–41.
42. ICJ Reports 1971, p. 131.

Declaration of Human Rights."[43] In other words, the Court has accepted that the human rights provisions of the Charter contain binding obligations and that they may be interpreted in light of subsequent human rights instruments adopted by the United Nations.[44]

The second subquestion concerns the extent to which the framers of the Charter intended to empower the United Nations to respond to violations of human rights. Reference must be made here not only to Article 55—which deals with the role of the United Nations—but also to Article 56—which provides that member states shall cooperate with the organization for the achievement of the purposes set forth in Article 55. It follows that as long as UN organs do not overstep the limitations set by Article 55, offending states not only cannot raise the claim of interference in their internal affairs, they even have a positive duty to cooperate.

So what role did the drafters of the Charter envisage for the United Nations? From the *travaux préparatoires* of the San Francisco Conference it appears again that delegations took a rather defensive position. They were much concerned that the wide-ranging new powers given to the organization in the economic and social field might cause interference in the internal affairs of member states. Accordingly, Committee II/3—the committee that drafted Articles 55 and 56—adopted the following statement:

> There were some misgivings that the statement of purposes now recommended implied that the Organization might interfere in the domestic affairs of member countries. To remove all possible doubt, the Committee agreed to include in its records the following statement:
> "The members of Committee 3 of Commission II are in full agreement that nothing contained in Chapter IX can be construed as giving authority to the Organization to intervene in the domestic affairs of member states."[45]

Although the statement adds little or nothing to the contents of Charter Article 2(7), it is illustrative of the fears of the majority of delegations. The framers of the Charter wished to provide the United Nations with extensive powers to deal with matters of international concern, but they also wished to exclude any interference—including discussion—in matters falling within domestic jurisdiction. This ambivalent approach was reflected in the juxtaposition of Article 2(7) and Articles 1(3), 55, and 56. Different solutions have been proposed

43. ICJ Reports 1980, p. 42.
44. See E. Schwelb, "The International Court of Justice and the Human Rights Clauses of the Charter," 66 *AJIL* (1972), pp. 337–51; F. C. Newman, "Interpreting the Human Rights Clauses of the UN Charter," 5 *HRJ* (1972), pp. 283–91; N. S. Rodley, *The Treatment of Prisoners Under International Law* (1987), pp. 66–69.
45. UNCIO, vol. 10, pp. 271–72. See Humphrey, *supra* note 41, p. 43.

to reconcile this contradiction. For example, Preuss has suggested that it should be assumed that the authors of the Charter intended to allow for general recommendations relating to matters within the scope of the Charter, but that they intended as well to exclude the possibility of recommendations addressed to specific member states and relating to matters within their domestic jurisdiction.[46] The best explanation is, however, that the founding fathers of the United Nations realized that they had created some highly flexible and contradictory provisions and that they hoped these would be reconciled in a satisfactory manner in the daily practice of the new organization. We must now turn our attention, therefore, to the way UN organs have interpreted these provisions since 1945.

2.1.3 Elaborating the Duty of Non-Interference

The UN General Assembly has invested considerable effort into attempts to further develop the duty of non-interference. It has adopted several resolutions on the subject. These resolutions were aimed primarily at clarifying the prohibition of interference by states (and groups of states) rather than by the United Nations itself. The starting point for these efforts was Charter Article 2(7). Although this provision, if taken literally, merely addresses the duty of non-interference by the United Nations itself, many member states took the view that Article 2(7) prohibits intervention not only by the United Nations but also by states.[47] The pronouncements made by the General Assembly on the subject of non-intervention may therefore also have repercussions for the United Nations as such. After all, the UN is, needless to say, an organization composed of states.

In 1965, the General Assembly adopted Resolution 2131 (XX), the Declaration on the Inadmissibility of Intervention in the Domestic Affairs of States and the Protection of Their Independence and Sovereignty.[48] The item had been inserted in the agenda at the request of the USSR, but the text finally adopted differed substantially from the text proposed by the Soviet Union.[49] In its preamble the declaration referred to the principle of non-intervention proclaimed in the char-

46. Preuss, *supra* note 18, pp. 584–87. See also Q. Wright, "Is Discussion Intervention?" 50 *AJIL* (1956), pp. 102–10.
47. Only the United States strongly insisted that Article 2(7) is not concerned with actions of states. See, e.g., Report of the Special Committee on Principles of International Law concerning Friendly Relations and Co-operation among States, 16 November 1964, UN Doc. A/5746, p. 143.
48. Resolution 2131 (XX) of 21 December 1965. Adopted with one abstention (United Kingdom).
49. UN Doc. A/5977 of 24 September 1965.

ters of the Organization of American States, the League of Arab States, and the Organization of African Unity. In fact, the first operative paragraph of the declaration took its inspiration from the most far-reaching of these provisions: Article 18 of the Charter of the Organization of American States:[50]

1. No State has the right to intervene, directly or indirectly, for any reason whatever, in the internal or external affairs of any other State. Consequently, armed intervention and all other forms of interference or attempted threats against the personality of the State or against its political, economic and cultural elements, are condemned.

The first sentence of this paragraph appears to be loosely based on Article 2(7) of the UN Charter. There are some major differences, however. While Article 2(7) is addressed to the United Nations, the paragraph in the declaration is addressed to states (the declaration indicates in its paragraph 7 that the term *State* covers both individual States and groups of states). Furthermore, the paragraph in the declaration purports to extend the prohibition to direct and indirect intervention as well as to internal and external affairs. The second sentence of the paragraph in the declaration is similar to Article 2(4) of the UN Charter in that it deals with the use of force between states. Again, however, it moves well beyond the Charter provision in several respects, not least because it condemns certain activities that do not involve the use of force.

Although the declaration apparently attempts to interpret extensively the scope of Charter Articles 2(4) and 2(7), the precise results of this attempt remain most unclear, as far as both their contents and their status under international law are concerned. The declaration suffers from the general defect of being hastily and imprecisely drafted; from the handicap that "all other forms of interference" are merely "condemned" and not "prohibited"; and from the fact that it was not adopted without a vote.

Perhaps to provide a balance for its ambitious non-intervention provisions, paragraph 6 of the declaration provides that states are required to exercise the right of self-determination "with absolute respect for human rights and fundamental freedoms." References to the need for "absolute" respect for human rights are few and far between in international instruments, especially in instruments on non-

50. Article 18 of the OAS Charter provides as follows: "No State or group of States has the right to intervene, directly or indirectly, for any reason whatever, in the internal or external affairs of any other State. The foregoing principle prohibits not only armed force but also any other form of interference or attempted threat against the personality of the State or against its political, economic and cultural elements."

intervention. In interpreting this provision, one author has suggested that it could be considered "radically interventionary."[51] This may be a misreading of the provision, however, since it merely says that states shall display absolute respect for human rights. It does not say that other states have a right to interfere if those rights are being violated.

Some of the rough edges of Resolution 2131 (XX) were removed when the General Assembly in 1970 adopted Resolution 2625 (XXV), the Declaration on Principles of International Law concerning Friendly Relations and Co-operation among States.[52] To begin with, this new declaration explicitly set out to progressively develop and codify a number of principles already contained in the UN Charter, including those in Articles 2(4) and 2(7). Moreover, unlike Resolution 2131 (XX) this new instrument was adopted without a vote. In spite of a number of shortcomings as far as its substantive provisions are concerned, it must therefore be regarded as an authoritative document reflecting the understanding of UN member states of their obligations under the Charter.[53] The non-intervention paragraph of the Declaration on Friendly Relations provides as follows:

No State or group of States has the right to intervene, directly or indirectly, for any reason whatever, in the internal or external affairs of any other State. Consequently, armed intervention and all other forms of interference or attempted threats against the personality of the State or against its political, economic and cultural elements, are in violation of international law.

This provision closely resembles its equivalent in Resolution 2131 (XX). The only substantial difference is that the activities referred to in the second sentence are said to constitute violations of international law instead of being merely "condemned."

The agreement reached on this provision should not obscure the fact that there were strong differences of opinion between member states. While the socialist and non-aligned states wished to maintain the formula contained in Resolution 2131 (XX), states belonging to the Western Group favored a much more restrictive provision that more explicitly would have allowed states to use diplomatic means to influence the policies of other states.[54] The United States in particular initially maintained that the prohibition contained in Charter Article 2(7) merely applied to the United Nations and not to inter-state relations.

51. R. J. Vincent, *Nonintervention and International Order* (1974), p. 240.
52. Resolution 2625 (XXV) of 24 October 1970.
53. See R. Rosenstock, "The Declaration of Principles of International Law Concerning Friendly Relations: A Survey," 65 *AJIL* (1971), pp. 713–16.
54. T. Mitrovic, "Non-Intervention in the Internal Affairs of States," in *Principles of International Law Concerning Friendly Relations and Cooperation* (1972), M. Sahovic (ed.), pp. 220–22.

According to the United States, the only restriction on inter-state interference was that contained in Charter Article 2(4), that is, the prohibition of the threat or use of force. One problem with this position was of course that the United States, as a party to the OAS Charter, had already accepted the further-reaching obligations contained in that instrument. It has been suggested[55] that the acceptance of the provision by the Western Group—and its upgrading from "political" to "legal" status—should be understood in light of the following interpretative statement by the British delegate, Sir Ian Sinclair:

> In considering the scope of "intervention," it should be recognized that, in an interdependent world, it is inevitable and desirable that States will be concerned with and seek to influence the actions and policies of other States, and that the objective of international law is not to prevent such activity but rather to ensure that it is compatible with the sovereign equality of States and self-determination of their peoples.[56]

Because of these fundamental disagreements between member states, it is hardly surprising that the Declaration on Friendly Relations obfuscates rather than clarifies the basic questions considered in this chapter. Its text does not help to explain the extent to which the implementation of human rights and fundamental freedoms is a matter of domestic jurisdiction or—in the terminology of the declaration—belongs to the "internal affairs" of states. The declaration refers to human rights merely in a cursory manner, which does not add to the human rights provisions of the Charter. Although the declaration provides that "[e]very State has an inalienable right to choose its political, economic, social and cultural systems, without interference in any form by another State," it can hardly be assumed that this constitutes a license to commit human rights violations without outside interference.

Neither does the declaration indicate with any precision what degree of pressure may be put on states that violate human rights, either by other states or by the United Nations itself. While it is apparent that the declaration does not look favorably upon coercive measures, its assertion that "all other forms of interference . . . are in violation of international law" is less than helpful. It remains quite unclear what could be intended by this assertion.

In the numerous summary records of the Sixth Committee of the General Assembly devoted to what was to become the non-interference provision of the declaration on Friendly Relations, references to

55. Rosenstock, *supra* note 53, p. 729.
56. Mr. Sinclair (United Kingdom), 10 April 1970, UN Doc. A/AC.125/SR.114, p. 73.

human rights are scarce indeed. Nevertheless, two schools of thought can be distinguished. Some delegates simply took the view that the principle of non-interference "could not be construed to mean that a country could violate the fundamental human rights of its citizens without that violation becoming the concern of the entire world community."[57] Other delegates argued that only certain categories of human rights violations did not fall within the area of domestic jurisdiction, such as denial of the right to self-determination, genocide, *apartheid* or more generally, violations threatening international peace and security.[58] Since none of these views found their way into the declaration, however, they can hardly be considered as authoritative interpretations of the Charter.

In 1981 the General Assembly made a third major attempt at redefining the principle of non-interference when it adopted Resolution 36/103, the Declaration on the Inadmissibility of Intervention and Interference in the Internal Affairs of States.[59] This ambitious instrument resulted from an initiative by a number of states belonging to the Non-Aligned Movement. It includes as part of the duty of non-interference numerous new elements, many of which are again imprecisely drafted.

According to paragraph l, for example, the principle of non-intervention and non-interference includes the following obligation: "The duty of a State to refrain from the exploitation and the distortion of human rights issues as a means of interference in the internal affairs of States." This is not a particularly helpful contribution. First of all, it is not very enlightening to be informed that the principle of non-interference includes the obligation not to interfere. Moreover, the subjective criteria proposed here ("exploitation" and "distortion") would of course provide any offending state with the perfect excuse to ward off legitimate expressions of concern by other states. Even if the concerns were presented politely and diplomatically, the offending state would always be in a position to argue that the underlying motives of the interceding state were dishonorable. It is hardly sur-

---

57. Mr. Brewer (Liberia), 17 November 1967, UN Doc. A/C.6/SR.1001, para. 2. In the same sense, Mr. Rossides (Cyprus), 9 October 1963, PV.1235, para. 49; Mr. Khelladi (Algeria), 12 November 1963, A/C.6/SR.809, para. 26; Mr. Saario (Finland), 29 November 1963, A/C.6/SR.822, para. 32; Mr. Mameri (Algeria), 18 November 1965, A/C.6/SR.878, para. 6; Mr. Kane (Senegal), 3 December 1965, A/C.6/SR.889, para. 20.

58. Mr. Okony (Nigeria), 12 November 1962, UN Doc. A/C.6/SR.757, para. 1; Mr. Anguelov (Bulgaria), 8 November 1963, A/C.6/SR.807, para. 27; Mr. N'Diaye (Mali), 24 November 1965, A/C.6/SR.882, para. 34; Mr. Sahinbas (Turkey), 7 December 1965, A/C.6/SR.892, para. 31; Mr. Panni (Pakistan), 9 December 1965, A/C.1/SR.1404, para. 5; Mr. Rawn (Pakistan), 17 November 1967, A/C.6/SR.1001, para. 16.

59. Resolution 36/103 of 9 December 1981.

prising, therefore, that a number of delegations made specific objections to this paragraph.[60]

In 1985, and again in 1990, abortive attempts were made by some
states to use this paragraph as the basis for a separate General Assembly resolution.[61] From the fact that these attempts were unsuccessful,
it may perhaps be deduced that there is not much enthusiasm among
states for the notion contained in it. Professor Christian Tomuschat
has observed with regard to Resolution 36/103 that such a text has
rarely been prepared with more haste.[62] The declaration was indeed
pushed through at record speed, and when it was put to a vote, one
hundred and twenty delegations voted in favor, twenty-two (mostly
members of the Western Group) against, and six abstained. The conclusion must be that Resolution 36/103 should be regarded as a document with little authority. The Declaration on Friendly Relations—
however unsatisfactory its provisions may be—remains the leading
text reflecting the current state of general international law on the
duty of non-interference in internal affairs.[63] This is apparently also
the view of the International Court of Justice. In the case concerning
Military and Paramilitary Activities in and Against Nicaragua, the Court
relied heavily on Resolutions 2131 (XX) and 2625 (XXV) but entirely
ignored Resolution 36/103.[64]

2.1.4 Elaborating the Duty to Promote Respect for Human Rights

In the preceding section an analysis has been made of the attempts
by the General Assembly to elaborate the duty of non-interference,
especially in the field of human rights. The underlying objective of
these efforts, based on the prohibitions contained in Charter Articles
2(4) and 2(7), was to put restrictions on the possibility of responses
by the United Nations and individual states to violations of human
rights. At the same time, however, the General Assembly and the Economic and Social Council have attempted to approach the issue from
a positive point of view, based on the human rights provisions of the

60. See Doc. A/C.1/36/PV.51, 3 December 1981: Mr. Adamson (United States),
p. 56; Mr. Megalokonomos (Greece), p. 57; Mr. Blomberg (Finland), p. 58; Mr. O'Con-
nor (Ireland), p. 61.
61. See the Preface to the present study.
62. Chr. Tomuschat, "Neuformulierung der Grundregeln des Völkerrechts durch
die Vereinte Nationen, Bewegung, Stillstand oder Rückschritt?" 38 *Europa-Archiv*
(1983), p. 732. Similarly, M. Vincineau, "Quelques commentaires à propos de la 'Déclaration sur l'inadmissibilité de l'intervention et de l'ingérence dans les affaires intérieures des états,'" in *Mélanges offerts à Charles Chaumont* (1984), pp. 555–77.
63. Tomuschat, *supra* note 62, p. 737. A. Verdross and B. Simma, *Universelles Völkerrecht,* 3d ed. (1984), pp. 305–6.
64. See *infra* Chapter 3, note 14.

Charter. The underlying idea in this second approach has been to define in general terms the way in which the United Nations should promote respect for human rights, in particular the way in which it should respond to violations.

At the center of the discussion on the appropriate UN response to human rights violations has been the question of how the United Nations should respond to so-called communications on violations.[65] Each year since its establishment, the United Nations has received thousands of messages from different sources alleging violations of human rights. From its first session in 1947, the Commission on Human Rights took the view that it had "no power to take any action in regard to any complaints concerning human rights."[66]

In 1959, the Economic and Social Council once again confirmed this position with Resolution 728 F (XXVIII), although this same resolution also established a procedure for handling the communications.[67] Members of the Commission were to be furnished with confidential lists containing a summary of the substance of each communication. At the same time, governments were to be furnished with copies of communications concerning territories under their jurisdiction, and any of their replies were to be presented to members of the Commission. In other words, under this procedure confidential information would be circulated but no action of any kind could be taken.

This unsatisfactory situation was changed only in 1967 when the Economic and Social Council adopted Resolution 1235 (XLII).[68] By this resolution, ECOSOC welcomed the decision of the Commission on Human Rights to give annual consideration to the question of the violation of human rights "in all countries." The resolution also authorized the Commission and its Sub-Commission on Prevention of Discrimination and Protection of Minorities to "examine information relevant to gross violations of human rights . . . contained in the communications listed by the Secretary-General pursuant to Economic and Social Council Resolution 728 F (XXVIII)." Finally, the resolution decided that the Commission could "make a thorough study of situations which reveal a consistent pattern of violations of human rights, as exemplified by the policy of *apartheid*." Although the reso-

---

65. On this issue, see J. Th. Möller, "Petitioning the United Nations," 1 *Universal Human Rights* (1979), pp. 57–72; T. J. M. Zuijdwijk, *Petitioning the United Nations* (1982); H. Tolley, "The Concealed Crack in the Citadel: The United Nations Commission on Human Rights' Response to Confidential Communications," 6 *HRQ* (1984), pp. 420–62.

66. UN Doc. E/259, para. 22.

67. Resolution 728 F (XXVIII) of 30 July 1959.

68. Resolution 1235 (XLII) of 6 June 1967.

lution contained repeated references to violations caused by policies of racial discrimination, it is clear from the text that the gross violations on which the Commission could act were not restricted to such abuses.[69] Most importantly, however, Resolution 1235 established the principle that UN action could be taken on the basis of communications from any source.

Although Resolution 1235 established a general procedure for examining "information" on gross violations—including information emanating from "communications"—it did not establish a machinery whereby the numerous communications could be scrutinized. In 1970 the Economic and Social Council began to correct this deficiency by establishing the so-called 1503-procedure.[70] Under this procedure, the UN Sub-Commission on Prevention of Discrimination and Protection of Minorities was requested to examine communications and to refer to the Commission on Human Rights "situations which appear to reveal a consistent pattern of gross and reliably attested violations of human rights requiring consideration by the Commission." The Commission became empowered to respond to this information by instituting a "thorough study" or an "investigation" by an ad hoc committee.

Resolutions 1235 and 1503 were both controversial. The former was adopted by twenty votes to four, with two abstentions; the latter was adopted by fourteen votes to seven, with five abstentions. The main objection of the opponents of the procedure laid down in Resolution 1503 was that it was incompatible with Charter Article 2(7).[71] The Soviet delegate argued that individuals were not subjects of international law and that accordingly they lacked the necessary standing to be able to submit complaints against governments; that members of the United Nations were not required to submit matters that were essentially within their domestic jurisdiction to settlement under the Charter; and that it did not follow from Charter Articles 55 and 56 that the United Nations should promote respect for human rights by carrying out investigations.[72] But the supporters of the proposal maintained, without further explanation, that a right balance had been struck between Charter Article 2(7) and Articles 55 and 56.[73]

Although in the Economic and Social Council the main focus of discussion has long been the question of how to respond to commu-

---

69. Möller, *supra* note 65, p. 60.
70. So called after ECOSOC Resolution 1503 (XLVIII) of 27 May 1970.
71. Mr. Tarassov (USSR), 18 May 1970, UN Doc. E/AC.7/SR.637, p. 124.
72. Mr. Tarassov (USSR), 20 May 1970, UN Doc. E/AC.7/SR.641, pp. 183–86.
73. Mr. Paolini (France), 20 May 1970, UN Doc. E/AC.7/SR.641, p. 182. Mrs. Chitty (United Kingdom), 21 May 1970, E/AC.7/SR.642, p. 195.

nications, in the General Assembly one of the major general questions has been whether or not a post of UN High Commissioner for Human Rights should be created. A principal objection of opponents of the proposal has been—and remains—that the High Commissioner might interfere in the internal affairs of states. Such a post, it has been maintained, would be fundamentally incompatible with the purposes and principles of the Charter.[74] When agreement on the establishment of a High Commissioner's office proved to be impossible, a more general discussion developed on conceptual questions in the field of human rights under an agenda item with the contorted title "Alternative Approaches and Ways and Means within the United Nations System for Improving the Effective Enjoyment of Human Rights and Fundamental Freedoms."

Under this heading the General Assembly in 1977 adopted the important Resolution 32/130.[75] The resolution contains a number of general "concepts" for future work by the United Nations with respect to human rights questions. One concept is that all human rights and fundamental freedoms are indivisible and interdependent and that equal attention should be given to the implementation, promotion, and protection of both civil and political, and economic, social, and cultural rights. Another concept is that the United Nations should accord priority to the search for solutions to "mass and flagrant" violations of human rights. According to the resolution, these include violations resulting from *apartheid*, racial discrimination, colonialism, foreign domination and occupation, aggression, and the refusal to recognize the right to self-determination.

Resolution 32/130 is a political resolution in the sense that it sets out to establish a number of priorities and policy objectives for the United Nations. It does not claim that it would be contrary to Charter Article 2(7) for the United Nations to respond to violations of human rights that do not amount to "mass and flagrant" violations. But it does claim that it would not be a priority for the United Nations to be concerned with such violations. This line was continued two years later by Resolution 34/175, in which the General Assembly reaffirmed that "mass and flagrant violations are of special concern to the United Nations."[76]

In 1982, states belonging to the Western Group made a successful attempt to broaden the stated scope of UN involvement. In Resolution

74. See, for example, Mr. Troyanovsky (USSR), 17 November 1977, UN Doc. A/C.3/32/SR.50, paras. 22 and 23. For a critique of this line of argument, see R. S. Clark, *A United Nations High Commissioner for Human Rights* (1972), pp. 111–37.

75. Resolution 32/130 of 16 December 1977. Adopted with 15 abstentions, no votes against.

76. Resolution 34/175 of 17 December 1979. Adopted without a vote.

37/200, the Assembly affirmed "that a primary aim of international co-operation in the field of human rights is a life of freedom and dignity for each human being." In the same resolution, the Assembly reaffirmed "that violations of human rights, *wherever they exist*, are of concern to the United Nations" (emphasis added).[77] This seems to imply, in other words, that the UN should take a priority interest in violations of the rights of the individual and that in any case UN concern should not be restricted to "mass and flagrant" violations. In a barely disguised reference to Charter Article 56, the Assembly also for the first time urged "all States to co-operate with the Commission on Human Rights in its study of violations of human rights in all parts of the world." Although this resolution was much more controversial than its predecessors (it was adopted by eighty-one votes in favor, thirty-eight against, and twenty abstentions), subsequent resolutions containing the same notions were adopted with very little dissent.

Clearly it is well established from this review of general resolutions attempting to define the appropriate UN response to violations of human rights that the United Nations may hold accountable states alleged to have perpetrated a "consistent pattern of gross violations of human rights" or to have committed "mass and flagrant violations of human rights." Violations within these categories cannot be claimed to belong to the area of domestic jurisdiction within the meaning of Charter Article 2(7). The precise scope of these two categories including any differences between them, has not been defined, however. Moreover, the view of the large majority of UN member states is that beyond this, the United Nations may also respond to violations of human rights not belonging to these two categories. As for the permitted UN action, these resolutions have established that the UN may respond to a "consistent pattern of gross violations" by instituting a "thorough study" or an "investigation" or by less far-reaching actions. Such responses, in such circumstances, cannot be considered "intervention" and are again not incompatible with Charter Article 2(7).

Beyond these generalities, few firm conclusions can be drawn from this review of "policy" resolutions. As might have been expected, the political organs that drafted them have been reluctant to give up their freedom of action by laying down precise guidelines on how to handle sensitive matters in the future. Therefore, a more detailed look needs to be taken at actual UN practice and the decisions taken by UN bodies in specific instances.

77. Resolution 37/200 of 18 December 1982.

2.2 UN Practice

During the past forty-five years, political organs of the United Nations—in particular the General Assembly, the Economic and Social Council, and the Commission on Human Rights—have in numerous specific instances been called upon to decide whether or not a certain member state should be held accountable for violations of human rights allegedly committed under its authority. In only one instance has such a question come indirectly before the International Court of Justice as the result of a request for an advisory opinion.[78] In all other instances the matter has been resolved by the political organ itself; moreover, the Commission and the Council have invariably received the subsequent approval of the parent body. Clearly, therefore, state practice in the political organs of the United Nations in this field must be regarded as an important potential source of customary international law in general and especially as important evidence for interpreting the Charter and the powers of UN organs.[79] This applies both to the decisions of the organs themselves and to the views expressed by individual member states.

As a matter of fact, state practice in itself may not be equated with a rule of law, even if it is frequently repeated by a large majority of states. Additional evidence that states consider themselves legally bound by the particular practice must be produced.[80] As will be seen, however, the researcher's burden in this respect is lightened by the possible reciprocal effect of decisions on accountability. In taking a position whether or not a state should be held accountable for violations of human rights, other states often show themselves acutely aware that a precedent may be created which may be invoked against themselves at some later stage. The same applies *a fortiori* to the attitude taken by the offending state. It may be taken for granted that such a state will carefully consider all arguments that might help to prevent it from being held accountable. The legal arguments employed by the offending state therefore deserve particular scrutiny. If the offending state does not invoke the argument of domestic jurisdiction or non-interference, the prima facie assumption must be that it has concluded that no such objection can be made. Thus in the review of the practice of UN organs, answers will be sought to the following questions:

78. *Infra* note 90.
79. On this question see, generally, R. Higgins, *The Development of International Law Through the Political Organs of the United Nations* (1963), pp. 1–10.
80. *North Sea Continental Shelf* case, ICJ Reports 1969, para. 77.

- Did the offending state at any stage invoke the principle of non-interference in internal affairs?
- Did other states support or reject the argument?
- On which legal grounds?
- What areas of state activity were labeled as strictly "domestic," and what UN actions were marked as "interference?"
- What decision was finally taken by the UN organ?

In the following review, a distinction will be made between the period before 1974, when the General Assembly adopted its first resolution on the protection of human rights in Chile, and the period after that time. For two reasons, the year 1974 may be considered a watershed.[81] First, the decisions taken with regard to Chile marked the beginning of an era in which the existence of an international element was no longer considered a necessary precondition for a response by the United Nations. Second, around 1974 the focal point for determining UN action vis-à-vis offending states gradually moved from the General Assembly to the Commission on Human Rights. Yet another reason for making this distinction is that UN practice before 1974 has been thoroughly researched by previous authors.[82] The present review will therefore concentrate on developments after 1974, after presenting a summary of the period before that time.

2.2.1 The Period Before 1974

As early as 22 June 1946, the Indian delegation at the United Nations wrote to the UN Secretary-General to complain of the *discriminatory treatment of Indians in South Africa*.[83] In response, South Africa invoked Charter Article 2(7) and took the view that the matter was essentially within its domestic jurisdiction. After a thorough discussion of the legal issues involved, the General Assembly rejected a South African proposal that the matter be referred to the International Court of Justice for an advisory opinion. Instead, it adopted a resolution—by thirty-two votes in favor, fifteen against, and seven ab-

81. For a different view, which places the beginning of the Commission's "interventionist" period in 1967, see J.-B. Marie, "La pratique de la Commission des Droits de l'Homme de l'ONU en matière de violation des droits de l'homme," 15 *Revue Belge de Droit International* (1980), p. 360.

82. M. S. Rajan, *United Nations and Domestic Jurisdiction*, 2d ed. (1961), pp. 228–96. R. Higgins, *supra* note 79, pp. 58–130. M. Milojevic, "Les droits de l'homme et la compétence nationale des états," in Institut International des Droits de l'Homme, *René Cassin Amicorum Discipulorumque Liber*, vol. IV (1972), pp. 331–72. A. A. Cançado Trindade, "The Domestic Jurisdiction of States in the Practice of the United Nations and Regional Organisations," 25 *ICLQ* (1976), pp. 715–65.

83. UN Doc. A/149.

stentions—expressing the opinion "that the treatment of Indians in the Union should be in conformity with the international obligations under the agreements concluded between the two governments[84] and the relevant provisions of the Charter."[85] An important precedent had been set.

On 27 May 1948, the Permanent Representative of Chile at the United Nations, relying on Charter Article 14, requested the General Assembly by letter to include in its agenda an item on the refusal of the Soviet Union to permit *Russian wives of foreign nationals* to leave the country.[86] In response, the Soviet Union claimed that the matter of exit visas was within its domestic jurisdiction. The General Assembly rejected the Soviet contention and referred the matter to its Sixth Committee. After a full discussion of the legal issues, the Assembly adopted a resolution—by thirty-nine votes in favor, six against, and eleven abstentions—declaring that the measures were not in conformity with the Charter and recommending that the Soviet Union withdraw them. The resolution's preamble invoked Charter Articles 1(3) and 55(c).[87] The resolution was remarkable in that at the time the Soviet Union was not bound by any rule of international law obliging it to allow its citizens to leave the country. The Soviet plea of domestic jurisdiction therefore had considerable merit and would probably have been accepted if submitted for an advisory opinion to the International Court of Justice.[88]

On 16 and 19 March 1949, Australia and Bolivia, in separate letters, requested the General Assembly to consider the question of the *observance of human rights in Bulgaria and Hungary* "in special relation to recent trials of church leaders."[89] Bulgaria and Hungary were not members of the United Nations at the time, but Poland and the Soviet Union claimed on their behalf that the matters referred to in the letters were within domestic jurisdiction in view of Charter Article 2(7). After a full discussion of the legal issues, the General Assembly decided by thirty votes in favor, seven against, and twenty abstentions to include the item in its agenda. On 30 April 1949, the Assembly adopted a resolution—by thirty-four votes in favor, six against, and

---

84. The agreements referred to were, according to the Indian letter referred to in the preceding note, a 1926 Cape Town agreement concerning the segregation of Indians in South Africa, as confirmed by a 1932 joint statement (apparently not registered with the Secretariat of the League of Nations). South Africa maintained that these instruments did not give rise to treaty obligations.

85. Resolution 44(I) of 8 December 1946.

86. UN Doc. A/560.

87. Resolution 285 (III) of 25 April 1949.

88. A. Verdross, "The Plea of Domestic Jurisdiction before an International Tribunal and a Political Organ of the United Nations," 28 *ZaöRV* (1968), p. 38.

89. UN Docs. A/820 and A/821.

nine abstentions—that "most urgently" drew the attention of the governments of Bulgaria and Hungary to their obligations under the peace treaties.[90]

On 12 September 1952, thirteen member states wrote to request inclusion in the agenda of the General Assembly "the question of *race conflict in South Africa* resulting from the policies of *apartheid* of the Government of the Union of South Africa" (emphasis added). This policy, the letter stated, was "creating a dangerous and explosive situation, which constitutes both a threat to international peace and a flagrant violation of the basic principles of human rights and fundamental freedoms which are enshrined in the Charter of the United Nations."[91]

In response to this initiative, the South African representative argued in considerable detail that to include this item on the agenda would be contrary to Charter Article 2(7). He stated that the term "nothing" in that provision meant exactly what it said and that the only exception permitted under that provision was that of enforcement measures under Chapter VII. If other exceptions would have been permitted, these would have been mentioned. He submitted that the ordinary dictionary meaning of "intervention" includes interference; the term should not be read as "dictatorial intervention." He argued that the change from "solely" (in the equivalent provision in the Covenant of the League of Nations) to "essentially" had the effect of widening the scope of the safeguard rather than restricting it. And finally, he maintained that "according to international law the relationship between a State and its nationals, including the treatment of these nationals, is a matter of exclusive domestic jurisdiction . . . subject only to any treaty obligations."

The South African representative moved that the Assembly pass the following motion: "Having regard to the provisions of Article 2, paragraph 7, of the Charter, the General Assembly decides that it is not competent to consider the item entitled 'The question of race conflict in South Africa resulting from the policies of *apartheid* of the Government of the Union of South Africa.'" The Australian and

90. Resolution 272 (III). On 22 October 1949, the General Assembly requested an advisory opinion from the International Court of Justice on the applicability of the procedure for the settlement of disputes contained in the peace treaties. One objection made against the Court's jurisdiction in this case was that the Assembly had been acting *ultra vires*, in view of Charter Article 2(7), because, in dealing with the question of the observance of human rights and fundamental freedoms in the three states, it was intervening in matters essentially within domestic jurisdiction. The Court did not confront this assertion directly, but it did note with apparent approval that the Assembly had justified its request for an advisory opinion with reference to Charter Article 55. See ICJ Reports 1950, p. 70.

91. UN Doc. A/2183, p. 3.

British representatives spoke in favor of this motion. Unfortunately, however, from the point of view of scholarly interest, the motion was not put to a vote. The Assembly reversed a ruling by its President that the South African motion was to be put to the Assembly before the proposal to include the question on the agenda. The Assembly then proceeded to place the item on the agenda by forty-five votes in favor, six against and eight abstentions.[92]

In the same year, the General Assembly decided to establish a commission, consisting of three members, "to study the racial situation in the Union of South Africa in the light of the Purposes and Principles of the Charter, with due regard to the provision of Article 2, paragraph 7, as well as the provisions of Article 1, paragraphs 2 and 3, Article 13, paragraph 1(b), Article 55(c), and Article 56 of the Charter."[93] The commission set up on the basis of this resolution produced a highly competent and authoritative report that took full account of the views of the South African Government and scholars such as Lauterpacht, Preuss, Kelsen, and René Cassin. The Commission concluded that, as explained by Lauterpacht, the term "intervention" in Article 2(7) meant dictatorial intervention; that as a result of the adoption of the Charter fundamental human rights no longer fell essentially within domestic jurisdiction; and that the principal UN organs were entitled to decide in every specific instance whether or not a matter fell within the domestic jurisdiction of a state. It should be noted that the commission's conclusions went beyond the area of racial discrimination. It took the view that in principle the organs of the United Nations were competent to deal with any alleged violations of human rights and to address recommendations to the offending state.[94] The commission also found that the philosophy on which the policy of *apartheid* was based, was "extremely dangerous to international peace and international relations."[95]

In 1953, in response to the Commission's report, the South African representative at the General Assembly again attempted to prevent discussion of the matter by invoking Article 2(7). He proposed a resolution by which the Assembly would have noted both that the matters discussed in the report were essentially within the domestic jurisdiction of a member state and that it had no competence to intervene in these matters. The draft resolution was decisively defeated by eight

92. 7 GAOR, plenary, pp. 53–69 (1952).
93. Resolution 616 (VII) A of 5 December 1952.
94. UN Doc. A/2505 of 3 October 1953, pp. 46–65. The members of the Commission were Hernán Santa Cruz (Chile), chairman-rapporteur; Dantès Bellegarde (Haiti); and Henri Laugier (France).
95. *Ibid.* p. 116.

votes in favor (Australia, Belgium, Colombia, France, Greece, Luxembourg, South Africa, and the United Kingdom), forty-two against, and ten abstentions (Argentina, Canada, Dominican Republic, the Netherlands, New Zealand, Panama, Peru, Turkey, the United States, and Venezuela).[96] The General Assembly then proceeded to adopt a resolution by which—although it did not explicitly endorse the commission's findings with respect to the UN's competence to respond to violations of human rights—it expressed its appreciation of the work of the commission and continued its mandate.[97]

In 1959, the General Assembly again ignored claims of domestic jurisdiction when it passed a resolution calling for respect for human rights in *Tibet*. Since the People's Republic of China was not a member of the United Nations at the time, these objections were raised on its behalf by Romania and the USSR. The resolution—which referred to the principles of human rights set out in the Charter—was carried by forty-five votes in favor, nine against, and twenty-six abstentions.[98] Similar resolutions were adopted in 1961 and 1965.[99]

A turning point occurred in 1963 when *South Viet Nam*, which was also not a member of the United Nations, offered to receive a UN mission to investigate allegations that it had violated the religious rights of its Buddhist community.[100] The speed with which this operation was carried out was remarkable. On 8 October 1963, the General Assembly decided to accept Viet Nam's invitation.[101] On 21 October, the mission, consisting of the representatives of seven member states and headed by the Chairman of the Commission on Human Rights, left for Viet Nam. On 7 December, the mission submitted an elaborate report[102] to the General Assembly, and on 13 December, the General Assembly decided to discontinue consideration of the matter because the government against which the allegations had been directed had in the meantime been overthrown.[103] No allegations of interference in internal affairs were raised, and the government was reported to have cooperated with the mission.

In 1968, the General Assembly decided to establish a Special Committee to Investigate Israeli Practices Affecting the Human Rights of

96. 8 GAOR, plenary, pp. 24–28, 432–36 (1953).

97. Resolution 721 (VIII) of 8 December 1953.

98. Resolution 1353 (XIV) of 21 October 1959. 14 GAOR, plenary, pp. 444–54 and 469–530 (1959).

99. Resolutions 1723 (XVI) of 20 December 1961 and 2079 (XX) of 18 December 1965.

100. Letter of 4 October 1963 to the President of the Assembly, UN Doc. A/PV.1232, para. 93.

101. UN Doc. A/PV.1234, para. 83.

102. UN Doc. A/5630.

103. UN Doc. A/PV.1280, para. 5.

the Population of the Occupied Territories.[104] The resolution was adopted by sixty votes to twenty-two, with thirty-seven abstentions. Israel rejected the resolution as being discriminatory and unbalanced. It also criticized the procedure that had been followed in adopting the resolution, and it refused to cooperate with the Special Committee.[105] The committee's subsequent reports, and UN resolutions based on them, have been frequently attacked by Israel on the grounds of their alleged selectivity, double standards, and prejudice. Unlike South Africa, however, Israel has not taken the view that the establishment of the Special Committee amounted, in itself, to interference in its internal affairs (as a matter of fact, it would have been difficult to maintain that its conduct in occupied territories constituted internal affairs). Israel has consistently argued that any violation of human rights in any part of the world is a matter of concern for the entire international community, so that a state could not evade its responsibilities by hiding behind the excuse of domestic jurisdiction.[106]

Until 1963, therefore, offending states invariably invoked the domestic jurisdiction rule, but in all these instances the General Assembly nevertheless decided to hold them accountable. It did so by placing the matter on the agenda, discussing it, addressing recommendations to the offending state, or establishing an investigation. In fact, it is difficult to identify any instances in which the claim of domestic jurisdiction was accepted.[107] In all cases, moreover, the General Assembly considered itself competent to decide on the accountability question. It has shown no inclination to submit it to the International Court of Justice for an advisory opinion, in spite of formal proposals to that effect, for example by South Africa. The decisions to hold offending states accountable were invariably taken by a large majority, after a thorough discussion of the legal implications. The relevant resolutions relied upon either the Charter in general terms or its Articles 1(3), 55, and 56 specifically.

2.2.2 The Case of Chile

Following the military coup in Chile in September 1973, serious and widespread violations of human rights occurred in that country. The nature of the UN responses to these violations and the attitude taken toward these responses by the Government of Chile constitute an important element of our investigation into the accountability of

---

104. Resolution 2443 (XXIII) of 19 December 1968.
105. UN Doc. A/8089, pp. 12–14.
106. E.g., Mr. Blum (Israel), 1 December 1978, UN Doc. A/C.3/33/SR.64, para. 25.
107. Higgins, *supra* note 79, p. 118.

states toward intergovernmental organizations, and will therefore be examined here in further detail.

In 1975, the UN Commission on Human Rights, urged by the General Assembly to study the reported violations of human rights in Chile, established an *Ad Hoc* Working Group, consisting of five of its members, "to inquire into the present situation of human rights in Chile." The resolution establishing the Working Group relied in general terms on the UN Charter and the Universal Declaration of Human Rights, and it was adopted without a vote.[108] Chile did not oppose the resolution. On the contrary, its representative welcomed the action "as an attempt to seek the truth without prejudice," and he promised that his government would lend its fullest support to the Working Group.[109]

Later that same year, the General Assembly had before it the *Ad Hoc* Working Group's first progress report.[110] Delegates were clearly aware of the importance of the decisions that now had to be taken and the precedents that would thereby be created. Previous investigations initiated by the Commission on Human Rights—those regarding Southern Africa[111] and the Israeli Occupied Territories[112]— had been based on the existence of an "international element" in the situation. This argument did not really apply to Chile. Although it could have been argued that General Augusto Pinochet had come to power partly owing to intervention by the United States, it was difficult to maintain that the situation of human rights in Chile was causing a continuing threat to international peace and security. The criterion for the establishment of the inquiry, therefore, was in effect the simple existence of a consistent pattern of gross violations of human rights. Under ECOSOC Resolution 1235 (XLII), the Commission on Human Rights had become authorized to make a thorough study of situations revealing a consistent pattern of violations of human rights. Although Commission Resolution 8 (XXXI) did not explicitly refer to Resolution 1235, the establishment of the *Ad Hoc* Working Group constituted in effect its first application.

Some delegations (including Nicaragua and Paraguay) opposed the proposed General Assembly resolution, which expressed appreciation to the *Ad Hoc* Working Group and called on the Chilean authorities

108. Resolution 8 (XXXI) of 27 February 1975. On the establishment of the Working Group see, generally, J.-B. Marie, "La situation des droits de l'homme au Chili: enquête de la Commission des droits de l'homme des Nations Unies," 22 *AFDI* (1976), pp. 305–35.
109. Mr. Diez (Chile), 27 February 1975, UN Doc. E/CN.4/SR.1323, p. 79.
110. UN Doc. A/10285 of 7 October 1975.
111. Resolution 2 (XXIII) of 6 March 1967.
112. Resolution 6 (XXV) of 4 March 1969.

to take certain measures to restore basic human rights, on the grounds that it constituted interference in the internal affairs of a sovereign state. Chile itself again took a more moderate line. Its representative quoted at length from the lectures on the subject of human rights and domestic jurisdiction delivered at the Hague Academy of International Law by Professor Felix Ermacora, one of the members of the *Ad Hoc* Working Group.[113] The Chilean representative stated explicitly that his government did not wish to take refuge in the principle of non-intervention in order to cover up the facts. He acknowledged that it was within the competence of the General Assembly to take cognizance of the situation of human rights in all countries. But he maintained that the *Ad Hoc* Working Group had interfered in Chile's internal affairs by calling for the termination of the state of siege, the abolition of military tribunals, the repeal of laws promulgated after September 1973, the abolition of military intelligence services, and the release of political prisoners.[114]

The views expressed by Chile on this occasion remained a constant feature of the attitude it maintained throughout the years. It frequently argued that certain elements in the resolutions adopted and certain elements in the reports produced by the *Ad Hoc* Working Group—and subsequently the special rapporteurs on Chile—were *ultra vires* and amounted to interference in Chile's internal affairs. It also suggested many times that the UN's treatment of Chile was discriminatory, selective, and proof of a double standard. Furthermore, it frequently used the tu quoque argument and charged its principal accusators at the UN with being worse offenders than itself.[115]

But Chile did not raise the preliminary objection that it was incompatible with Charter Article 2(7) for UN bodies to adopt resolutions on the human rights situation in Chile or to create special bodies to investigate this situation. At the 1976 session of the Commission on Human Rights, the Chilean delegate stated that his government had decided to accept "the competence of the Working Group and had given it freedom to travel because it had not wished to set a precedent whereby the accused country arrogated itself the right to determine whether or not mass violations of human rights had occurred on its territory."[116] The argument repeatedly and authoritatively made by Chile that it did not wish to invoke Article 2(7) and that it did not

113. F. Ermacora, "Human Rights and Domestic Jurisdiction (Article 2, par. 7, of the Charter)," 124 *RCADI* (1968), pp. 375–451.
114. Mr. Diez (Chile), 10 November 1975, UN Doc. A/C.3/Sr. meeting 2153, paras. 22–27.
115. E.g., Mr. Diez (Chile), 11 November 1976, UN Doc. A/C.3/31/SR.46, para. 17.
116. Mr. Diez (Chile), 20 February 1976, UN Doc. E/CN.4/SR.1359, para. 4. The Working Group was only permitted to visit Chile for the first time in 1978, however.

contest the competence of UN bodies to decide on their response to alleged violations of human rights must be regarded as an important precedent.

The remaining controversial area, therefore, is Chile's contention that some of the actions taken in its regard by the United Nations, especially certain recommendations addressed to it by the General Assembly, the Economic and Social Council, and the Commission on Human Rights, amounted to interference in its internal affairs. The areas of public administration touched upon in these recommendations—including the right to proclaim a state of emergency, the choice of the type of government, the administration of justice, and the acquisition and loss of nationality—had until then been presented in the literature as examples of matters that are in principle within domestic jurisdiction.[117] It is true that Chile was bound by a number of treaties in which some of these matters are regulated, including the International Covenant on Civil and Political Rights. But it would have been difficult to maintain that Chile was under any obligation to comply with these particular urgings, which went far beyond the undertakings contained in these treaties. UN support for such far-reaching recommendations nevertheless gradually increased. In 1987 the Commission on Human Rights adopted one of its most sweeping resolutions yet, without a vote.[118] Given this unanimous backing, some of the recommendations contained in this particular resolution deserve closer scrutiny.

First, this resolution "urges the Chilean Government to honour the requests from various social and political sectors for the *peaceful re-establishment of a pluralist democracy*" (emphasis added). The implication here seems to be that a major UN body considers unanimously that a pluralist democracy is the type of government a UN member state ought to adopt. Though one need not necessarily disagree with this view, it is not easy to see on which legal grounds it could be based. Certainly there is no indication in the Charter of the United Nations that its members must be pluralist democracies. As we have seen above, the Declaration on Friendly Relations provides that "[e]ach State has the right to freely choose and develop its political, social, economic and cultural systems." Following the same line of thought, the *Ad Hoc* Working Group on Chile in 1977 took the view that "the form of régime which Chile wishes to adopt . . . is a matter for the Chilean people exclusively to decide; the group may not, either di-

---

117. E.g., J. E. S. Fawcett, "Human Rights and Domestic Jurisdiction," in *The International Protection of Human Rights* (1967), E. Luard (ed.), pp. 286–87 and 297–99.
118. Resolution 1987/60 of 12 March 1987.

rectly or indirectly, interfere in such a question which is one of domestic policy unconnected with its mandate."[119] The adoption,
without a vote, of an appeal in favor of the establishment of a pluralist
democracy should therefore be regarded as a significant innovation.

Second, the resolution appeals to the Chilean Government "*to put
an end to . . . states of emergency*" (emphasis added). Appeals addressed
to the Chilean Government to terminate various states of emergency
have been a frequent feature of General Assembly and Commission
on Human Rights resolutions on Chile since 1976. Chile has long
maintained that declaring a state of emergency and suspending certain rights is a sovereign right of the state concerned. It has argued
that UN bodies had a role to play with regard to states of emergency
only if nonderogable rights had been violated.[120] Chile's view that it
constitutes unacceptable interference in a state's internal affairs for a
UN body to call for the termination of a state of emergency has received explicit support from a number of governments, including
Australia and Costa Rica.[121]

Third, the resolution appeals to the Chilean Government "*to reorganize the police and security forces*, including organizations such as the
National Information Center, so as to help to put an end to persistent
problems of human rights violations" (emphasis added). The organization of state machinery, and particularly of security forces, has also
traditionally been considered a national prerogative. An appeal by a
UN body, adopted without a vote, to reorganize security forces must
therefore be regarded as a further exceptional action that in the past
would have been considered unacceptable.

These appeals were not only adopted without a vote, Chile itself
did not object to them. The Chilean representative listed ten objections to the resolution, but the claim that any of the appeals contained in it amounted to interference in Chile's internal affairs was

119. UN Doc. E/CN.4/1221, para. 46. Ironically, the Soviet Union has long been one
of the prime advocates of this rule: "There are internal questions which are completely
out of bounds for other states and which under no circumstances are or may be subject
to regulation under international law. Such questions fall within the sphere of *exclusive*
internal jurisdiction of each state. Appertaining to the exclusive internal competence
of states are indisputably the socio-political system, questions of the socio-economic
order and *system of government*" (emphasis added). *Kurs mezhdunarodnogo prava* (Soviet
Course of International Law), vol. II, p. 183. Quoted in Mitrovic, *supra* note 54, p. 246.
120. E.g., Mr. Diez (Chile), 10 March 1977, UN Doc. E/CN.4/SR.149, para. 7.
121. Mr. Barreiro (Paraguay), 18 November 1976, UN Doc. A/C.3/31/SR.54, para.
17; Mr. Mosquera Chaux (Colombia), 23 November 1976, A/C.3/31/SR.58, para. 5; Mr.
Albomoz (Ecuador), 23 November 1976, A/C.3/31/SR.58, para. 26; Mr. Varela (Costa
Rica), 2 March 1981, E/CN.4/SR.1617, para.47; Mr. Davis (Australia), 2 March 1981,
E/CN.4/SR. 1617, para. 50.

not among them.[122] Chile thus acquiesced in recommendations to which in the past it had strongly and repeatedly objected.

2.2.3 The Attitude of Other Offending States

A systematic survey of the debates of and the actions taken by the General Assembly and the Commission on Human Rights since 1974 reveals that Chile's attitude is no longer exceptional. During this period the Commission launched public investigations, of one kind or another, into violations of human rights in Equatorial Guinea (1979), El Salvador (1981), Bolivia (1981), Guatemala (1982), Poland (1982), Iran (1982), Afghanistan (1984), Cuba (1988), Romania (1989), and Iraq (1991).[123] As will be seen below, only a few of these states have claimed, at any time, that these investigations amounted in themselves to interference in their internal affairs in breach of Article 2(7) of the Charter.

When in 1979 the Commission on Human Rights decided that a Special Rapporteur should be appointed to make a thorough study of the human rights situation in *Equatorial Guinea*, the government of that country did not oppose the decision on the grounds of interference in its internal affairs.[124]

Similarly, *El Salvador* has not taken the view that the appointment in 1981 of a Special Representative to investigate the situation of human rights in the country constituted interference in its internal affairs. It has argued, however, that certain elements in the reports of the Special Representative and certain elements in the resolutions adopted on El Salvador amounted to such interference. In 1983, El Salvador's representative in the Third Committee of the General Assembly stated that his delegation interpreted Charter Article 2(7) as meaning "not that the United Nations was not empowered to deal with human rights but that it should do so with due care and tact, so as not to interfere in matters which were strictly the internal concern of nations."[125] El Salvador's strongest criticism was reserved for the 1984 resolution of the Commission on Human Rights,[126] which it said contained "value judgments on elections held in El Salvador,

122. Mr. Calderon (Chile), 16 March 1987, UN Doc. E/CN.4/1987/SR.57, paras. 10–13.
123. For a general overview of these investigations until 1985, see M. J. Bossuyt, "The Development of Special Procedures of the United Nations Commission on Human Rights," 6 *HRLJ* (1985), pp. 179–210.
124. UN Doc. E/CN.4/SR.1519, p. 20.
125. Mr. Lovo-Castelar (El Salvador), 8 December 1983, UN Doc. A/C.3/38/SR.68, para. 46.
126. Resolution 1984/52 of 14 March 1984.

on the internal policy making procedures and on the implementation of economic measures."[127] The resolution inter alia recommended the effective application of agrarian reform in El Salvador and urged all states to suspend any type of military assistance to the country. El Salvador's objections to these clauses received little support, however. The resolution was adopted by twenty-four votes to five (Bangladesh, Brazil, Pakistan, United States, Uruguay), with thirteen abstentions.

In 1981, *Bolivia* did not object to the appointment of a Special Envoy charged with making a thorough study of the human rights situation in the country. In an earlier letter to the UN Secretary-General, the government had already indicated that it was ready to receive a delegation from the Commission on Human Rights.[128]

Guatemala did not maintain that the decision in 1982 to establish a Special Rapporteur on Guatemala constituted per se interference in its internal affairs. But in 1983 it protested that a paragraph in a resolution of the Commission on Human Rights, calling on states to refrain from supplying arms to Guatemala as long as serious human rights violations continued, represented such interference.[129] In 1984 its representative maintained that an appeal addressed to it by the Commission to allow international humanitarian organizations (that is, the International Committee of the Red Cross) to investigate the fate of disappeared persons, visit detainees, and bring assistance to the civilian population in areas of conflict, amounted to interference in its internal affairs.[130]

The Islamic Republic of *Iran* has put forward a number of sophisticated arguments to frustrate the efforts of the Commission on Human Rights to investigate serious and large-scale violations of human rights on its territory. It has repeatedly stated that it will only comply with its obligations under international human rights law to the extent that these are consistent with Islamic law. It has also criticized resolutions adopted on the situation of human rights in Iran for their "prejudicial" language. But it has not suggested that the establishment in 1984 of a Special Representative on Iran constituted interference in its internal affairs.[131] In 1990 the government increased its

127. Mr. Lovo-Castelar (El Salvador), 14 March 1984, UN Doc. E/CN.4/1984/SR.58, para. 11.
128. Letter of 29 October 1980, UN Doc. A/C.3/35/9.
129. Mr. Fagardo-Maldonado (Guatemala), 8 March 1983, UN Doc. E/CN.4/1983/SR.52, para. 11.
130. Mr. Fagardo-Maldonado (Guatemala), 14 March 1984, UN Doc. E/CN.4/1984/SR.58, para. 69.
131. See, in particular, Mr. Nasseri (Iran), 5 March 1987, UN Doc. E/CN.4/1987/SR.48/Add.1, para. 28. Also, E/CN.4/1988/12, para. 40.

cooperation with the UN by permitting the Special Representative to visit the country for the first time.

A major exception to this pattern was the response by *Poland* to two resolutions adopted by the Commission on Human Rights in 1982 and 1983. These resolutions expressed deep concern at the continued reports of widespread violations of human rights in Poland and requested the Secretary-General or a person designated by him to undertake a thorough study of the human rights situation in Poland.[132] Both resolutions were adopted by relatively small margins.[133] The question whether they interfered in Poland's internal affairs was extensively debated by the Commission, both in 1982 and in 1983 (as of 1984, no further draft resolutions on Poland were put to a vote). Poland's representatives took the very restrictive view that the United Nations was only entitled to consider human rights violations in member states whenever the following criteria had been met:

1. The situation constituted a gross, massive, and flagrant violation of human rights and fundamental freedoms.
2. The situation constituted a consistent pattern of such violations.
3. The situation endangered international peace and security.
4. The consideration was without prejudice to the functions and powers of organs already in existence.[134]

According to the Polish representatives, none of these criteria had been met. There was no consistent pattern of gross violations in Poland, and there was no threat to international peace and security. In accordance with the relevant provisions of the International Covenant on Civil and Political Rights, the proclamation of a state of martial law on 13 December 1981 had been duly notified to the other states parties to the Covenant. In the Polish view, the reporting procedure under Article 40 of the Covenant now prevailed over the general procedures applicable at the Commission.[135]

In 1982, the representatives of the Netherlands and the Soviet Union engaged in an interesting exchange that further clarified the East European philosophy. The Netherlands' delegate pointed out that arguments of non-interference had not prevented the Commis-

132. Resolutions 1982/26 of 10 March 1982 and 1983/30 of 8 March 1983.
133. In the case of the former, nineteen votes to thirteen, with ten abstentions; in the case of the latter, nine votes to fourteen, with ten abstentions.
134. Mr. Sokalski (Poland), 28 February 1983, UN Doc. E/CN.4/1983/SR.40/Add.1, para. 56.
135. Mr. Lopatka (Poland), 5 March 1982, UN Doc. E/CN.4/1982/SR.51/Add.1, pp. 18–21.

sion from taking action in 1974 with regard to Chile.[136] The Soviet delegate responded that the action taken on Chile had been justified because the events there constituted an international problem, since they had involved a coup d'état engineered by a foreign power. In Poland, on the other hand, there had been no coup d'état and no massive violations of human rights.[137]

Likewise, the 1984 decision by the Commission on Human Rights to appoint a Special Rapporteur on the situation of human rights in *Afghanistan* was regarded by the Afghan Government as interference in its internal affairs.[138] The government maintained that the mere consideration of the situation of human rights in Afghanistan by the Commission on Human Rights or the Economic and Social Council represented a clear violation of Charter Article 2(7).[139] Accordingly, it refused to cooperate with the Special Rapporteur. By early 1987, however, Afghanistan's attitude toward the Special Rapporteur had changed radically. From then on, it no longer took the view that his appointment or his activities constituted interference in its internal affairs, and it even invited him to visit the country.[140]

In 1988, *Cuba* similarly agreed to accept a visit by the Chairman and five members of the Commission on Human Rights to observe the human rights situation there.[141]

In 1989, however, in response to a decision by the Commission on Human Rights to appoint a Special Rapporteur to examine the human rights situation in *Romania*,[142] the Romanian Government maintained that the resolution represented "brutal interference" in the internal affairs of the Romanian people. It rejected "methods of inquiry and control" as incompatible with the principles of sovereignty and non-interference in the internal affairs of states.[143] But the new Romanian Government established after the overthrow of the Ceaucescu regime in December 1989 welcomed the Special Rapporteur's reports and has supported the continuation of his mandate.

In 1991, *Iraq* responded to the decision to establish a Special Rapporteur to make a thorough study of the violations of human rights

---

136. Mr. Kooijmans (Netherlands), 5 March 1982, UN Doc. E/CN.4/1982/SR.51/Add.1, para. 34.
137. Mr. Zorin (USSR), 10 March 1982, UN Doc. E/CN.4/1982/SR.57, pp. 12–13.
138. Mr. Kherad (Afghanistan), 13 March 1985, UN Doc. E/CN.4/1985/SR.48/Add.1, para. 14.
139. UN Doc. E/CN.4/1985/21, para. 29.
140. UN Doc. E/CN.4/1987/56.
141. Decision 1988/106 of 10 March 1988.
142. Resolution 1989/75 of 9 March 1989.
143. Mr. Dolgu (Romania), 9 March 1989, UN Doc. E/CN.4/1989/SR.56, paras. 21 and 22.

by Iraq[144] by invoking the tu quoque argument. It accused the sponsors of the resolution of having infringed the rights of Iraqi citizens by their blockade and by their bombardment of civilian targets. But it did not raise the argument of interference in internal affairs.[145]

Thus, in response to the eleven major, public, country-related investigations launched by the Commission on Human Rights since 1975, only three of the offending states (Afghanistan, Poland, and Romania) maintained at one time or another that these investigations were per se incompatible with Charter Article 2(7). Moreover, these three states subsequently changed their attitude. Afghanistan dramatically altered its position in 1987 and has cooperated with the Special Rapporteur ever since. The new Romanian Government, established after the overthrow of the Ceaucescu regime in December 1989, has welcomed the Special Rapporteur's reports and has supported the continuation of his mandate. Poland was only under investigation in 1982 and 1983, and subsequent changes in its attitude therefore cannot be established with certainty. It seems fair to assume, however, that if currently confronted with a similar investigation by the UN, the present Polish Government would not again invoke the non-interference rule in a similar fashion.[146]

A similar pattern of decreasing reliance by offending states on the principle of non-interference in internal affairs may be perceived under the Commission's other monitoring procedures. Because of its confidential character, no definite conclusions can be drawn with regard to the communications procedure under ECOSOC Resolutions 728F and 1503. From the files that have been made public so far, however, it appears that it is very rare indeed for offending states to invoke the principle of non-interference to oppose the procedure per se, although it may still be invoked to oppose particular decisions taken under the procedure.[147] The same applies to the so-called thematic procedures of the Commission on Human Rights that were set up during the 1980s (Working Group on Enforced or

144. Resolution 1991/74 of 6 March 1991.
145. Mr. Madhour (Iraq), 6 March 1991, UN Doc. E/CN.4/1991/SR.54, pp. 14–16.
146. See the statement by President Wojciech Jaruzelski at the 46th session of the UN Commission on Human Rights, in which he expressed understanding for the criticisms made by members of the Commission regarding his declaration of martial law nine years earlier. UN Doc. E/CN.4/1990/SR.12, pp. 3–5.
147. Equatorial Guinea repeatedly invoked Charter Article 2(7) to oppose decisions taken under the 1503-procedure by the Commission on Human Rights during the late 1970s. UN Doc. E/CN.4/1371, paras. 8, 12, and 20. Uruguay twice "rejected" communications made by Amnesty International under the 1503-procedure on the grounds of their alleged interference in its internal affairs. But Uruguay's objections were not directed against the 1503-procedure itself. See the letter of 21 May 1979, E/CN.4/GR.80/1/Add.1 and the letter of 13 August 1981, E/CN.4/GR.81/8.

Involuntary Disappearances, Special Rapporteur on Summary or Arbitrary Executions, Special Rapporteur on Torture, and Special Rapporteur on Religious Intolerance).[148] Few if any states have, as a matter of principle, explicitly refused to cooperate with the thematic procedures.[149]

The principle of non-interference in internal affairs may of course also be invoked in response to simple allegations made at UN meetings. Here again the sharply decreasing reliance on the principle appears significant. When at the 1986 session of the Commission on Human Rights Turkey criticized Bulgaria for its treatment of its Turkish minority, the Bulgarian and Soviet representatives did not respond by claiming that this was a matter within domestic jurisdiction. Instead, they responded by using the tu quoque argument.[150] Representatives of some (Western) states have gone a step further by explicitly indicating that they did not wish to invoke the principle of non-interference in response to allegations made against them. In 1982, the British representative at the Commission on Human Rights stated that his government did not regard discussions of Northern Ireland in the Commission as unwarranted interference.[151] In 1986, the U.S. representative at the Commission on Human Rights said that his delegation considered it no interference to have a frank discussion in the Commission of human rights issues within its borders.[152]

2.2.4 The Response to Individual Cases

Some states have maintained that the United Nations is only entitled to respond to large-scale patterns of human rights violations and not to individual instances of such violations. In general, the Soviet

148. On the thematic procedures see, generally, D. Weissbrodt, "The Three 'Theme' Special Rapporteurs of the UN Commission on Human Rights," 80 *AJIL* (1986), pp. 685–99; N. Rodley, "U.N. Action Procedures Against 'Disappearances', Summary or Arbitrary Executions and Torture," 8 *HRQ* (1986), pp. 700–730; and M. T. Kamminga, "The Thematic Procedures of the UN Commission on Human Rights," 34 *NILR* (1987), pp. 299–323. A Working Group on Arbitrary Detention was established by Commission Resolution 1991/42 of 5 March 1991.

149. Kamminga, *supra* note 148, p. 322. A rare exception was the response made in 1988 by Saudi Arabia to a letter by the Special Rapporteur on Torture expressing concern about a case of flogging. The Saudi Government responded that "the Special Rapporteur's interpretation of the international law *vis-à-vis* the sovereignty of a State Member of the United Nations was entirely unacceptable and, hence, rejected." See UN Doc. E/CN.4/1989/15, p. 18.

150. N Doc. E/CN.4/1986/SR.46/Add.1, pp. 22 and 31.

151. Viscount Colville of Culross (United Kingdom), 26 March 1982, UN Doc. E/CN.4/1982/SR.55, para. 37.

152. Mr. Schifter (United States), 27 February 1986, UN Doc. E/CN.4/1986/SR.35, para. 75.

Union has been the leading proponent of the view that it would be incompatible with the principle of non-interference in internal affairs for the United Nations to be concerned with violations of the human rights of specific individuals. This attitude was most clearly articulated by its representative at the 1975 session of the Commission on Human Rights:

[I]n accordance with the United Nations Charter and with established practice, it was the Commission's right and duty to examine questions connected with consistent patterns of gross violations of human rights. Only in such cases was it possible to speak of failure of States to fulfill the obligation, laid down in the Charter, to respect human rights. The examination of communications or complaints relating to single cases of violation of individual rights of particular persons did not fall within the competence of UN bodies, but was entirely a domestic affair of each State.[153]

The assertions made here are not very convincing. Although under ECOSOC Resolutions 1235 and 1503 special procedures have been created to respond to consistent patterns of (gross) violations, it does not follow that UN responses to violations of the human rights of single individuals are thereby ruled out. The UN Charter certainly contains no support for the view that UN organs may only respond to violations of human rights if they add up to a consistent pattern. According to Charter Article 55, the United Nations shall promote universal respect for human rights and fundamental freedoms *for all*. UN practice does not support the Soviet thesis either. Although the large majority of UN human rights resolutions have been concerned with general situations rather than with named individuals, there have been a considerable number of exceptions.[154]

As early as 1948, the Security Council twice called upon the Netherlands Government to release immediately *President Ahmed Sukarno* of Indonesia.[155] In 1961, the Council decided to hold an investigation into the killing of the Congolese leader *Patrice Lumumba* and two of his colleagues.[156] It is probably fair to say that these decisions were prompted more by concern about the promotion of self-determination and the preservation of international peace and security than by concern about the human rights of the individuals concerned. This does not apply, however, to subsequent decisions by the Security Council on individual cases. During the 1980s, the Council repeatedly called

153. Mr. Zorin (USSR), 17 February 1975, UN Doc. E/CN.4/SR.1308, p. 169.
154. Cf. also B. G. Ramcharan, *The Concept and Present Status of the International Protection of Human Rights* (1989), pp. 80–101.
155. Resolutions 63 (1948) of 24 December 1948 and 64 (1948) of 28 December 1948.
156. Resolution 161 (1961) of 21 February 1961.

on the South African authorities to commute death sentences imposed on certain named *members of the African National Congress.*[157] These resolutions all relied not only on the Charter of the United Nations and relevant resolutions of the Security Council, but also on unspecified "relevant international instruments." The United States has explained its understanding that this term comprises the Universal Declaration of Human Rights. In the American view, therefore, these appeals were motivated not only by concern about international peace and security but also by concern about the human rights of the individuals in question.[158]

The General Assembly has been more reluctant to adopt resolutions on named individuals, but here again there have been a few cases. In 1981, the Assembly called for the release of *Ziad Abu Eain,* a Palestinian extradited to Israel by the United States.[159] The Israeli Government responded that this resolution was *ultra vires* and incompatible with Charter Article 2(7) on the grounds that the bringing to justice of an individual accused of criminal offences is clearly within the domestic jurisdiction of the prosecuting state.[160] Like the Security Council, the General Assembly has furthermore occasionally called on South Africa to commute death sentences imposed on certain named *members of the African National Congress.*[161]

The largest number of decisions on individual cases has been taken by the Commission on Human Rights. In 1974, the Commission decided to send a telegram to the Government of Chile in which it expressed concern about five named individuals whose lives were reported to be in imminent danger: *Clodomiro Almeida, Luis Corvalán, Enrique Kirberg, Pedro Felipe Ramires,* and *Anselmo Sule.*[162] Although some delegations considered it discriminatory merely to express concern about the safety of certain prominent individuals and not others, the decision was adopted without a vote.

In 1975, the Commission on Human Rights decided, without a vote, to appeal to the Government of the United Kingdom, in its capacity as the administering authority of what was then Southern Rho-

157. E.g., Resolutions 503 (1982), 525 (1982), 533 (1983), and 547 (1984).

158. The Soviet Union would have preferred to restrict the justification for the actions taken to the fact that *apartheid* threatens international peace and security. See UN Doc. S/PV.2351, pp. 8–12. South Africa contended on at least one occasion that consideration by the Security Council of a common law murder case constituted unwarranted interference in South Africa's internal affairs. See UN Doc. S/16271.

159. Resolution 36/171 of 16 December 1981. Adopted by seventy-five votes in favor, twenty-one against, and forty-three abstentions.

160. UN Doc. A/36/35, Annex I.

161. Resolutions 37/1 of 1 October 1982 and 37/68 of 7 December 1982.

162. Decision of 1 March 1974, Commission on Human Rights, Report on the 30th Session, UN Doc. E/CN.4/1154, p. 56.

desia, to intervene and secure the immediate release of the Reverend *Ndabaningi Sithole* from detention by the Smith regime.[163] Prior to the decision's adoption, the United Kingdom had declared itself willing to study such a message most carefully.[164]

In 1976, the Commission on Human Rights decided to send a telegram in which it urged the Government of Chile to release thirteen individuals who had been in detention for over two years: *José Cademartori, Luis Corvalán, Fernando Flores, Alfredo Joignant, Leopoldo Luna, Jorge Montes, Tito Palestro, Aníbal Palma, Pedro Felipe Ramírez, Eric Schnake, Andrés Sepúlveda, Daniel Vergara, and Sergio Vuskovic.*[165] The decision was taken without a vote. Chile responded that the telegram constituted interference in matters that were specifically within the competence of local authorities.[166]

Also in 1976, the Commission on Human Rights decided to send a telegram to request that the UN Secretary-General employ whatever means he might deem most appropriate to save the lives of South West Africa People's Organization (SWAPO) leaders *Aaron Mushimba* and *Hendrik Shikongo*, who were in danger of being executed in South Africa. The decision was taken unanimously.[167]

In 1979, the Commission on Human Rights decided to send a telegram to the Government of Guatemala expressing profound regret at the assassination of former Foreign Minister *Dr. Alberto Fuentes Mohr* and inviting information on the matter before its next session.[168] The decision was taken without a vote, and Guatemala did not object to it. Interestingly enough, however, the Soviet representative expressed some reservations. He stated that his delegation would have no objection to the telegram being adopted without a vote, on the understanding that the action taken related to the general situation in Guatemala.[169]

In 1980, a similar message was proposed which would have expressed concern about the administrative measures taken against academician *Andrei Sakharov* and which would have requested the Soviet Union to provide information on this case to the Commission's next session.[170] The Soviet Union and several of its allies argued that the

---

163. Decision 15 (XXXI) of 6 March 1975.
164. Sir Keith Unwin (United Kingdom), 6 March 1975, UN Doc. E/CN.4/SR.1333, p. 165.
165. Decision 1 (XXXII) of 19 February 1976.
166. Letter from Chile's Minister of Foreign Affairs to the Chairman of the Commission on Human Rights, 14 May 1976, UN Doc. E/CN.4/1216.
167. Decision 2 (XXXII) of 15 February 1976.
168. Decision 12 (XXXV) of 14 March 1979.
169. Mr. Zorin (USSR), 14 March 1979, UN Doc. E/CN.4/SR.1520, para. 73.
170. UN Doc. E/CN.4/L.1534 of 7 March 1980.

case was a domestic matter.[171] Senegal took the more utilitarian view that the Commission could not be an organ for individual recourse. The Commission should only deal with emergencies constituting a serious threat to the life of a person.[172] The Commission decided without a vote to defer a decision on the message until its following session, but the proposal was never reintroduced.

In 1983, the Commission's Sub-Commission on Prevention of Discrimination and Protection of Minorities decided to ask the Chairman of the Commission to transmit a message to the Uruguayan Government requesting it to release *José Luis Massera*, a professor of mathematics and a former member of parliament, on humanitarian grounds.[173] The decision was adopted without a vote.

In 1984, the Commission decided to transmit a telegram appealing to the President of Malawi to commute the death sentences imposed on former minister of justice *Orton Chirwa and his wife Vera*.[174] The decision was again taken without a vote. The representatives of the Soviet Union and the German Democratic Republic explained their reluctance to go along with the decision and repeated their view that the Commission should not concern itself with individual cases. They had nevertheless agreed to it, they said, because the African Group had raised no objection and because it was understood that no precedent would be created.[175]

It may be concluded that while resolutions on the violation of the human rights of named individuals have been relatively scarce, they have in almost all cases been adopted without a vote, in spite of occasional claims of domestic jurisdiction by the offending state. The reason such resolutions have not been adopted more frequently has not been that they are considered incompatible with the prohibition of interference in internal affairs or with the requirement that action may only be taken on "consistent patterns" of violations, but because of the political difficulties involved in the process of selecting certain cases and rejecting others. Only the Soviet Union has repeatedly raised objections of principle against the adoption of such resolutions.

171. UN press releases HR/871–873 (no summary records were prepared of this session).

172. Mr. M'baye (Senegal), UN press release HR/872, p. 6.

173. Decision 1983/3 of 31 August 1983. In 1979, the Human Rights Committee, set up under the International Covenant on Civil and Political Rights, had already established, in response to a communication submitted under the Optional Protocol procedure, that Professor Massera had been subjected inter alia to torture and unfair trial. See communication No. 5/1977, view of 15 August 1979, *Selected Decisions under the Optional Protocol* (1985), UN Doc. CCPR/C/OP/1, p. 40.

174. Decision 1984/102 of 14 February 1984.

175. Mr. Chernichenko (USSR), 14 February 1984, UN Doc. E/CN.4/1984/SR.11, para. 12; Mr. Klenner (GDR), 14 February 1984, E/CN.4/1984/SR.11, para. 11.

Finally, and most significantly, it should be pointed out that the Commission on Human Rights has permitted its thematic procedures to act on individual cases without requiring the prior establishment of a consistent pattern of violations. The mandates of these procedures do not restrict their activities to consistent patterns of violations, and in practice also they have not followed a "threshold" policy. This is in spite of the fact that the establishment of these procedures by the Commission must have been based on ECOSOC Resolution 1235 (XLII).[176] The annual reports of the Working Group on Enforced or Involuntary Disappearances, the Special Rapporteur on Summary or Arbitrary Executions, and the Special Rapporteur on Torture and Other Cruel, Inhuman or Degrading Treatment or Punishment abound with names of individuals on behalf of whom action has been taken. Indeed, action is frequently taken on the basis of a single reported case in a particular country. For example, the 1989 report of the Working Group on Enforced or Involuntary Disappearances indicated that the group had acted upon single cases of "disappearance" in China, Cuba, Egypt, Mozambique and Zimbabwe.[177] No objections to this type of action, by this time a well-established practice, are known to have been raised by members of the Commission on Human Rights.[178]

In fact, it seems more than likely that the somewhat decreasing frequency with which the Commission on Human Rights has adopted decisions on individuals during the 1980s can be fully attributed to the corresponding expansion of activities by the thematic procedures. By delegating the task of acting upon individual cases to its thematic procedures, the Commission has wisely rid itself of the task of having to make impossible choices. The thematic procedures offer the advantage of being able to respond throughout the year, away from the limelight, and on the basis of consistently applied criteria.

2.2.5 The Case of China

So far, we have considered primarily the attitude adopted by offending states directly affected by decisions of the UN General Assembly and the UN Commission on Human Rights. For the purposes of determining the status of general international law on accounta-

176. See *supra* note 68.
177. UN Doc. E/CN.4/1989/18.
178. P. H. Kooijmans, "Bescherming van de Mensenrechten: de effectiviteit van het VN Beleid" [Protection of Human Rights: The Effectiveness of UN Policy], 1 *VN Forum* (1988), No. 2, p. 6. Kamminga, *supra* note 148, p. 307.

bility toward international organizations, special significance should be attached to this category of states.[179] Since the United Nations has now taken decisions on the situation of human rights in a large number of states belonging to different political and regional groupings, the information thus collected must be regarded as having considerable authority. Some significance may also be attached to the attitude taken by states not directly affected, however, especially if it can be established that the views taken by such states were consistently held and not influenced by ad hoc political considerations.

As we have seen above, some of the most sweeping resolutions of the Commission on Human Rights were adopted without a vote. This is an obvious indication of the wide-ranging support these resolutions received. There have nevertheless been instances in which states demonstrated their disapproval of "interventionist" elements in UN human rights resolutions by voting against them or abstaining. Even without a detailed analysis, it is fair to assume that such dissenting votes were often motivated more by political opportunism than by consistently held convictions of what is legally unacceptable. But there is one clear exception to this general pattern. Of all member states, the People's Republic of China has had one of the most consistently "anti-interventionist" voting records on human rights questions, even before China itself became the subject of a UN resolution.

Since its admission to the United Nations in 1971, whenever a vote was taken in the General Assembly on the situation of human rights in Bolivia, Chile, El Salvador, Guatemala, or Iran, China has either not participated in the vote or abstained. At the same time, it has consistently voted in favor of resolutions on the situation of human rights in Afghanistan, the Israeli Occupied Territories, and Southern Africa. It must be considered remarkable that China has been unwilling to vote in favor of resolutions on, for example, the situation of human rights in Chile under the Pinochet regime, in spite of political considerations.

Since China is not in the habit of explaining its vote, it has until recently been difficult to appreciate fully the reasons for this behavior. This lack of assertiveness has long made it difficult to grant China the status of "persistent objector" to the principle that the United Nations may act on alleged violations of human rights in any part of the world. By restricting its positive support to responses to the situation of human rights in Afghanistan, the Israeli Occupied Territories, and Southern Africa, however, it may have been guided by the

---

179. *North Sea Continental Shelf* case, ICJ Reports 1969, paras. 73 and 74.

old theory that the United Nations may only respond to violations of human rights that threaten international peace and security or the right to self-determination.[180]

Over the course of 1989, China was forced to state its position more clearly when confronted with the UN reaction to its violent suppression of the pro-democracy movement. In August 1989, the UN Sub-Commission on Prevention of Discrimination and Protection of Minorities adopted a very moderate resolution in which it appealed for clemency and requested the UN Secretary-General to transmit relevant information to the Commission on Human Rights.[181] China responded by claiming that this resolution constituted "brutal interference in China's internal affairs while hurting the feelings of the Chinese people."[182] It also asserted that "[p]unishment of criminals in accordance with the law is a matter within the realm of a country's sovereignty, and no foreign country or international organization has the right to interfere in it."[183] In an important speech in the Third Committee of the UN General Assembly, China's representative had earlier argued in more general terms that different views on the concept and interpretation of human rights should be allowed; that the principal responsibility for promoting and protecting human rights rests with the sovereign state; and that the principle of non-interference in the internal affairs of other countries should also apply to the issue of human rights.[184]

China has thereby taken over the role of the Soviet Union as the champion at the UN of the principle of non-interference in connection with human rights violations. Like the Soviet Union in the past, it takes the view that international human rights standards do not apply everywhere in the same manner and that the implementation

180. Cf. the statement by Mr. Wang (China) in the Third Committee of the General Assembly in 1979: "[T]he legislation of many countries incorporated individual rights in the form of the rights of citizens. Such rights varied from State to State in accordance with social systems and actual conditions. Such matters fell within the internal responsibility of each State and brooked no interference by outsiders. His delegation therefore supported the view that the United Nations should focus its attention on the search for solutions to the problem presented by the mass and flagrant violations of human rights which were inseparable from the policies of colonialism, racism, racial discrimination, *apartheid*, expansionism, aggression and hegemonism followed by certain countries." See UN Doc. A/C.3/34/SR.25, para. 45. See also Shen Baoxiang, Wang Chenquan and Li Zerui, "On the Question of Human Rights in the International Realm," *Beijing Review*, 1982, No. 30, pp. 13–22; and Guo Shan, "China's Role in Human Rights Field," *Beijing Review*, 1987, nos. 5 and 6, pp. 25–26.

181. Resolution 1989/5 of 31 August 1989, UN Doc. E/CN.4/1990/2, p. 23.

182. Letter from the Permanent Representative of the People's Republic of China to the UN Office at Geneva, 1 December 1989, UN Doc. E/CN.4/1990/52, p. 2.

183. Letter from the Permanent Representative of the People's Republic of China to the UN Secretary-General, 12 January 1990, UN Doc. E/CN.4/1990/55.

184. Mr. Ding (China), 24 November 1989, UN Doc. A/C.3/44/SR.53, pp. 12–14.

of these standards should be left to the states concerned. From the point of view of consistency, China has been more impressive than the Soviet Union because its philosophy, unlike that of the Soviet Union, has for many years been reflected in its voting record. Interestingly, however, China's objections apparently do not apply to the thematic procedures of the UN Commission on Human Rights. Indeed, China has been cooperating with these procedures for a number of years. For example, it responded in detail and without invoking the non-interference rule to cables from the Special Rapporteur on Summary or Arbitrary Executions concerning the killings of demonstrators and bystanders on Tiananmen Square in June 1989.[185]

3. Other Intergovernmental Organizations

A brief look at some other intergovernmental organizations suggests that in striking a balance between the duty of non-interference and the duty of the international protection of human rights no uniform solutions have been established. Some organizations, such as the International Labour Organisation (ILO), have a long tradition of holding their members accountable for violations of international standards adopted under their auspices. Within the limited area of its mandate, the ILO has gone further, in this respect, than the United Nations in the area of human rights. Other organizations, such as the Organization of African Unity (OAU), have been more restrictive than the UN. The Organization of American States (OAS) has a somewhat contradictory record.

The Constitution of the International Labour Organisation does not contain a prohibition of interference in internal affairs, and the ILO's supervisory procedures in the field of human rights are among the most incisive anywhere. Although all activities of the ILO could be said to be related to human rights in a broad sense, "human rights" in the context of the ILO usually refers to the right to freedom of association[186] and the prohibition of forced labor.[187]

Of the different supervisory procedures, the Governing Body's Committee on Freedom of Association is especially noteworthy.[188]

185. UN Doc. E/CN.4/1990/22, pp. 18–23.
186. As reflected chiefly in Convention No. 87 on Freedom of Association and Protection of the Right to Organise (1948) and Convention No. 98 on the Right to Organise and Collective Bargaining (1949).
187. As reflected chiefly in Convention No. 29 on Forced Labour (1930) and Convention No. 105 on Abolition of Forced Labour (1957).
188. See, generally, G. von Potobsky, "Protection of Trade Union Rights: Twenty Years' Work by the Committee on Freedom of Association," 105 *International Labour Review* (1972), pp. 69–83; and A. J. Pouyat, "The ILO's freedom of association

The Committee examines complaints of violations of trade union rights submitted to it by workers' and employers' organizations and by governments. It is not required that the state complained against be a party to any of the ILO conventions on freedom of association. The Committee on Freedom of Association has developed an extensive body of case law.[189] It has frequently addressed highly specific "requests" to governments, including requests that certain trade unionists be either released or promptly brought to trial; requests that judicial inquiries be conducted into killings or the "disappearance" of trade unionists; and requests to be informed of the outcome of such trials and investigations. The reports of the Committee indicate that governments on many occasions complied with such requests by supplying the information requested and by taking the necessary corrective measures.[190] It has been suggested that a widely held view exists among states that they are under an obligation to account to the ILO for their behavior in the field of freedom of association, even if they have not ratified the conventions in question.[191]

Criticisms of the ILO's supervisory procedures, however, have been directed especially at its machinery for the supervision of the application of conventions and recommendations.[192] This machinery consists of the Committee of Experts on the Application of Conventions and Recommendations and the Conference Committee on the Application of Conventions and Recommendations. The Committee of Experts produces an annual report on the extent to which member states have complied with their ILO obligations. This report is then considered by the Conference Committee, which is set up each year by the International Labour Conference. The whole procedure tends to be a model of prudence and scrupulousness. Nevertheless, in 1983, a group of socialist states, motivated apparently by the machinery's critical attitude toward Czechoslovakia, Poland, and the USSR, called for a reexamination of the supervisory machinery. The group alleged that tendentious and one-sided assessments had been made of the law and practice of socialist and developing countries and that the ma-

---

standards and machinery: a summing up," 121 *International Labour Review* (1982), pp. 287–302.

189. See the ILO publication *Freedom of Association: Digest of decisions and principles of the Freedom of Association Committee of the Governing Body of the ILO*, 3d ed. (1985).

190. The reports of the Committee on Freedom of Association are reproduced in the ILO's *Official Bulletin*, Series B.

191. N. Valticos, "Droit international du travail et souverainités étatiques," in *Mélanges Fernand Dehousse* (1979), vol. 1, p. 130. *Id., Droit International du Travail*, 2d ed. (1983), p. 618.

192. For a description of the system, see, generally, N. Valticos, "Un système de contrôle international: la mise en oeuvre des conventions internationales de travail," 123 *RCADI* (1968), pp. 315–407.

chinery had become a kind of supranational tribunal.[193] This echoed criticisms made by the USSR as early as 1959.[194] In response, the ILO's Director-General issued a characteristically spirited and confident defense of the supervisory system.[195] Significantly, as in the past, the criticisms found little support among the other member states, and no changes of any consequence were made as a result of this attack.

In contrast to the ILO, the Charter of the Organization of African Unity prominently lists non-interference in the internal affairs of states among the principles of the organization.[196] This is no coincidence. The strict inter-state structure of the OAU and the organizations's emphasis on non-interference reflects the fragility of African states and their fear of outside intervention.[197] Unlike the Charter of the United Nations, which starts with the words "We the Peoples of the United Nations," and the Charter of the Organization of American States, which starts with "The peoples of the Americas," the Charter of the Organization of African Unity begins with "We, the Heads of African States and Governments." Against this background, it comes as no surprise that the political organs of the OAU have in the past frequently refused even to discuss large-scale violations of human rights, including the genocidal massacres in Biafra, Burundi, and Rwanda. OAU practice in this regard has been exceptionally restrictive.[198]

This laissez faire attitude has been strongly criticized, both in the literature and by some African leaders. It remains to be seen whether the adoption, in 1981, of the African Charter on Human and Peoples' Rights[199] reflects a significant shift in favor of the principle of inter-

193. Memorandum submitted by the Byelorussian SSR, Bulgaria, GDR, Cuba, Mongolia, Czechoslovakia, Hungary, Ukrainian SSR, and the SSR. See International Labour Conference, *Record of Proceedings*, 1983, p. 7/18.

194. See E. A. Landy, *The Effectiveness of International Supervision: Thirty Years of I.L.O. Experience* (1966), pp. 193–94.

195. International Labour Conference, 70th session (1984), *Report of the Director-General*, p. 5.

196. Art. III (2).

197. F. Borella, "Le système juridique de l'OUA," 17 *AFDI* (1971), p. 236. O. Okongwu, "The O.A.U. Charter and the Principle of Domestic Jurisdiction in Intra-African Affairs," 13 *Indian Journal of International Law* (1973), pp. 589–93.

198. O. Umozurike, "The Domestic Jurisdiction Clause in the OAU Charter," 78 *African Affairs* (1979), at pp. 198–202. See also, A. B. Akinyemi, "The OAU and the Concept of Non-Interference in Internal Affairs," 46 *BYIL* (1972–73), pp. 393–400; Ph. Kunig, *Das völkerrechtliche Nichteinmischungsprinzip: Zur Praxis der Organisation der afrikanischen Einheit (OAU) und des afrikanischen Staatenverkehrs* (1981), pp. 180–88; O. Ojo and A. Sesay, "The O.A.U. and Human Rights: Prospects for the 1980s and Beyond," 8 *HRQ* (1986), p. 92.

199. Reproduced in 21 *ILM* (1982), pp. 59–68. Entered into force 21 October 1986.

national protection of human rights.[200] In 1986, President Yoweri Kaguta Museveni of Uganda declared at a session of the OAU's Assembly of Heads of State and Government:

> [I] must state that Ugandans were unhappy and felt a deep sense of betrayal that most of Africa kept silent while tyrants killed them. The reason for not condemning such massive crimes has supposedly been a desire not to interfere in the internal affairs of a member state, in accordance with the Charters of the OAU and the United Nations. . . .
> While we accept and recognise the validity of the principle of non-interference in the internal affairs of a member state, we strongly hold that this should never be used as a cloak to shield genocide from just censure.[201]

Of the constituent instruments of all intergovernmental organizations, the Charter of the Organization of American States contains the most radical prohibition of interference in the internal affairs of states.[202] At the same time, the American Convention on Human Rights[203] contains some of the strongest human rights provisions of any general human rights treaty. This apparent contradiction can be explained as a reaction to the long-standing policy of United States intervention in Latin America. Interestingly, the Latin American founders of the OAS did not regard the establishment of a regional system for the protection of human rights primarily from the point of view of the threat it might offer to their national sovereignty. Rather, they considered it as a method to oppose U.S. interference in their internal affairs under the guise of the traditional international law for the protection of aliens.[204] F. V. García Amador, the International Law Commission's first rapporteur on state responsibility, was a representative of this school of thought, which proposed that the traditional international law of injury to aliens should be replaced by the new international law of human rights.[205] According to a famous reso-

---

200. On the African Charter see, e.g., R. Gittelman, "The African Charter on Human and Peoples' Rights: A Legal Analysis," 22 *Virginia Journal of International Law* (1981), pp. 668–714; U. O. Umozurike, "The African Charter on Human and Peoples' Rights," 77 *AJIL* (1983), pp. 902–12; R. M. D'Sa, "Human and Peoples' Rights: Distinctive Features of the African Charter," 29 *Journal of African Law* (1985), pp. 72–81. The first activity report of the African Commission on Human and Peoples' Rights may be found in 9 *HRLJ* (1988), p. 326.

201. Address by President Yoweri Kaguta Museveni of Uganda, 22d ordinary session of the Assembly of Heads of State and Government, Addis Ababa, 29 July 1986.

202. Art. 18.

203. Reproduced in 9 *ILM* (1970), pp. 99–122.

204. M. M. Ball, "Issue for the Americas: Non-Intervention v. Human Rights and the Preservation of Democratic Institutions," 15 *International Organization* (1961), pp. 21–37. J. A. Cabranes, "The Protection of Human Rights by the Organization of American States," 62 *AJIL* (1968), pp. 891–93.

205. *YILC*, 1956, vol. II, pp. 202–3.

lution adopted at the Inter-American Conference held in Mexico City in 1945:

International protection of the essential rights of man would eliminate the misuse of diplomatic protection of citizens abroad, the exercise of which has more than once led to the violation of the principles of non-intervention and of equality between nationals and aliens, with respect to the essential rights of man.[206]

The dilemmas caused by the organization's emphatic commitment to both non-interventionism and the international protection of human rights appear, for example, in the tensions between the OAS General Assembly and the Inter-American Commission on Human Rights. The Assembly has generally failed to give appropriate political backing to the Commission; it has generally not, for instance, included in its resolutions specific references to the countries singled out in the annual reports of the Commission. The ambivalence may also be perceived in the attitude the organization has adopted toward member states that are repressive dictatorships. According to Article 3(d) of the 1948 OAS Charter, "[t]he solidarity of the American States and the high aims which are sought through it require the political organization of those States on the basis of the effective exercise of representative democracy." But in practice the OAS has often been reluctant to promote the effective fulfillment of this principle. In 1959, a committee established by the Inter-American Conference expressed strong doubts about the capacity of the organization to "set itself up as the judge of the democratic nature of this or that government."[207]

In spite of this, in 1979 one of the political bodies of the OAS took one of the most interventionist actions ever taken by an intergovernmental organization. In response to serious and widespread violations of human rights in Nicaragua, the Meeting of Consultation of Ministers of Foreign Affairs called for the "immediate and definitive replacement of the Somoza regime" and the "installation in Nicaraguan territory of a democratic government."[208] One may wonder how such a call for the removal of a head of state of a member state may be reconciled with the Charter's strict non-intervention provision. Ac-

206. Resolution XL of 7 March 1945. Report of the Delegation of the United States of America to the Inter-American Conference on Problems of War and Peace, Mexico City, February 21-March 8, 1945, Department of State Publication No. 2497, p. 108.

207. Eleventh Inter-American Conference, *Study on the Juridical Relationship Between Respect for Human Rights and the Exercise of Democracy*, OEA/Ser.E/XI.1, Doc. 16 (1959), pp. 6–7. Quoted in Ball, *supra* note 204, pp. 34–35.

208. Resolution II of the Seventeenth Meeting of Consultation, 23 June 1979. Quoted in the case concerning *Military and Paramilitary Activities in and Against Nicaragua*, ICJ Reports 1986, p. 89.

cording to one author who has studied the case in detail, it should be assumed that in the Americas the principle of non-intervention applies only vis-à-vis states that are representative democracies.[209] But this can hardly be considered a satisfactory explanation.

It follows from this brief review of the practice of three intergovernmental organizations that there are no universally applicable rules on accountability toward international organizations in the field of human rights. There are simply no common constitutional principles upon which all organizations rely. What is considered perfectly acceptable in one organization is deemed inadmissible interference in another. Contrary to conventional wisdom, regional organizations are not necessarily more advanced than global ones in this respect. If there is a common element, it is only that in all organizations there is a steady tendency toward greater rather than less accountability. Pragmatic considerations, such as the degree of confidence enjoyed by the organization's supervisory machinery, seem to be the main driving force in this regard.

4. Conclusions

The oldest and most consistently held justification for inter-state accountability for violations of human rights is that such violations may cause a threat to international peace and security.[210] Evidence of this justification may be found, for example, in the peace treaties of Westphalia and in the peace treaties concluded after World War I and World War II. The view that future wars might be prevented by making states with minorities accountable to the international community was the underlying idea of the system for the protection of minority rights set up under the League of Nations. The Charter of the United Nations similarly reflects the view that respect for human rights is a necessary precondition for the preservation of international peace. Violations that threaten the peace cease to be the sole concern of the offending state and give rise to accountability to the world organization. A closely connected justification, also recognized at the San Francisco Conference, is that human rights violations that are clearly incompatible with specific provisions of the Charter like-

209. Chr. Cerna, "Human Rights in Conflict with the Principle of Non-Intervention: The Case of Nicaragua before the Seventeenth Meeting of Consultation of Ministers of Foreign Affairs," in Inter-American Commission on Human Rights, *Human Rights in the Americas: Homage to the Memory of Carlos A. Dunshee de Abranches* (1984), pp. 102–3.

210. O. Schachter, "International Law in Theory and Practice," 178 *RCADI* (1982), pp. 328–29.

wise give rise to accountability to the United Nations.[211] This applies, for example, to the Charter provisions on non-discrimination and self-determination.

Some governments and authors have maintained that a UN response to violations of human rights in a member state could only be justified on these limited grounds. When such grounds are absent, mere discussion by a UN body of alleged violations of human rights would constitute interference in the offending state's internal affairs.[212] In the practice of the United Nations, the threat to international peace and security as a specific justification for UN action on human rights violations has been particularly reflected in resolutions on the system of *apartheid* in South Africa.[213] More recently, the Security Council has held that the consequences of the repression of the civilian population in many parts of Iraq threaten international peace and security in the region, and it has demanded that Iraq, as a contribution to international peace and security in the region, immediately end this repression.[214] It is important that it has thereby become recognized that human rights violations may reach such a level of severity that they threaten international peace and security and thereby qualify for corresponding enforcement action by the Security Council.

On the other hand, it is also abundantly clear that the UN's authority to respond to human rights violations is not limited to such extreme situations. As early as 1949, the General Assembly adopted a resolution on violations of human rights in the Soviet Union which by no stretch of the imagination could be considered a response to a threat to international peace and security.[215] The competence of the United Nations to respond to violations *not* representing a threat to international peace and security was formally recognized in 1967 when the Economic and Social Council adopted Resolution 1235 (XLII). Under this resolution, the Commission on Human Rights was authorized to investigate "situations which reveal a consistent pattern of violations of human rights." Although the resolution mentioned the South African policy of *apartheid* as an example of such a situa-

211. UNCIO, vol. 6, p. 705.

212. B. Graefrath, *Die Vereinte Nationen und die Menschenrechte* (1956), p. 44. See also the view taken by Poland in 1983, *supra* note 134.

213. According to several Security Council resolutions, South Africa's policy of *apartheid* "seriously disturbs" international peace and security. E.g., Resolutions 392 (1976) of 19 June 1976 and 473 (1980) of 13 June 1980.

214. Resolution 688 (1991) of 5 April 1991. It is debatable whether, according to this resolution, the internal repression alone had caused a threat to international peace and security or whether this threat had only materialized through the resulting massive exodus of refugees.

215. Resolution 285 (III) of 25 April 1949 (Russian wives case).

tion, it did not require the existence of a threat to international peace and security as a precondition for the establishment of an investigation. The criterion of "a consistent pattern of gross and reliably attested violations of human rights," not necessarily amounting to a threat to international peace and security, was also the triggering mechanism used in ECOSOC Resolution 1503 (XLVIII), which established the confidential communications procedure.

ECOSOC Resolutions 1235 and 1503 reflected the formal recognition of states that they are entitled to be concerned with human rights violations committed in another state even if their own material interests have not been affected. Under these two resolutions, the legitimacy of UN involvement no longer depended on the question whether the security of other states was being threatened but simply on the seriousness and scale of the violations being committed. Because of this implication, it is not surprising that some states strongly opposed the adoption of these resolutions.

In 1977, in an apparent attempt by its sponsors to counteract the effects of resolutions 1235 and 1503, the General Assembly adopted Resolution 32/130, which introduced the more restrictive concept of "mass and flagrant" violations. The resolution gave as examples of such abuses violations resulting from *apartheid*, racial discrimination, colonialism, foreign domination and occupation, aggression, and the refusal to recognize the right to self-determination (curiously enough, genocide does not appear on this list). According to this resolution, the United Nations was to accord "priority" to the search for solutions to such violations. The resolution did not attempt to alter the fact that UN action could continue to be taken on consistent patterns of gross violations, however. Accordingly, Resolution 32/130 has not significantly affected practice under ECOSOC Resolutions 1235 and 1503.

Although this raises the inevitable question as to what should be understood by "a consistent pattern of gross violations," especially since the UN itself has not defined the concept,[216] a precise definition is not needed since the political organs of the United Nations have on numerous occasions demonstrated that they do not consider themselves restricted by this category. A "pattern" obviously requires the

216. One author has recently proposed the following definition: "Gross, systematic violations of human rights are those violations, instrumental to the achievement of governmental policies, perpetuated in such a quantity and in such a manner as to create a situation in which the rights to life, to personal integrity or to personal liberty of the population as a whole or of one or more sectors of the population of a country are continuously infringed or threatened." See C. Medina Quiroga, *The Battle of Human Rights* (1988), p. 16. For a discussion of this concept in the context of state responsibility, see *infra*, Chapter 3, text accompanying note 143.

occurrence of more than one case. Nevertheless, under the thematic procedures of the Commission on Human Rights, countless actions have been taken on individual cases not alleged to be part of a consistent pattern. This practice has not been controversial. Moreover, a number of resolutions have been adopted, particularly by the Commission on Human Rights, that have expressed concern about violations of the human rights of a single individual. This development arguably received the seal of approval through General Assembly Resolution 37/200, which affirmed "that violations of human rights, wherever they exist, are of concern to the United Nations." It follows that in practice UN concern with violations of human rights has moved from the highly restricted category of violations threatening international peace and security, to the wider category of gross violations constituting a consistent pattern, to the present broad category of violations of any UN human rights standard.

Country-related resolutions now routinely commence with the following preambular paragraph: "*Guided* by the principles embodied in the Charter of the United Nations, the Universal Declaration of Human Rights, the International Covenants on Human Rights and the humanitarian rules set out in the Geneva Conventions of 1949," or words to that effect. The apparent implication is that a state may be held accountable by the United Nations if it has committed infringements of one or more of these core instruments, whether or not the offending state has specifically consented to be bound by them. Offending states have not—with one or two temporary exceptions—objected to being held accountable on this basis. The reason for this flexible attitude does not appear to be that offending states accept that these instruments reflect customary international law. Rather, this attitude can be explained by the fact that these instruments have not been cited to formally invoke the offending states' international responsibility.[217] They have been employed not for the purpose of determining the occurrence of an internationally wrongful act, but merely as a benchmark in the accountability process. That this has indeed been the intention appears already from the gentle words "guided by."

The standards contained in these instruments include not only civil and political rights, but also economic, social, and cultural rights. In practice, however, UN action in response to violations of the latter rights has tended to be limited to instances in which rights belonging to both categories were infringed. Appeals and recommendations

217. Cf. also, Ramcharan, *supra* note 154, p. 59.

aimed at correcting abuses of economic, social, and cultural rights have also tended to be more global and less specific than those prompted by infringements of civil and political rights.

Although these developments have not always been immediately welcomed by all states, the objectors have been fighting no more than a rear guard action. In spite of initial objections by some states to ECOSOC Resolutions 1235 and 1503, subsequent action taken under these resolutions has often been approved unanimously. Of the eleven states which have so far been subjected to a public investigation of their human rights record by the Commission on Human Rights, only three (Afghanistan, Poland, and Romania) have at some point taken the view that these investigations constituted, in and of themselves, interference in their internal affairs. None of these states is likely to maintain those objections today. In spite of initial objections by some states against the thematic procedures, the mandates of these procedures have for many years been renewed without a vote. In spite of principled objections by some states (especially the Soviet Union) against the adoption of resolutions on violations of the human rights of named individuals, such resolutions have in almost all cases been adopted without a vote.

The change in attitude adopted by the offending states themselves is noteworthy. Initially, states held accountable for human rights abuses through General Assembly resolutions invariably and without exception invoked Charter Article 2(7). In 1974 one author could still observe: "There is no instance in the history of the United Nations where a government which has been called to account for its domestic policies or actions conceded the legitimacy of such intervention, even for the most worthy of ends."[218] But a year after this was written, the Chilean Government in effect started a new trend by its positive reaction to the establishment of the *Ad Hoc* Working Group on Chile. It welcomed the resolution of the Commission on Human Rights "as an attempt to seek the truth without prejudice," and it promised its fullest support to the Working Group.[219] Reluctant acceptance by offending states of their accountability toward the United Nations has since become the rule rather than the exception.

Especially in view of this general attitude of states most directly affected, it can be confidently asserted that in current UN practice a violation of a UN human rights standard is no longer "essentially within domestic jurisdiction" under the terms of Charter Article 2(7). Although the objection is still raised occasionally, it is simply not taken

218. M. Moskowitz, *International Concern with Human Rights* (1974), p. 62.
219. *Supra* note 109.

seriously anymore. Whether human rights violations are of legitimate concern to the United Nations is no longer determined solely by assessing their possible international repercussions or their magnitude.

This does not mean that any response by a UN body is permissible, however. Even though the violations acted upon may not be within domestic jurisdiction and a UN reaction may therefore be legitimate, the nature of the response remains subject to the restrictions of Article 2(7). At the one end of the scale, it has long been accepted in the practice of the United Nations that placing human rights violations on the agenda and discussing them does not constitute intervention within the meaning of Article 2(7).[220] At the other end of the scale, it has long been equally uncontroversial that the sending of a fact-finding mission into the territory of a state without its permission does represent such intervention.[221] No examples are known of clandestine visits by UN bodies to investigate human rights abuses. But what has long remained unclear is the gray area in between: What kinds of UN investigations and what kinds of recommendations addressed to states should be regarded as interventionist? Actions by the Commission on Human Rights that might prima facie be considered interventionist include the following appeals and recommendations addressed to member states:

- To give "active consideration" to becoming a party to certain human rights instruments (Equatorial Guinea,[222] Haiti[223])
- To terminate a state of emergency (Chile,[224] Paraguay[225])
- To reorganize certain named branches of the security forces (Chile[226])
- To become a pluralist democracy (Chile[227])

The Commission on Human Rights has also occasionally seen fit to declare certain laws or even the constitution of a state "null and void"

220. Fawcett, *supra* note 117, p. 291. L. M. Goodrich, E. Hambro, and A. P. Simons, *Charter of the United Nations*, 3d ed. (1969), pp. 67–68.

221. H. Lauterpacht, *International Law and Human Rights* (1950), p. 171. V. Leary, "When Does the Implementation of International Human Rights Constitute Interference into the Essentially Domestic Affairs of a State?" in *International Human Rights Law and Practice* (1978), J. C. Tuttle (ed.), p. 21. Mr. Ermacora (Austria), in the UN Commission on Human Rights, 28 February 1978, UN Doc. E/CN.4/SR.1457, para. 24. A significant exception to the rule has recently been accepted in the context of the CSCE. See *supra* Chapter 1, note 165.

222. Resolution 1988/52.

223. Resolution 1988/51.

224. Resolution 1983/38.

225. Resolution 1984/46.

226. Resolution 1987/60.

227. Resolution 1987/60.

(Israeli Occupied Territories,[228] Namibia,[229] South Africa[230]). It is possible to question whether each of these actions constitutes unacceptable interference in domestic affairs.

Whether to become a party to a treaty is of course a sovereign decision of the state concerned. While a state may not be coerced into accepting a treaty,[231] this does not explain what lesser degree of pressure may be put on it to encourage its adherence to a convention. International organizations have long employed various techniques to promote wider acceptance of treaties adopted under their auspices. One method has been the adoption of general appeals to states to become parties to certain treaties; a more successful method has been the use of reporting procedures. Under the Constitution of the International Labour Organisation, member states are obliged to report periodically on the difficulties that have prevented or delayed the ratification of conventions adopted by the organization.[232] Within the United Nations, a Working Group on Universal Acceptance of Human Rights Instruments—set up in 1979 by the Sub-Commission on Prevention of Discrimination and Protection of Minorities—for a number of years operated a similar system under which governments were requested to provide periodic information on the reasons that had prevented them from becoming parties to the major UN human rights treaties.[233] Neither method interferes with the sovereign discretion of states to adhere or not to adhere to a treaty; states are merely encouraged to use this discretion.[234] Although the adoption of specific appeals addressed to specific states would appear to be a relatively novel method, the same consideration applies here. Because the states concerned are merely urged to give "active consideration" to becoming parties to certain treaties, their sovereign discretion is not interfered with.

Similarly, whether or not to declare a state of emergency and to derogate from certain human rights is in principle a sovereign right of the state concerned, within the limitations set by the relevant human rights treaties. The supervisory bodies set up under these treaties have shown considerable restraint in judging the legitimacy of

228. Resolution 1986/2.
229. Resolution 1987/8.
230. Resolution 1987/7. Similarly, Security Council Resolution 554 (1984) of 17 August 1984.
231. Arts. 51 and 52, Vienna Convention on the Law of Treaties.
232. Art. 19(5), ILO Constitution.
233. See D. Weissbrodt, "A New United Nations Mechanism for Encouraging the Ratification of Human Rights Treaties," 76 *AJIL* (1982), pp. 418–29.
234. See O. Schachter, M. Nawaz, and J. Fried, *Toward Wider Acceptance of UN Treaties* (1971), p. 52.

such a decision. Although individual members of the Human Rights Committee established under the International Covenant on Civil and Political Rights have not hesitated to question state representatives on the need for a (continuing) state of emergency with accompanying derogations, the Committee has been careful not to conclude that the proclamation of a state of emergency had been unjustified.[235] The European Commission and European Court of Human Rights have permitted states parties to the European Convention on Human Rights a "wide margin of appreciation" in judging the application of this right.[236] One may wonder, therefore, whether a political organ of the United Nations has the competence to address an appeal to a state to terminate its state of emergency, especially if, as in the case of Chile, the state in question is being "urged" to do so.[237] On balance, however, this possibility should probably be admitted.[238]

With regard to the appeals addressed by the UN Commission on Human Rights to Chile "to reorganize the police and security forces, including organizations such as the National Information Center" and to re-establish "a pluralist democracy," the question must be asked whether this is compatible with the paragraph in the Declaration on Friendly Relations which provides that "[e]ach State has the right to freely choose and develop its political, social, economic and cultural systems without interference in any form by another State." This question arises *a fortiori* with regard to the call by the OAS Meeting of Consultation of Ministers of Foreign Affairs for the "immediate and definitive replacement of the Somoza regime" and the "installation in Nicaraguan territory of a democratic government." Is there indeed a primary norm of international law that imposes on states a duty to be pluralist democracies, or is this a matter of domestic jurisdiction?

On a regional level, it could probably be argued that such an obligation rests on members of the Council of Europe and the Organiza-

---

235. See J. A. Walkate, "The Human Rights Committee and Public Emergencies," 9 *Yale Journal of World Public Order* (1982), No. 1, pp. 133–46.

236. *Ireland v. UK*, European Court of Human Rights, Series A, No. 25, p. 79. See R. St. J. MacDonald, "The Margin of Appreciation in the Jurisprudence of the European Court of Human Rights," in *International Law at the Time of its Codification: Essays in Honour of Roberto Ago* (1987), vol. III, pp. 187–208.

237. Unlike Chile, Paraguay has merely been invited "to consider" ending its state of siege. Paraguay did not object to this appeal on the grounds of its alleged interference in internal affairs. See Mr. González Alsina (Paraguay), 12 March 1984, UN Doc. E/CN.4/1984/SR.50, para. 16. On 13 June 1986, in a statement on behalf of the members of the Security Council, the President of the Council called on South Africa to lift its state of emergency.

238. See M. Bossuyt, "The United Nations and Civil and Political Rights in Chile," 27 *ICLQ* (1978), pp. 462–71.

tion of American States.[239] Parties to the International Covenant on Civil and Political Rights are under an obligation to hold genuine periodic elections by secret ballot,[240] but this is not a rule of customary international law.[241] Many UN member states are not pluralist democracies, and it would be difficult to identify any evidence of *opinio juris* that this is considered unlawful. In the case concerning *Military and Paramilitary Activities in and Against Nicaragua*, the International Court of Justice observed forcefully, "adherence by a State to any particular doctrine does not constitute a violation of customary international law; to hold otherwise would make nonsense of the fundamental principle of State sovereignty."[242]

Most of the above appeals and recommendations were couched in advisory language, and for this reason alone it could be argued, in Lauterpacht's footsteps, that they do not amount to impermissible interference. But one may have serious doubts about the competence of a political body of the United Nations to "declare" that certain national laws are null and void.[243] It is difficult to escape the impression that by making such a "declaration," a political body of the United Nations has attempted to arrogate itself a semijudicial role. This may therefore be regarded as a rare example of impermissible "legislative interference" (defined by Lauterpacht as "an attempt to impose upon States rules of conduct as a matter of legal right"[244]).

By way of general conclusion, it can therefore be observed that in striking a balance between the non-interference provisions and the human rights provisions of the Charter, UN practice has been much more liberal than may have been expected by the framers of the Charter. This confirms the findings of earlier students of UN practice.[245] As envisaged by the framers of the Charter, the political organs themselves have invariably assumed the right to decide whether or not an offending state could be held accountable. No requests for an ad-

239. See preamble, Statute of the Council of Europe, and Art. 3(d), Charter of the Organization of American States. See also, in the context of the CSCE, the Charter of Paris for a New Europe, 30 *ILM* (1991), p. 193.

240. Art. 25, International Covenant on Civil and Political Rights.

241. American Law Institute, *Restatement (Third) of the Foreign Relations Law of the United States* (1987), § 702, Reporters' Note 10.

242. ICJ Reports 1986, para. 263.

243. On 13 December 1984, Sir John Thompson (British Permanent Representative at the United Nations) declared in a Security Council debate on *apartheid* in South Africa: "It does not lie within the competence of any organ of the United Nations to reject or declare null and void the constitution of a Member State." See 55 *BYIL* (1984), p. 417. South Africa itself has also made this objection.

244. H. Lauterpacht, *International Law and Human Rights* (1950), p. 171.

245. E.g., E. Hambro, in *Report of the 46th Conference of the International Law Association* (1954), p. 143; Fawcett, *supra* note 117, pp. 292–93; Verdross, *supra* note 88, p. 35; Schwelb, *supra* note 44, p. 341.

visory opinion have been addressed to the International Court of Justice in this regard. But contrary to the expectations of the framers, UN practice on human rights questions has narrowly interpreted the injunction against intervention in matters belonging to domestic jurisdiction and liberally interpreted the UN's duty to promote the protection of human rights.

In other words, the initial controversy between commentators such as Kelsen and Graefrath on the one hand and Lauterpacht on the other has been decisively settled in favor of the latter. In view of the elasticity of the relevant Charter provisions, this causes no problems with regard to the kinds of abuses to which the UN has assumed the right to respond. But questions remain regarding some of the actions taken in response to these abuses, especially given the simultaneous efforts by the General Assembly to further define and elaborate the general duty of states to refrain from interference in internal affairs.

The question therefore arises as to which legal value should be attached to UN practice in the field of human rights. Is it mere usage or does it amount to custom?[246] What about the actions by UN organs that are arguably *ultra vires*? Does it matter that they were invariably either decided upon without a vote or adopted by a large majority? Does it matter that offending states to which controversial appeals and recommendations were addressed in most cases did not object to them? In a remarkable article, J. S. Watson has suggested that at the United Nations a state's vote in favor of a proposition does not entail its solid commitment to it and that "the inconsistency and high political content of the practice of the Organization's organs are such as to render it completely useless as a source of law."[247] In Watson's view, the power to make authoritative interpretations of Charter Article 2(7) has not been yielded to the political organs of the United Nations but still rests with the member states.

In response, Professor Rosalyn Higgins has observed that the political organs of the UN *are* the member states and that there has been no significant resistance by states to the practice that Article 2(7) may be interpreted by these organs with regard to their own functions.[248] This latter observation is certainly confirmed by the present study. Offending states have almost invariably accepted the notion that the political organs could decide on the applicability of Article 2(7). Going

246. On the difference, see the *North Sea Continental Shelf* cases, ICJ Reports 1969, para. 77.
247. J. S. Watson, "Autointerpretation, Competence, and the Continuing Validity of Article 2(7) of the UN Charter," 71 *AJIL* (1977), p. 76.
248. R. Higgins, "Reality and Hope in International Human Rights: A Critique," 9 *Hofstra Law Review* (1981), pp. 1495–96.

a step further, offending states have increasingly and in recent years almost without exception accepted the idea that the political organs could discuss, investigate, and make recommendations on alleged violations committed within their territory, although they have not always immediately felt bound to cooperate with the investigation. Few if any states have consistently opposed UN responses to certain types of human rights abuses (with two exceptions: China's apparent resistance to the consideration of situations that do not amount to a threat to international peace and security, and the Soviet Union's resistance to the consideration of individual cases). There is therefore little evidence of *opinio juris* that militates *against* the established practice summarized above.

In a speech delivered in 1985, UN Secretary-General Javier Pérez de Cuéllar made the following observation:

Some Member States have insisted that action by the United Nations with regard to alleged human rights violations in their territory was an infringement of their sovereignty and contrary to the Charter. However, the history of the United Nations during its first 40 years has increasingly denied the tenability of this argument. As I have said, the Universal Declaration of Human Rights has universal applicability. It is now accepted in practice that infringements, wherever they may be, are of common concern.[249]

This is a remarkably emphatic statement on an issue that has long been considered highly sensitive. It represents a volte-face from the view held for almost three centuries (from the peace of Westphalia until and including the time of the adoption of the UN Charter) that states could only be held accountable if abuses threatened international peace and security. Any remaining controversy is no longer about the circumstances under which the United Nations may hold states accountable, but about the manner in which it may do so.

249. Address to the United Nations Association of the United States, 30 April 1985, 22 *UN Chronicle* (1985), No. 1, p. 23.

Chapter 3
Aspects of State Responsibility

> The fact must also be recognized that kings, and those who possess rights equal to those kings, have the right of demanding punishments not only on account of injuries committed against themselves or their subjects, but also on account of injuries which do not directly affect them but excessively violate the law of nature or of nations in regard to any persons whatsoever.
>
> Hugo Grotius, *De Jure Belli ac Pacis* (1625)

In the preceding chapters we have examined the increasing willingness of states to hold other states accountable for violations of the human rights of persons who are nationals of the offending state. This willingness is evident both through diplomatic action on behalf of such persons (examined in Chapter 1) and through the activities of intergovernmental organizations (examined in Chapter 2). We have also noted an increasing willingness of offending states to be held internationally accountable in this manner. At the same time, however, we found that interceding states have shown a marked lack of enthusiasm for couching their démarches in terms of formal legal claims against the offending state. In other words, interceding states have been reluctant to invoke the offending state's formal responsibility under international law to treat its citizens in accordance with its international obligations. The question to be considered in the present chapter is whether, in spite of this lack of state practice, an offending state may nevertheless be formally held responsible for a breach of its international human rights obligations.

The international law of human rights and the international law of state responsibility are both established fields of international law.

Both have their recognized experts and specialists. But perhaps as a result of the increasing compartmentalization of international law, there has been little interaction between the two fields. Experts in international human rights law have tended to remain within the narrow confines of their own specialty and they have, at least until recently, not written much on state responsibility for violations of human rights.[1] Conversely, the International Law Commission's work on state responsibility demonstrates little awareness of UN practice in the area of human rights. In view of the lack of both state practice and scholarly interest, an examination of state responsibility for violations of human rights must therefore have a more tentative and speculative character than that of the topics considered in the preceding two chapters.

The subject of state responsibility has been under consideration by the International Law Commission since the 1950s. Although the Commission's work has not met with universal approval and is still far from finished, it represents the most authoritative effort so far to codify and progressively develop this particular area of international law. It therefore constitutes a convenient starting point for our inquiry. The Commission has suggested that a distinction should be drawn between *primary* rules, which impose specific obligations on states, and *secondary* rules, which determine the legal consequences of a failure to comply with those obligations. The breach of a primary obligation constitutes an internationally wrongful act if the breach is attributable to the offending state. *State responsibility* then refers to the new legal relationship that is the result of an internationally wrongful act. Under this new relationship, the injured state may be entitled to pursue certain remedies against the offending state, including a right to claim reparation and a right to take reprisals.[2]

It is not our intention here to examine exhaustively all aspects of state responsibility for violations of human rights. In particular, we will not go deeply into the subject of reprisals, sanctions, or other coercive measures that might be taken in response to a state's breach of its human rights obligations. Continuing the line of inquiry started

1. Favorable exceptions include F. Ermacora, "Über die Völkerrechtliche Verantwortlichkeit für Menschenrechtsverletzungen," in *Ius Humanitatis: Festschrift für Alfred Verdross* (1980), H. Miehsler et al. (eds.), pp. 357–78; B. G. Ramcharan, "State Responsibility for Violations of Human Rights Treaties," in *Contemporary Problems of International Law: Essays in Honour of Georg Schwarzenberger* (1988), Bin Cheng and E. D. Brown (eds.), pp. 242–61; D. Shelton, "State Responsibility for Aiding and Abetting Flagrant Violations of Human Rights," in *Essays on the Concept of a 'Right to Live'* (1988), D. Prémont (ed.), pp. 222–32; Th. Meron, *Human Rights and Humanitarian Norms as Customary Law* (1989), pp. 136–245; *id.*, "State Responsibility for Violations of Human Rights," 83 *Proceedings of the ASIL* (1989), pp. 372–85.

2. Cf. *YILC*, 1975, Vol. II, pp. 55–56.

in Chapter 1, we will investigate whether under general international law a state is entitled to bring a valid international claim against another state on the grounds that the latter has committed an internationally wrongful act consisting of a breach of its international human rights obligations, even though the interceding state's material interests or those of its nationals have not been affected. In particular, we will consider some of the preliminary objections that might be raised against such a claim if it were submitted to an international tribunal (based on some general title of jurisdiction). From the survey of state practice carried out in the preceding two chapters, we can identify what the two principal objections against such a submission are likely to be: first, that the alleged breaches are within the area of domestic jurisdiction, and second, that the interceding state lacks *locus standi*. The first objection refers to the primary rules, the second to the secondary rules.

1. Primary Rules

Obligations in the field of human rights may seriously undermine a government's freedom to manoeuvre and even its ability to stay in power. Governments have therefore long insisted that matters such as these could not be subject to any foreign interference whatsoever. This applied *a fortiori* to any matters that might be submitted for settlement to an international tribunal. Thus, prior to World War I, international agreements providing for compulsory arbitration by an international tribunal commonly excluded from such arbitration matters affecting "national honor," "vital interests," or "national independence." It was generally accepted that states that had made such reservations had retained the right to decide for themselves whether in a given situation such matters were at stake (automatic reservations). This obviously deprived compulsory international arbitration of much of its value.[3]

These clauses may be regarded as the precursors of the reservations currently included in declarations accepting the compulsory jurisdiction of the International Court of Justice in accordance with Article 36(2) of its Statute. Of the fifty-one states that have made such a declaration, twenty have made specific reservations with regard to matters within their domestic jurisdiction. Five of these reservations are still automatic (Liberia, Malawi, Mexico, the Philippines, and Sudan).[4]

3. See R. R. Wilson, "Reservation Clauses in Agreements for Obligatory Arbitration," 23 *AJIL* (1929), pp. 68–93.
4. See *YICJ*, 1989–1990, pp. 62–98.

The first question arising in this connection is whether it is at all necessary to make such a reservation with regard to matters within domestic jurisdiction. Would the Court not in any case refuse to pronounce on matters that are within domestic jurisdiction? The answer is yes. Professor C. H. M. Waldock has stressed that the role of the Court is determined by its Statute, not by the UN Charter. Whether the Court has *jurisdiction* depends on the terms of the instrument conferring jurisdiction on it, not on Charter Article 2(7).[5] As a *substantive* defense, however, the objection of domestic jurisdiction could certainly be raised even if it had not been referred to in such instrument. As Lauterpacht has put it, "if a matter is exclusively within the domestic jurisdiction of a State, not circumscribed by any obligation stemming from a source of international law as formulated in Article 38 of its Statute, the Court must inevitably reject the claim as being without foundation in international law."[6]

This raises the question as to the actual content of the prohibition of intervention in matters within domestic jurisdiction. As we have seen in Chapter 2, the political organs of the United Nations have so far been unable to give clear guidance with regard to the scope of this rule in the field of human rights. Has the World Court done any better? In one of the first cases brought before the Permanent Court of International Justice, the Council of the League of Nations requested an advisory opinion on the question whether a dispute between France and Great Britain concerning nationality decrees issued by the French Government in Tunis and Morocco was a matter of domestic jurisdiction within the terms of Covenant Article 15(8). In response, the Court inter alia made the following observations:

The words "solely within domestic jurisdiction" seem . . . to contemplate certain matters which, though they may very closely concern the interests of more than one State, are not, in principle, regulated by international law. As regards such matters, each State is sole judge.
The question whether a certain matter is or is not solely within the jurisdiction of a State is an essentially relative question; it depends upon the development of international relations. Thus, in the present state of international law, questions of nationality are, in the opinion of the Court, in principle within the reserved domain.[7]

The approach taken by the Permanent Court in this case was confirmed in a number of subsequent cases presented to the Interna-

5. C. H. M. Waldock, "The Plea of Domestic Jurisdiction Before International Legal Tribunals," 31 *BYIL* (1954), pp. 122–24.
6. *Interhandel* case, diss. op. Lauterpacht, ICJ Reports 1959, p. 122.
7. *Nationality Decrees in Tunis and Morocco*, PCIJ, Series B, No. 4 (1923), pp. 23–24.

tional Court of Justice.[8] In 1949, the Court was invited by the UN General Assembly to give an advisory opinion on the applicability of the procedure for the settlement of disputes contained in the peace treaties with Bulgaria, Hungary, and Romania. The request had been prompted by the refusal of these countries to heed appeals by the Assembly to comply with their human rights obligations under the peace treaties.[9] The Court did not directly respond to an objection that the Assembly, by dealing with the question of the observance of human rights and fundamental freedoms, was "interfering" or "intervening" in matters essentially within the domestic jurisdiction of states. It did, however, offer a confirmation of the observations the Permanent Court had made in the *Nationality Decrees in Tunis and Morocco* case. It stated that "the interpretation of the terms of a treaty . . . could not be considered as a question essentially within the domestic jurisdiction of a State. It is a question of international law which, by its very nature, lies within the competence of the Court." [10]

This advisory opinion was not unanimous. In an interesting but not entirely convincing dissenting opinion, Judge S. B. Krylov challenged the Court's view that the observations by the Permanent Court in the *Nationality Decrees* case were still applicable. He pointed out that the word "exclusively" (*sic*) in Article 15(8) of the Covenant of the League of Nations had been replaced by the word "essentially" in Article 2(7) of the Charter of the United Nations. Consequently, in Krylov's view, a matter could now be within the domestic jurisdiction of a state "despite the fact that it has been dealt with in a treaty." According to Krylov:

The question of human rights and fundamental freedoms, which it is alleged, Bulgaria, Hungary and Romania have failed to observe is after all no more than the problem of the functioning of the judicial and administrative authorities of these States. There is no doubt that the question so defined belongs to the essentially domestic jurisdiction of the State and, as such, is out of the jurisdiction of this Court.[11]

In 1979, in the case *US Diplomatic and Consular Staff in Tehran*, the Court responded as follows to the Iranian objection that the repercussions of the Islamic Revolution were "essentially and directly within the national sovereignty of Iran":

8. *Anglo-Iranian Oil Co.* case, ICJ Reports 1951, p. 93. *Interhandel* case, ICJ Reports 1959, p. 24.

9. *Supra* Chapter 2, note 90.

10. *Peace Treaties* case, ICJ Reports 1950, pp. 70–71.

11. *Peace Treaties* case, diss. op. Krylov, ICJ Reports 1950, pp. 111–12. For an elaboration of Krylov's views, see 43 *Annuaire de l'Institut de Droit International* (1950), vol. I, pp. 33–35.

Whereas it is no doubt true that the Islamic revolution of Iran is a matter "essentially and directly within the national sovereignty of Iran"; whereas however a dispute which concerns diplomatic and consular premises and the detention of internationally protected persons, and involves the interpretation or application of multilateral conventions codifying the international law governing diplomatic and consular relations, is one which by its very nature falls within international jurisdiction.[12]

Finally, in 1986, in the case *Military and Paramilitary Activities in and against Nicaragua*, the Court specifically addressed itself to the scope and content of the principle of non-intervention, which it said was "part and parcel of customary international law." Pointedly basing itself on UN General Assembly Resolutions 2131 (XX) and 2625 (XXV) rather than Resolution 36/103,[13] the Court made the following helpful observations:

A prohibited intervention must accordingly be one bearing on matters in which each State is permitted, by the principle of sovereignty, to decide freely. One of these is the choice of a political, economic, social and cultural system, and the formulation of foreign policy. Intervention is wrongful when it uses methods of coercion in regard to such choices which must remain free ones. The element of coercion, which defines, and indeed forms the essence of, prohibited intervention, is particularly obvious in the case of an intervention which uses force.[14]

Some clear conclusions can be drawn from this brief review of World Court rulings. A matter is within domestic jurisdiction if it is not subject to an international obligation. On such a matter a state is sole judge, and an international tribunal cannot pronounce on it. The extent of domestic jurisdiction in a particular context depends on the treaty obligations of the state concerned and on the status of customary international law. This is a straightforward and workable scheme. A matter is either within domestic jurisdiction or it is regulated by international law. Only in the latter situation can there be a breach of an international obligation and can state responsibility ensue. It is therefore of key importance to determine what are at a given moment a state's international obligations in the field of human rights. With regard to treaty obligations, the answer will usually be clear-cut (although problems of interpretation may arise with regard to vague provisions, such as those concerning human rights in the UN Charter). But what may be regarded as the customary international law of human rights?

12. *US Diplomatic and Consular Staff in Tehran*, ICJ Reports 1979, pp. 15–16.
13. See *supra* Chapter 2, section 2.1.3.
14. *Military and Paramilitary Activities in and Against Nicaragua*, ICJ Reports 1986, para. 205.

There is some evidence that the Universal Declaration of Human Rights as such constitutes customary international law. In 1968, the International Conference on Human Rights, held in Tehran, solemnly proclaimed that "[t]he Universal Declaration of Human Rights states a common understanding of the peoples of the world concerning the inalienable and inviolable rights of all members of the human family and constitutes *an obligation for the members of the international community*" (emphasis added).[15] In 1988, UN Secretary-General Javier Pérez de Cuéllar declared that "[the Universal Declaration's] gradual and growing acceptance by the international community have led to the conclusion that the Declaration constitutes *binding law as international custom, in accordance with Article 38 of the Statute of the International Court of Justice*" (emphasis added).[16]

With all due respect to the authors of these statements, the proposition that states are bound by each and every provision of the Universal Declaration may be somewhat of an overstatement. It seems doubtful whether an international tribunal would be willing to adopt such an approach. It is certainly correct that UN bodies have frequently used the Universal Declaration as a yardstick for judging the behavior of states. But this has always been merely for the purpose of holding states accountable rather than for formally invoking their international responsibility. As a matter of fact, the Universal Declaration may be used as important evidence for interpreting the UN Charter's human rights provisions and as important evidence of state practice for determining the existence of a rule of customary international law. But it does not, in itself and in toto, represent customary international law.[17]

The International Court of Justice has so far determined that the following practices are prohibited by customary international law: genocide,[18] racial discrimination,[19] and "[w]rongfully to deprive hu-

---

15. Proclamation of Tehran, 13 May 1968, UN Doc. A/CONF.32/41.

16. Address on receiving an honorary degree, Leiden University, 7 September 1988.

17. Remarkably, the International Law Commission observed as recently as 1977 that "today, the international obligations of the State in regard to the treatment of its own nationals are almost exclusively of a conventional nature." See *YILC*, 1977, vol. II, Part Two, p. 46. For a contrary view, see, for example, J. P. Humphrey, "The Universal Declaration of Human Rights: Its History, Impact and Juridical Character," in *Human Rights: Thirty Years After the Universal Declaration* (1979), B. Ramcharan (ed.), p. 29. Cf. also the question whether the Universal Declaration constitutes *jus cogens, infra,* notes 109 and 110.

18. Case concerning *Reservations to the Genocide Convention*, ICJ Reports 1951, p. 23.

19. *Namibia* case, ICJ Reports 1971, p. 57.

man beings of their freedom and to subject them to physical constraint in conditions of hardship."[20] This is obviously not an exhaustive list, if only because the Court has had only a few occasions to pronounce on the issue. The American Law Institute, an authoritative institution representing lawyers in the United States, has in its *Restatement (Third) of the Foreign Relations Law of the United States* suggested the following:

A state violates international law if, as a matter of state policy, it practices, encourages or condones
   (a) genocide,
   (b) slavery or slave trade,
   (c) the murder or causing the disappearance of individuals,
   (d) torture or other cruel, inhuman, or degrading treatment or punishment,
   (e) prolonged arbitrary detention,
   (f) systematic racial discrimination, or
   (g) a consistent pattern of gross violations of internationally recognized human rights.[21]

The *Restatement*'s catalogue may of course be criticized on various grounds. For example, one may wonder whether, in addition to the practices cited, customary international law does not also prohibit the imposition of the death penalty on a person who was under eighteen years of age when committing his or her offence.[22] But on the whole, Section 702 of the *Restatement* represents a serious effort to bring some clarity in a controversial area of international law, and it will be adopted here as a working hypothesis.

2. Secondary Rules

In view of the complexity of some of the issues arising from state responsibility for violations of human rights, it may be useful first to introduce some of the basic concepts and questions. The following issues will be discussed briefly in this section: (1) the alleged nonreciprocal character of human rights treaties; (2) the absence of inter-state "damage" in case of a breach of an international human rights obli-

20. Case concerning *US Diplomatic and Consular Staff in Tehran*, ICJ Reports 1980, p. 42.
21. American Law Institute, *Restatement (Third) of the Foreign Relations Law of the United States* (1987), § 702.
22. This prohibition is overwhelmingly reflected in state practice. See N. S. Rodley, *The Treatment of Prisoners Under International Law* (1987), p. 186 and sources cited there. See particularly, D. Weissbrodt, "Execution of Juvenile Offenders by the United States Violates International Human Rights Law," 3 *American University Journal of International Law and Policy* (1988), pp. 339–82. For some other suggested additions to the list, see Th. Meron, *Human Rights and Humanitarian Norms as Customary Law* (1989), pp. 95–98.

gation; (3) the difficulty of identifying the injured state and the requirement of *locus standi*; and (4) the problem of imputing to the state violations committed by unofficial groups.

1. Most treaties are based on the principle of *reciprocity*. The performance of a treaty obligation by one party depends on the corresponding performance by the other parties. A breach may be invoked by the other parties as a ground for terminating or suspending the operation of a treaty. But in the case of a human rights treaty the reciprocal character is less obvious. For one thing, a serious breach by one party does not entitle one or more of the other parties to respond by terminating the treaty or by committing corresponding breaches, either against their own nationals or even against nationals of the offending state. Accordingly, Article 60(5) of the Vienna Convention on the Law of Treaties provides that the measures of termination or suspension of the operation of a treaty that may be taken in response to a material breach of a treaty by one of the parties "do not apply to provisions relating to the protection of the human person contained in treaties of a humanitarian character."

It has therefore been suggested by some observers that if a state violates the human rights of its own citizens, the direct interests of other states are not thereby affected. Proponents of this view rely on actual state practice. They point out that states are much more likely to respond to breaches affecting their own nationals than to breaches affecting foreigners. Consequently, in this view, human rights treaties differ substantially from ordinary treaties: "[r]ather than being a reciprocal bargain by states, a human rights treaty is closer to being a series of unilateral adoptions of a common standard." States have no incentive to induce other parties to comply with such treaties.[23]

According to a more moderate and more authoritative view, a party to a human rights treaty has undertaken obligations, not toward the other parties but toward some "collective interest" of the parties. In the words of Sir Gerald Fitzmaurice: "The obligation has an absolute rather than a reciprocal character—it is so to speak an obligation towards all the world rather than towards particular parties."[24] This view was clearly expressed, for example, by the International Court of Justice when it observed with regard to the Genocide Convention:

In such a convention the contracting States do not have any interests of their own; they merely have, one and all, a common interest, namely, the accom-

---

23. J. S. Watson, "The Limited Utility of International Law in the Protection of Human Rights," 74 *Proceedings of the ASIL* (1980), pp. 3–4.
24. Second Report on the Law of Treaties, by the Special Rapporteur, G. G. Fitzmaurice, *YILC*, 1957, vol. II, p. 54.

plishment of those high purposes which are the raison d'être of the convention. Consequently, in a convention of this type one cannot speak of individual advantages or disadvantages to States, or of the maintenance of a perfect contractual balance between rights and duties.[25]

Although this observation was no doubt intended to be generous, the Court's categorical statement that "in such a convention the contracting States do not have any interests of their own" seems rather unfortunate. If quoted out of context, it could be taken to mean that remedies against an offending state could only be exercised by the states parties collectively. In fact, states generally do not become parties to human rights treaties to bind themselves unilaterally or to bind themselves toward some abstract common interest. After all, if this were all they wished to do, it would be sufficient to issue a unilateral statement. Instead, what they usually hope to achieve by becoming a party to a human rights treaty is to put pressure on other states to do the same.[26] Or, conversely, they become a party because they have been put under pressure to do so by one or more of the existing parties. In other words, each party to a human rights treaty has an individual interest in compliance by all the others, and even human rights treaties are therefore based on reciprocal interests. Such interests should not be discounted merely on the grounds that they are of a nonmaterial character. In their international relations, states have not only material but also immaterial interests, and these are just as legitimate.[27]

A good illustration of the interest states take in the human rights obligations undertaken by other states is the way they react to reservations to multilateral human rights treaties. Reservations may be objected to by the existing parties on the grounds that they are incompatible with the object and purpose of a treaty.[28] If it is true that parties to human rights treaties do not have an interest of their own in fulfillment by the other parties, one would not expect them to object individually to reservations that do not directly affect their interests. This is not the case, however. Under the International Covenant on Civil and Political Rights, the Federal Republic of Germany and the

25. Case concerning *Reservations to the Genocide Convention*, ICJ Reports 1951, p. 23.

26. An exception to this general rule would be a government that decided to become a party to a human rights treaty mainly in order to bind any future government of the same state to certain human rights standards (cf. the French Government's decision in 1986 to become a party to Protocol No. 6 to the European Convention on Human Rights concerning the abolition of the death penalty).

27. See B. Simma, *Das Reziprozitätselement im Zustandekommen Völkerrechtlicher Verträge* (1972), pp. 194–98. See also M. Hanz, *Zur Völkerrechtlichen Aktivlegitimation zum Schutze der Menschenrechte* (1985), p. 86.

28. Arts. 19 and 20, Vienna Convention on the Law of Treaties.

Netherlands have objected to reservations made by India and by Trinidad and Tobago; Belgium and the Netherlands have entered objections to a reservation made by the Congo; and the Netherlands has formally requested further information on reservations made by Australia. The Federal Republic of Germany, Mexico, and Sweden have objected to a large number of reservations made to the Convention on the Elimination of All Forms of Discrimination Against Women. Czechoslovakia, Norway, Pakistan, Sweden, and Yugoslavia have objected to the reservations made by Guatemala and Spain to certain provisions of the Convention on the Political Rights of Women.[29]

The significance of these objections lies not only in the fact that they were made although the material interests of the objecting states had not been affected. They also reflect the apparent view of states of virtually all regional and political groupings that they have not merely a collective but also an individual interest in full observance of human rights treaties by the other parties. With one possible exception,[30] none of the objecting states indicated that it was acting exclusively on behalf of the common interest rather than on its own behalf. Moreover, none of the reserving states appear to have responded that the objections were not admissible because the interests of the objecting state had not been affected. On the other hand, it should be pointed out that in none of the cases cited here did the objecting state indicate specifically that it considered a reservation so objectionable that it precluded the entry into force of the treaty as between the objecting and the reserving state. On the contrary, objecting states repeatedly indicated that this was not the result they wished to obtain, probably because they had decided that on the whole their interest in promoting wider adherence to the treaty was more important than their objections to the reservations in question.

2. Since states do not normally have a material interest in the observance of human rights obligations by other states, it follows that if such obligations are violated, other states generally do not suffer harm or *damage* that can be expressed in financial or physical terms. Although it could be argued that a state suffers some kind of "moral" damage if another violates human rights, in fact this applies to any violation of an international obligation. As the International Law Commission has put it, "any breach of an obligation towards another

29. *Human Rights: Status of International Instruments* (1987), UN Doc. ST/HR/5, Sales No. E.87.XIV.2, pp. 18–19, 49–52, 167–71, and 326–28.

30. In its objections to reservations made to the Convention on the Elimination of All Forms of Discrimination Against Women, Sweden included the following justification for its intercession: "It is in the common interest of States that treaties to which they have chosen to become parties are also respected, as to object and purpose, by other parties." *Ibid.*, p. 171.

State involves some kind of 'injury' to that State."[31] Accordingly, damage is not a distinctive constituent element of an internationally wrongful act and therefore of state responsibility.[32] It is precisely this reasoning with regard to human rights that has led the International Law Commission, in its draft articles on state responsibility, to produce a definition of an internationally wrongful act that does not include the element of damage:

There is an internationally wrongful act of a State when:
   (a) conduct consisting of an action or omission is attributable to the State under international law; and
   (b) that conduct constitutes a breach of an international obligation of the State.[33]

The omission of "damage" from the definition of an internationally wrongful act met with little opposition in the Sixth Committee of the UN General Assembly. The Netherlands specifically supported the proposal.[34] It may therefore be taken for granted that the absence of inter-state damage is no impediment to invoking a state's international responsibility in the field of human rights. State responsibility simply arises if an international obligation has been breached and can be attributed to the offending state.

   3. Closely connected with the confusion about the alleged nonreciprocal character of human rights obligations and the absence of material damage in case of a breach, is the difficulty of identifying *the entity entitled to bring a claim.* The direct victim of a human rights violation is usually an individual. Since an individual is not entitled to bring a claim under international law against a state (unless the state in question has specifically admitted this possibility), however, the claiming entity will generally be another state. One of the basic prin-

   31. *YILC*, 1973, vol. II, p. 183.

   32. See, generally, B. Bollecker-Stern, *Le préjudice dans la théorie de la responsabilité internationale* (1973). See also, P. Reuter, "Le dommage comme condition de la responsabilité internationale," in *Estudios de Derecho Internacional: Homenaje al Professor Miaja de la Muela* (1979), vol. II, p. 844; B. Graefrath, "Responsibility and Damages Caused: Relationship Between Responsibility and Damages," 185 *RCADI* (1984), pp. 34–37; A. Tanzi, "Is Damage a Distinct Condition for the Existence of an Internationally Wrongful Act?" in *United Nations Codification of State Responsibility* (1987), M. Spinedi and B. Simma (eds.), pp. 1–33.

   33. *YILC*, 1973, vol. II, p. 179.

   34. "The Netherlands Government also agrees with the Commission's decision not to make damage a constituent element of a wrongful act. This decision ensues, indeed, from the structure of the draft; whether or not damage is required is a matter of primary rules. The Commission's decision is also correct from another point of view: a State could have a legitimate interest in the fulfillment of an international obligation which has been breached in a specific case even though it has suffered no damage." See *YILC*, 1980, vol. II, Part One, p. 102.

ciples of international law is that "only the party to whom an international obligation is due can bring a claim in respect of its breach."[35] In other words, only the state that has suffered an injury is entitled to bring a claim under international law. In case of a breach of a human rights obligation, the question that needs to be answered is, therefore, which state or states—if any—have been injured by the breach.

This question would arise specifically if a claim arising out of a breach of an international human rights obligation were to be submitted to an international tribunal. Neither the Statute nor the Rules of Procedure of the International Court of Justice provide that a claimant state must be able to demonstrate some kind of interest in a claim. Nevertheless, it is generally assumed that this is one of the conditions of admissibility. The maxim *point d'intérêt—point d'action* tends to be cited as a justification for the rule. The underlying purpose of the principle apparently is no more sophisticated than the wish to prevent both tribunals and defendants from being burdened with "unnecessary" law suits.[36]

Terms frequently used in this context are *locus standi* and *actio popularis*. These terms have been derived from municipal (English and American) law and can easily cause confusion. The term *locus standi* may refer to different requirements which cannot always be easily distinguished: (a) the requirement of the capacity to sue; (b) the requirement of a special capacity or status; (c) the requirement of an interest to sue. Under the *actio popularis*, a complainant may present a claim to a tribunal without having been injured and without having to demonstrate any special status or special interest.[37] The concepts of *locus standi* and *actio popularis* played an important part in the 1962 and 1966 *South West Africa* cases and in the 1970 *Barcelona Traction* case. The observations made in these cases by the International Court of Justice will be examined below.

4. The question of *imputability* may also pose special difficulties in the context of violations of human rights, since governments frequently deny responsibility for such abuses. It is a well-established rule of international law that acts by persons acting on behalf of the state may be attributed to that state. Conduct by such persons acting

---

35. *Reparation for Injuries* case, ICJ Reports 1949, pp. 181–82.

36. See P. van Dijk, *Judicial Review of Governmental Action and the Requirement of an Interest to Sue* (1980), p. 21. See also K. Mbaye, "L'intérêt pour agir devant la CIJ," 209 *RCADI* (1988), pp. 231–36.

37. Van Dijk, *supra* note 36, pp. 18–25. The term *actio popularis*, as employed in this sense, is somewhat of a misnomer. Under Roman law, *actiones populares* served primarily to protect the interests of the complainant, rather than the public interest. See F. Casavola, *Studi sulle azioni populari romanae: Le "Actiones Populares"* (1958), pp. 1–22, as referred to by Van Dijk, *supra* note 36, p. 19, note 36.

outside their competence or contrary to instructions is also attributable to the state.[38] The fact that an official has acted in contravention of domestic law therefore does not discharge a state from its responsibility.

The American Law Institute's *Restatement (Third) of the Foreign Relations Law of the United States* takes the view, on unexplained grounds, that although in general a state is responsible for the acts of its officials even if they were acting *ultra vires*, a different regime applies if a government violates its human rights obligations under customary international law. In the latter case, a state could only be held responsible if the violations were "practiced, encouraged, or condoned by the government of a state as official policy."[39] This proposition, if accepted, would of course make it easy for governments to evade responsibility simply by claiming that the violations in question had not been committed by way of official policy. To prove otherwise would usually be very difficult. There does not appear to be any good reason for introducing this exception to the general rule, however.[40]

In any case, the exception clearly does not apply under treaty law, such as under the European Convention on Human Rights. According to the European Court of Human Rights, a state cannot evade responsibility by claiming either ignorance of infringements committed by its officials or inability to control them. In the case of *Ireland v. the United Kingdom*, the European Court of Human Rights observed with regard to a systematic practice of ill-treatment:

It is inconceivable that the higher authorities of a State should be, or at least should be entitled to be, unaware of the existence of such a practice. Furthermore, under the Convention those authorities are strictly liable for the conduct of their subordinates; they are under a duty to impose their will on subordinates and cannot shelter behind their inability to ensure that it is respected.[41]

Special difficulties arise with regard to abuses committed by so-called death squads or similar unofficial groups acting with the apparent but unacknowledged agreement of the authorities. The use of such groups is a device employed by certain governments precisely

38. See Art. 10 of the ILC's draft articles on state responsibility and accompanying commentary, in *YILC*, 1975, vol. II, pp. 61–70.
39. American Law Institute, *Restatement (Third) of the Foreign Relations Law of the United States* (1987), § 702, Comment b.
40. See Th. Meron, "State Responsibility for Violations of Human Rights," 83 *Proceedings of the ASIL* (1989), pp. 375–76.
41. *Ireland v. UK*, 18 January 1978, European Court of Human Rights, Series A, vol. 25, p. 64.

to avoid international scrutiny. Although these groups may partly consist of (off-duty) security personnel, this will not necessarily be the case. Can their conduct nevertheless be attributed to the state?

The International Court of Justice, following the approach taken by the International Law Commission in its draft articles on state responsibility, has laid down strict criteria that need to be met before acts by unofficial groups may be imputed to a state. In the case *US Diplomatic and Consular Staff in Tehran* the Court found that the initial conduct of the militants who had occupied the embassy could not be imputed to the Iranian state because there was insufficient evidence to conclude that the militants had been charged by some competent organ of the Iranian state to carry out this operation. Only the subsequent approval of the occupation by the Iranian authorities and their decision to perpetuate the situation translated the occupation into an act of the Iranian state for which it could be held internationally responsible.[42] In the case *Military and Paramilitary Activities in and Against Nicaragua*, the Court held that the United States could not be held responsible for violations of human rights and humanitarian law committed by the Contras, in spite of the high degree of dependence of this group on the United States. The Court took the view that "for [their] conduct to give rise to legal responsibility of the United States, it would in principle have to be proved that that State had effective control of the military or paramilitary operations in the course of which the alleged violations were committed."[43] The close parallel between these two cases has been pointed out by Judge Roberto Ago in his separate opinion in the latter case.[44]

This strict standard of proof—actual orders having been given or effective control of the operation—has not been required by an international tribunal charged specifically with the supervision of the fulfillment of human rights obligations. In the *Velásquez Rodríguez* case, the Inter-American Court of Human Rights held that a government could be held responsible for a "disappearance," even if the perpetrators had been private individuals not acting on official orders. The Court based this view on the primary rule contained in Article 1(1) of the American Convention on Human Rights, according to which states parties undertake not only to "respect" certain rights and freedoms, but also to "ensure" the free and full exercise of these rights and freedoms to persons within their jurisdiction. As the Court put it:

42. Case concerning *United States Diplomatic Staff in Tehran*, ICJ Reports 1980, pp. 29 and 35.

43. Case concerning *Military and Paramilitary Activities in and Against Nicaragua*, ICJ Reports 1986, p. 65.

44. ICJ Reports 1986, p. 180.

An illegal act which violates human rights and which is initially not directly imputable to a State (for example, because it is the act of a private person or because the person responsible has not been identified) can lead to international responsibility of the State, not because of the act itself, but because of the lack of due diligence to prevent the violation or to respond to it as required by the Convention.[45]

A tendency to extend the imputability of the state for abuses committed ostensibly by private individuals may also be perceived in other primary rules. The 1975 UN General Assembly Declaration against Torture still defined torture as "pain or suffering . . . inflicted by or at the instigation of a public official."[46] The 1984 UN Convention against Torture, however, defines the same concept as "pain or suffering . . . inflicted by or at the instigation of *or with the consent or acquiescence* of a public official or other person acting in an official capacity" (emphasis added).[47] It follows that under the new definition, acts of brutality committed by members of unofficial groups with the consent or acquiescence of the authorities are imputable to the state and may give rise to state responsibility.[48] Similarly, the draft declaration on disappearances, as adopted by the UN Sub-Commission on Prevention of Discrimination and Protection of Minorities, refers to disappearances "practised, permitted or tolerated by a Government."[49] Clearly, these instruments, in combination with the decisions by the European and Inter-American Courts of Human Rights referred to above, represent a more adequate response to the way some governments operate to take advantage of nongovernmental entities than the more aloof attitude adopted by the World Court.[50]

45. Inter-American Court of Human Rights, Judgment in *Velásquez Rodríguez* case, 29 July 1988, Annual Report of the Inter-American Court of Human Rights, 1988, p. 971. Also reproduced in 28 *ILM* (1989), pp. 326–27. See D. Shelton, "Private Violence, Public Wrongs and the Responsibility of States," 13 *Fordham International Law Journal* (1989–1990), pp. 1–34.

46. Art. 1, UN Declaration on the Protection of All Persons from Being Subjected to Torture and Other Cruel, Inhuman or Degrading Treatment or Punishment, UN General Assembly Resolution 3452 (XXX) of 9 December 1975.

47. Art. 1, UN Convention against Torture and Other Cruel, Inhuman or Degrading Treatment or Punishment, UN General Assembly Resolution 39/46 of 10 December 1984.

48. See the first report by the UN Special Rapporteur on Torture and Other Cruel, Inhuman and Degrading Treatment or Punishment, Mr. P. Kooijmans, UN Doc. E/CN.4/1986/15, p. 11; Rodley, *supra* note 22, pp. 90–91; J. H. Burgers and H. Danelius, *The United Nations Convention against Torture* (1988), pp. 119–20.

49. Art. 1(1), draft Declaration on the Protection of All Persons from Enforced or Involuntary Disappearance, UN Doc. E/CN.4/Sub.2/1990/32, p. 12.

50. See also G. A. Christenson, "Attributing Acts of Omission to the State," 12 *Michigan Journal of International Law* (1991), pp. 312–70.

In sum, the following acts contrary to international human rights law may be imputed to the state:

a. Abuses committed by officials, even if they were acting *ultra vires*.
b. Abuses committed by private individuals acting on the direct orders or under the direct control of the authorities.
c. Abuses committed by private individuals in response to which the authorities failed to exercise due diligence by taking adequate preventive and repressive measures.

2.1 Jurisdiction of International Tribunals

The central question addressed in this chapter is whether a state could bring a formal human rights claim against another state and in particular whether such a claim might be declared admissible by an international tribunal on the basis of some general title of jurisdiction. It seems pertinent, therefore, to examine the existing case law of international tribunals. Before doing so, however, some consideration must be given to the jurisdiction of such tribunals. International tribunals do not have automatic jurisdiction. Cases can only be considered by them with the express consent of the states concerned. It is possible to distinguish three broad categories of instances in which claims arising from breaches of international human rights obligations may be considered by international tribunals.

First, cases may be submitted to special, ad hoc or permanent bodies with a judicial or quasi-judicial character set up under particular conventions.[51] Examples include the following:

- The *ad hoc* Commissions of Inquiry, which may be established under the Constitution of the International Labour Organisation (1919)
- The Human Rights Committee, set up under the International Covenant on Civil and Political Rights (1966)
- The Committee on the Elimination of Racial Discrimination, set up under the International Convention on the Elimination of All Forms of Racial Discrimination (1965)
- The Committee against Torture, set up under the UN Convention against Torture and Other Cruel, Inhuman or Degrading Treatment or Punishment (1984)

51. See, generally, S. Leckie, "The Inter-State Complaints Procedure in International Human Rights Law: Hopeful Prospects or Wishful Thinking?" 10 *HRQ* (1988), pp. 249–303.

- The European Commission and European Court of Human Rights, set up under the European Convention on Human Rights (1950)
- The Inter-American Commission and Inter-American Court of Human Rights, set up under the American Convention on Human Rights (1969)
- The African Commission on Human and Peoples' Rights, set up under the African Charter on Human and Peoples' Rights (1981)

Second, the following provisions in UN human rights treaties provide that disputes relating to the interpretation or application of the treaty may be referred for decision to the International Court of Justice at the request of any one of the parties to the dispute: [52]

- Article 8, Slavery Convention (1926)
- Article 9, Convention on the Prevention and Punishment of the Crime of Genocide (1948)
- Article 22, Convention for the Suppression of the Traffic in Persons and of the Exploitation of the Prostitution of Others (1949)
- Article 38, Convention Relating to the Status of Refugees (1951)
- Article 9, Convention on the Political Rights of Women (1952)
- Article 5, Convention on the International Right of Correction (1952)
- Article 34, Convention Relating to the Status of Stateless Persons (1954)
- Article 10, Supplementary Convention on the Abolition of Slavery, the Slave Trade, and Institutions and Practices Similar to Slavery (1956)
- Article 10, Convention on the Nationality of Married Women (1957)
- Article 14, Convention on the Reduction of Statelessness (1961)
- Article 22, International Convention on the Elimination of All Forms of Racial Discrimination (1965)
- Article 29, Convention on the Elimination of All Forms of Discrimination Against Women (1979)
- Article 30, Convention against Torture and Other Cruel, Inhuman or Degrading Treatment or Punishment (1984)

Third, cases may be submitted to the International Court of Justice if the applicant and the defendant state have both accepted the Court's jurisdiction under some general title of jurisdiction. Forty-six

52. The text of these instruments may be found in the UN publication *Human Rights: A Compilation of International Instruments*, Doc. ST/HR/1/Rev.3, Sales No. E.88. XIV.1.

states have currently accepted, under Article 36(2) of its Statute, the jurisdiction of the International Court of Justice in all legal disputes, in relation to any other state accepting the same obligation. A similar general formula may be found, for example, in instruments for the pacific settlement of disputes and in friendship treaties.[53]

At first sight, this may seem like an impressive array of possibilities for submitting a human rights dispute to an international tribunal without the consent of the offending state. There are, however, numerous restricting factors, both in law and in practice, which explain why few inter-state applications have been lodged so far.

With regard to the first category, the procedures under the International Covenant on Civil and Political Rights, the American Convention on Human Rights, and the Convention against Torture are merely optional and require a separate declaration of acceptance. Relatively few states have been prepared to make such a declaration. It is remarkable, in this context, that twice as many states have accepted the right of individual petition under the Optional Protocol to the International Covenant on Civil and Political Rights as have accepted the right of inter-state complaint under Article 41. Contrary to conventional wisdom, states are apparently more inclined to admit complaints from individuals than from other states. This attitude has been reflected in the American Convention on Human Rights, under which individual applications may be submitted against each state party, but inter-state applications can only be made if the applicant and the defending state have specifically accepted this facility.

With regard to the second category, lack of acceptances should not have presented a problem, since the provisions on the referral of disputes to the International Court of Justice are an integral part of the treaties concerned. Some states, however, have circumvented these provisions by registering reservations against the ICJ jurisdiction clause when becoming parties. In the absence of a provision on the admissibility of reservations in the convention itself, the question arose after the adoption of the Genocide Convention in 1948 whether such reservations should not be considered inadmissible. In response to a request for an advisory opinion on this issue addressed to it by the UN General Assembly, the International Court of Justice advised that

a State which has made and maintained a reservation which has been objected to by one or more of the parties to the Convention but not by others, can be regarded as being a party to the Convention if the reservation is com-

---

53. For a list containing many of these instruments, see *YICJ*, 1989–1990, pp. 98–115.

patible with the object and purpose of the Convention; otherwise that State cannot be regarded as being a party to the Convention.[54]

The criterion of compatibility with the object and purpose of a convention initially did not solve the controversy. Reservations continued to be made against ICJ jurisdiction clauses contained in UN human rights treaties, and some states parties continued to take the view that such reservations were incompatible with the object and purpose of these treaties.[55] From the late 1950s, however, the ambiguity was resolved by the inclusion of specific provisions in human rights treaties containing dispute settlement procedures to the effect that reservations against the jurisdiction clause were permitted. In view of the fact that the subject matter of these later treaties does not differ significantly from the earlier ones, it should probably be accepted that under current international law a state can become a party to a UN human rights treaty even if it does not accept the ICJ jurisdiction clause contained in it.

It is interesting to note the shifting attitudes of states toward this question. Initially, the controversy had an East-West character, with especially (though not exclusively) the Soviet Union and other East European states taking exception to the ICJ jurisdiction clause and especially (though again not exclusively) a number of Western states maintaining that reservations against the clause were not acceptable. But in 1986, the United States became a party to the Genocide Convention subject to a reservation similar to the one that had hitherto been maintained by the Soviet Union: a dispute could only be considered by the International Court of Justice with the specific consent of the United States.[56] To their credit, some Western states (Italy, the Netherlands, and the United Kingdom) formally objected, in accordance with their previous practice, that they were unable to accept such a reservation.[57] The development came almost full circle when in 1989 the Soviet Union lifted all reservations it had thus far maintained to the ICJ jurisdiction clause in all UN human rights treaties to which it was a party, including the Genocide Convention.[58]

Even when it is possible to file an inter-state human rights appli-

54. *Reservations to the Genocide Convention,* ICJ Reports 1951, p. 23.
55. See objections made to reservations to the Convention on the Prevention and Punishment of the Crime of Genocide (1948); the Convention for the Suppression of the Traffic in Persons and of the Exploitation of the Prostitution of Others (1949); and the Convention on the Political Rights of Women (1952). Reproduced in *Human Rights: Status of International Instruments, supra* note 29, pp. 187–90, 227, 326–28.
56. Reproduced in 80 *AJIL* (1986), p. 612.
57. *Multilateral Treaties Deposited with the Secretary-General: Status as at 31 December 1989,* pp. 102–04.
58. Reproduced in 83 *AJIL* (1989), p. 457.

cation with an international tribunal, states tend to be most reluctant to do so. Witness the failure of states to submit an application to the International Court of Justice in response to one of the clearest cases of genocide since World War II: Democratic Kampuchea from 1975 to 1978.[59] It has been estimated that "somewhere between one-seventh and one-third of the Cambodian people died as a result of Khmer Rouge policy and practice."[60] An application to the International Court of Justice could have been lodged under Article 9 of the Genocide Convention; Cambodia acceded to the convention in 1950 without reservations. It could also have been lodged under Article 36(2) of the Statute of the International Court of Justice; Cambodia accepted the Court's compulsory jurisdiction in 1957, and genocide constitutes a breach of customary international law.[61] So why has no such application yet been filed? The reasons suggested by one author are remarkably prosaic:

The Association of South East Asian Nations (ASEAN) have expressed concern that an application to the International Court of Justice would, by attacking one of the members of the CGDK,[62] indirectly support the continuing Vietnamese occupation of Cambodia by weakening the opposition forces. Other states in the region, such as Australia, fear that filing a case against Democratic Kampuchea might somehow constitute recognition of the CGDK government or query the technical difficulties . . . European and other states simply defer to those closest to the situation, and all seem wary of combining issues of self-determination and human rights.[63]

2.2 Leading Cases

In spite of the reluctance of states to accept the jurisdiction of international tribunals and to file complaints with such tribunals, even if the possibility to do so exists, there have been some instances in which applications have been made. The procedure under Article 26 of the ILO Constitution has so far been invoked six times, the procedure under Article 24 of the European Convention on Human Rights twenty times. Some of the verdicts resulting from these applications shed light on the questions occupying us in this chapter. There are also some relevant rulings by the International Court of Justice.

59. See, generally, H. Hannum, "International Law and Cambodian Genocide: The Sounds of Silence," 11 *HRQ* (1989), pp. 82–138; D. Hawk, "International Human Rights Law and Democratic Kampuchea," 16 *International Journal of Politics* (1986), No. 3, pp. 3–38.
60. Hawk, *supra* note 59, p. 26.
61. Case concerning *Reservations to the Genocide Convention*, ICJ Reports 1951, p. 23.
62. Coalition Government of Democratic Kampuchea (note supplied).
63. Hannum, *supra* note 59, p. 136.

Although six complaints have been filed so far under Article 26 of the ILO Constitution, Commissions of Inquiry have been established only in response to the first two complaints. The other cases were resolved before they reached this stage.[64] Commissions of Inquiry have a judicial or at least semi-judicial character. Their members tend to be senior judges and upon taking office they make a declaration comparable to the one made by members of the International Court of Justice. Their findings are binding and can only be appealed to the International Court of Justice. The conclusions and recommendations of Commissions of Inquiry therefore have considerable authority.[65]

The first Commission of Inquiry was appointed in 1962 to consider a complaint by Ghana concerning alleged nonobservance by Portugal of ILO Convention No. 105 on Forced Labour.[66] The second Commission of Inquiry was appointed in 1963 to consider a complaint by Portugal concerning alleged nonobservance by Liberia of ILO Convention No. 29 on Forced Labour.[67] Neither of the offending states contested the admissibility of the complaint on the grounds that the complaining state lacked the required degree of legal interest or that it had not suffered any damage as a result of the alleged breaches. Nevertheless, in the second case the Commission took the opportunity to point out that the right provided for in Article 26 is a constitutional right. It observed that the language of Article 26 is "broad, clear and precise: it gives rise to no ambiguity and permits no exception."[68] These terms were clearly borrowed from the verdict by the International Court of Justice in the 1962 *South West Africa* case.[69] The Commission quoted with apparent approval Judge Philip Jessup's

64. Leckie, *supra* note 51, pp. 277–89.

65. See Arts. 26–34 of the Constitution of the International Labour Organisation, and N. Valticos, "Les commissions d'enquête de l'Organisation internationale du Travail," 91 *RGDIP* (1987), pp. 847–79.

66. Report of the Commission Appointed under Article 26 of the Constitution of the International Labour Organisation to Examine the Complaint Filed by the Government of Ghana concerning the Observance of the Government of Portugal of the Forced Labour Convention, 1957 (No. 105), 45 *ILO Official Bulletin* (1962), No. 2, Supp. II.

67. Report of the Commission Appointed under Article 26 of the Constitution of the International Labour Organisation to Examine the Complaint Filed by the Government of Portugal concerning the Observance by the Government of Liberia of the Forced Labour Convention, 1930 (No. 29), 46 *ILO Official Bulletin* (1963), No. 2, Supp. II.

68. *Ibid.*, p. 154. Art. 26(1) provides: "Any of the Members shall have the right to file a complaint with the International Labour Office if it is not satisfied that any other Member is securing the effective observance of any Convention which both have ratified in accordance with the foregoing articles."

69. *Infra* note 84.

concurring opinion in this case, in which he stated with respect to the first complaint (*Ghana v. Portugal*):

The fact which this case establishes is that a State may have a legal interest in the observance, in the territories of another State, of general welfare treaty provisions and that it may assert such interest without alleging any impact upon its own nationals or its direct so-called tangible or material interests.[70]

It appears clear, therefore, that it is not a prerequisite of the procedure set out in Article 26 of the ILO Constitution that the state filing the complaint must have suffered any direct damage either to itself or to its nationals.[71] Moreover, the applicant state does not need to demonstrate any special interest beyond being a party to the convention in question.

Case law under the European Convention on Human Rights points in a similar direction. Under Article 25 of the Convention, persons and organizations exercising the right of individual petition must themselves be victims of a violation of the Convention. But this condition does not apply to inter-state applications under Article 24, which simply empowers "any High Contracting Party" to refer an alleged breach of the Convention to the European Commission of Human Rights. In the *Pfunders* case (Austria v. Italy), the Commission emphasized that the Convention did not constitute a system of reciprocal rights and obligations between the states parties. The Commission pointed to the "objective character" of the Convention "being designed rather to protect the fundamental rights of individual human beings from infringement by any of the High Contracting Parties than to create subjective and reciprocal rights for the High Contracting Parties themselves." The Commission furthermore observed that through Article 24,

the High Contracting Parties have empowered any one of their number to bring before the Commission any alleged breach of the Convention, regardless of whether the victims of the alleged breach are nationals of the applicant State or whether the alleged breach otherwise particularly affects the interests of the applicant State; whereas it follows that a High Contracting Party, when it refers an alleged breach of the Convention to the Commission under Article 24, is not to be regarded as exercising a right of action for the purpose of enforcing its own rights, but rather as bringing before the Commission an alleged violation of the public order of Europe.[72]

70. *Supra* note 67, p. 155. ICJ Reports 1962, p. 428.
71. Valticos, *supra* note 65, pp. 860–61.
72. *Austria v. Italy*, 11 January 1961, 4 *YECHR* (1961), p. 140.

The same line of thought has been followed by the Inter-American Court of Human Rights.[73] In 1978, however, in the case of *Ireland v. the United Kingdom*, the European Court of Human Rights apparently realized that it might have gone too far in emphasizing the nonreciprocal character of the obligations undertaken under the Convention. The Court specifically acknowledged that the Convention also creates reciprocal rights and obligations between the parties:

Unlike the international treaties of the classic kind, the Convention comprises *more than mere reciprocal engagements between Contracting States*. It creates, *over and above a network of mutual, bilateral undertakings*, objective obligations which, in the words of the Preamble, benefit from a "collective enforcement."

By virtue of Article 24, the Convention allows Contracting States to require the observance of those obligations without having to justify an interest deriving, for example, from the fact that a measure they complain of has prejudiced one of their own nationals.[74] (emphasis added)

According to this latest pronouncement, therefore, a state bringing an inter-state complaint under the European Convention on Human Rights may either be enforcing its own rights or be acting on behalf of the common good. Most important, however, is that states bringing applications under Article 26 of the ILO Constitution or Article 24 of the European Convention on Human Rights are not required to demonstrate that they have in any way been directly affected by the breaches complained of. This conclusion is not detracted from by the fact that of all applications brought so far under these two provisions, only in the two Greek cases[75] and in the Turkish case[76] did the applicant states clearly have no such direct interest in the matter. What is significant is that the test of having to demonstrate a direct interest was not applied in any of these cases and that it was specifically rejected in some. The same would apply, no doubt, if applications were lodged under any of the other inter-state complaint procedures established under any of the other human rights treaties.

But of course it cannot automatically be presumed that the position under general international law is the same as under conventional

---

73. Advisory Opinion on the Effect of Reservations on the Entry into Force of the American Convention, 24 September 1982. Reproduced in 22 *ILM* (1983), pp. 46–48.

74. *Ireland v. UK*, 18 January 1978, European Court of Human Rights, Series A, vol. 25, pp. 89–91. The European Commission of Human Rights, however, appears to continue to prefer the language it used in the *Pfunders* case to the more balanced language used by the Court in *Ireland v. UK*. See *Denmark, France, the Netherlands, Norway and Sweden v. Turkey*, 26 YECHR (1983), pp. 30–31.

75. *Denmark, the Netherlands, Norway and Sweden v. Greece*, 11 *YECHR* (1968), p. 690. *Denmark, Norway and Sweden v. Greece*, 13 *YECHR* (1970), p. 108.

76. *Denmark, France, the Netherlands, Norway and Sweden v. Turkey*. 26 YECHR (1983), Part Two, p. 1.

law. Early precursors of the view that states may bring a legal claim against an offending state even if their own direct interests have not been harmed may already be found among publicists in previous centuries. Hugo Grotius wrote in 1625 that states "have the right of demanding punishments not only on account of injuries committed against themselves or their subjects, but also on account of injuries which do not directly affect them but excessively violate the law of nature or of nations in regard to any persons whatsoever."[77] J. C. Bluntschli, writing in 1878, took the view that if a breach of international law is *gemeingefährlich* (that is, represents a danger to the international community as such), all states are equally entitled to insist on compliance with the international legal order. As examples of such breaches he cited inter alia slavery and religious intolerance.[78]

Elihu Root, writing in 1916, was still speaking *de lege ferenda* when he suggested that a parallel should be drawn with municipal law, where a distinction exists between ordinary wrongs which may be addressed only at the instance of the person directly injured, and serious wrongs by which every citizen is deemed to be injured because it affects everyone's safety. Accordingly, under international law, violations that threatened the peace and order of the community of nations should be considered as a legal injury to every nation, entitling every nation to protest and be heard. Examples of such violations were in his view breaches of the law protecting the independence of nations, the inviolability of their territory, and the lives and property of their citizens.[79] Similar suggestions were made by Clyde Eagleton in 1950.[80]

Such views were by no means limited to Western scholars. Tunkin, writing in 1965, took the view that states not directly affected may respond not only to violations threatening international peace and security; they may also take specific measures in response to certain other violations, including violations of the principle of freedom of the high seas and of the principle of conserving living maritime resources.[81] In 1974, he added to this open-ended list the principle of self-determination and the Nuremberg principles.[82]

The International Court of Justice was most clearly confronted with these questions in the 1962 and 1966 *South West Africa* cases. One

---

77. Hugo Grotius, *De Jure Belli ac Pacis*, vol. 2, chap. 20, para. 40, Carnegie Classics of International Law (1925).

78. J. C. Bluntschli, *Das Moderne Völkerrecht der Civilisirten Staten*, 3d ed. (1878), pp. 265–66.

79. E. Root, "The Outlook for International Law," 10 *AJIL* (1916), pp. 7–9.

80. C. Eagleton, "International Organization and the Law of Responsibility," 76 *RCADI* (1950), p. 423.

81. G. I. Tunkin, *Droit International Public* (1965), p. 223.

82. G. I. Tunkin, *Theory of International Law* (1974), p. 419.

of the central issues was whether Ethiopia and Liberia were entitled to bring a claim against South Africa based on the 1920 mandate for German South West Africa. Was the required legal right or interest to bring such a claim vested in individual members of the League of Nations, or did it appertain exclusively to the League itself?[83] In 1962 the Court decided that the applicant states had *locus standi* and that it had jurisdiction to adjudicate upon the merits of the dispute. This was simply because under Article 7(2) of the mandate agreement "any dispute whatever" relating to its interpretation or application could be submitted to the Permanent Court of International Justice by a member of the League of Nations. As the International Court observed, "The language used is broad, clear and precise: it gives rise to no ambiguity and it permits of no exception."[84] But in 1966— euphemistically called the "second phase"—the Court decided that the applicant states lacked the necessary legal right or interest to pursue the claim.[85] The controversial character of the matter appears from the fact that in each case the decision was taken by a majority of one.

In his separate opinion in the 1962 case, Judge Jessup argued in some detail that "[i]nternational law has long recognized that States may have legal interests in matters which do not affect their financial, economic, or other 'material', or, say, 'physical' or 'tangible' interests." As examples he cited the procedures created by the minorities treaties at the end of World War I; the Genocide Convention; and the ILO Constitution. Jessup also referred to "the right of a State to concern itself, on general humanitarian grounds, with atrocities affecting human beings in another country." He cited precedents in state practice consisting of intercessions based not only on treaty provisions but also on general principles of international law.[86]

In the 1966 case, the Court avoided answering the question whether in general a legal right or interest may have been infringed even though no material damage has been suffered (though it did not exclude this possibility). It simply observed that, in any case, "such rights or interests, in order to exist, must be clearly vested in those who claim them, by some text or instrument, or rule of law."[87] The Court disposed of the case on the grounds that this condition had not been met. It admitted that South Africa's mandate obligations were still in force, but maintained that these obligations were no longer due

83. ICJ Reports 1966, p. 22.
84. ICJ Reports 1962, p. 343.
85. ICJ Reports 1966, p. 51.
86. ICJ Reports 1962, pp. 425–27.
87. ICJ Reports 1966, p. 32.

to any (still existing) subject in particular. It asserted that "[i]n the international field, the existence of obligations that cannot in the last resort be enforced by any legal process, has always been the rule rather than the exception."[88]

If by "any legal process" the Court meant the exercise of any legal remedy, including the presentation of legal claims, this assertion is of questionable validity. An entirely different—and in the opinion of this writer more convincing—view was taken by the International Law Commission in 1976. Following the opinion of its special rapporteur on state responsibility, Professor Roberto Ago, the Commission maintained categorically that unlike in municipal law, "in international law there is always a correlation between the obligation of one subject and the subjective right of another."[89] It follows that an international obligation cannot exist without it being due to one or more subjects of international law.

The Court furthermore observed that the equivalent of an *actio populariis* "is not known to international law as it stands at present."[90] As Judge Jessup pointed out in his dissenting opinion, however, while it is true that there is no generally established *actio popularis* in international law, "international law has accepted and established situations in which States are given a right of action without any showing of individual prejudice or individual substantive interest as distinguished from the general interest."[91]

The Court's judgment in the 1966 *South West Africa* case was widely criticized.[92] In 1970, in the *Barcelona Traction* case, the Court apparently reacted to this criticism by modifying the line it had taken in 1966. In an *obiter dictum* it made the famous observation that

an essential distinction should be drawn between the obligations of a State towards the international community as a whole, and those arising vis-à-vis another State in the field of diplomatic protection. By their very nature the former are the concern of all States. In view of the importance of the rights involved, all States can be held to have a legal interest in their protection; they are obligations *erga omnes*.

Such obligations derive, for example, in contemporary international law, from the outlawing of acts of aggression, and of genocide, as also from the principles and rules concerning the basic rights of the human person, including protection from slavery and racial discrimination. Some of the cor-

88. ICJ Reports 1966, p. 46.
89. *YILC* 1976, vol. II, Part Two, p. 76.
90. ICJ Reports 1966, p. 47.
91. ICJ Reports 1966, pp. 387–88. See also E. Schwelb, "The 'Actio Popularis' in International Law," 2 *Israel Yearbook on Human Rights* (1972), pp. 46–56.
92. Judge Jessup's dissenting opinion, in which he expressed the view that the judgment was "completely unfounded in law," probably remains its most eloquent and effective critique. See ICJ Reports 1966, pp. 323–442.

responding rights of protection have entered into the body of general international law . . . ; others are conferred by international instruments of a universal or quasi-universal character." [93]

As pointed out by Professor Higgins, these paragraphs 33 and 34 of the judgment represent a significant evolution from the 1966 *South West Africa* verdict. While in 1966 the Court had taken the view that Ethiopia and Liberia lacked the necessary legal right or interest to pursue a claim that South Africa had breached an international obligation not to commit or tolerate racial discrimination, in 1970 the same Court took the view that this very obligation has an *erga omnes* character. Even though it seems fair to assume that the Court's changed composition had enabled it to take this step,[94] this does not fully explain the near unanimity with which the Court endorsed the new approach. Although the significance of the change could hardly have escaped the attention of individual judges, only one, Willem Riphagen, in a dissenting opinion made some marginal critical comments on the concept of obligations *erga omnes*.[95] One reason for this lack of dissent may have been that in paragraph 91 the judgment contains the following obscure and apparently contradictory observation:

However, on the universal level, the instruments which embody human rights do not confer on States the capacity to protect the victims of infringements of such rights irrespective of their nationality. It is therefore still on the regional level that a solution to this problem has had to be sought; thus, within the Council of Europe . . . , the problem of admissibility encountered by the claim in the present case has been resolved by the European Convention on Human Rights, which entitles each State which is a party to the Convention to lodge a complaint against any other contracting State for violation of the Convention, irrespective of the nationality of the victim.[96]

Unlike paragraphs 33 and 34, this paragraph deals exclusively with human rights obligations based on treaties. Its first sentence has puzzled the commentators, since it is difficult to reconcile with paragraphs 33 and 34.[97] The impression it creates is that parties to univer-

93. ICJ Reports 1970, p. 32.
94. R. Higgins, "Aspects of the Case Concerning the Barcelona Traction, Light and Power Company, Ltd.," 11 *Virginia Journal of International Law* (1971), p. 330. See also O. Schachter, "International Law in Theory and Practice," 178 *RCADI* (1982), p. 341.
95. ICJ Reports 1970, pp. 339–40.
96. ICJ Reports 1970, p. 47.
97. See, in particular, Bollecker-Stern, *supra* note 32, pp. 85–90. See also I. Seidl-Hohenveldern, "Actio Popularis im Völkerrecht?" 14 *Communicazioni e Studi Milano* (1975), pp. 803–13; B. Simma, "Fragen der zwischenstaatlichen Durchsetzung verträglich vereinbarter Menschenrechte," in *Festschrift für Hans-Jürgen Schlochauer* (1981), I. von Münch (ed.), pp. 642–43; J. A. Frowein, "Die Verpflichtungen erga omnes im

sal human rights instruments, such as the international covenants on human rights, have no remedy against a state party that commits a breach. This would be a disconcerting result since, as Professor Jochen Frowein has put it, "[h]uman rights guarantees which cannot be protected by some action, however weak, are not worth the ink with which they are written."[98]

One suggestion has been to interpret "capacity to protect" as "capacity to exercise diplomatic protection."[99] Such an interpretation would allow for less far-reaching action against offending states parties. But this interpretation must be rejected as incompatible with the rest of paragraph 91, since it is unlikely that the Court would have wished to suggest that the European Convention on Human Rights permits the exercise of diplomatic protection (in the traditional sense) on behalf of foreign nationals.

A more likely key to understanding the apparent contradiction between paragraphs 33 and 34 on the one hand and 91 on the other is that while the former refers to the limited category of "basic rights of the human person" (and cites only the prohibitions of slavery and racial discrimination as examples), the latter refers to the wider category of "human rights" generally. Perhaps the Court wished to indicate that the right to exercise protection on behalf of foreign victims of infringements could be used only in response to infringements of rights in the former category and not in response to infringements of all human rights contained in the covenants on human rights.[100]

Moreover, and perhaps most importantly, it should be emphasized that paragraph 91 states that universal human rights instruments do not specifically *confer* (French: *reconnaissent*) the capacity to protect foreign victims of infringements. This is no more than a simple statement of fact: the international covenants on human rights indeed do not contain any specific inter-state remedies other than purely optional ones. Such an interpretation finds support in the explanation offered by Judge Sture Petrén in his separate opinion in the *Nuclear Tests* case. Petrén acknowledged that an impression had been created "of a self-contradiction which had not escaped the attention of writ-

Völkerrecht und ihre Durchsetzung," in *Festschrift für Hermann Mosler* (1983), R. Bernhardt et al. (eds.), pp. 243–44.

98. J. A. Frowein, "The Interrelationship between the Helsinki Final Act, the International Covenants on Human Rights, and the European Convention on Human Rights," in *Human Rights, International Law and the Helsinki Accord* (1977), Th. Buergenthal (ed.), p. 71.

99. Simma, *supra* note 97, pp. 642–43.

100. Th. Meron, "On a Hierarchy of International Human Rights," 80 *AJIL* (1986), pp. 10–11.

ers," and he took the opportunity to explain that paragraph 91 of the *Barcelona Traction* judgment had no other intention than to clarify that *erga omnes* obligations on human rights could only be invoked before some international tribunal if there was a relevant title of jurisdiction.[101] This, of course, goes without saying. The paragraph therefore does not affect the remedies owed to states parties to human rights treaties under general international law.

What remains to be considered, therefore, are the implications of paragraphs 33 and 34 of the *Barcelona Traction* judgment. As will be seen below, these paragraphs have been generally welcomed by writers, and perhaps more importantly, they have been accepted and further built upon by the International Law Commission in its work on state responsibility. This has been useful, since the paragraphs constitute *obiter dicta*, and it is therefore difficult to assess their meaning from the context of the judgment itself. Questions arising from the paragraphs include: Which human rights obligations have an *erga omnes* character? Which entity or entities are injured by a breach of such obligations? And which legal remedies are the injured parties entitled to employ? These questions cannot always be easily distinguished, but they will be discussed here separately in the following three sections.

2.3 Obligations *Erga Omnes*

The International Law Commission has aptly summarized the implications of the *erga omnes* dictum in the *Barcelona Traction* judgment in the following terms:

In the Court's opinion, there are in fact a number, albeit a small one, of international obligations which, by reason of the importance of their subject-matter for the international community as a whole, are—unlike the others—obligations in whose fulfilment all States have a legal interest. It follows, according to the Court, that the responsibility engaged by the breach of these obligations is engaged not only in regard to the State which was the direct victim of the breach; it is also engaged in regard to all the other members of the international community, so that, in the event of a breach of these obligations, every State must be considered justified in invoking—probably through judicial channels—the responsibility of the State committing the internationally wrongful act.[102]

We must therefore examine the question of which international obligations in the field of human rights have such importance for the

101. ICJ Reports 1974, p. 303.
102. *YILC*, 1976, vol. II, Part Two, p. 99.

international community as a whole that all states have an interest in their fulfillment. The *Barcelona Traction* judgment does not define such obligations. The judgment simply suggests that "[i]n view of the importance of the rights involved" there are certain obligations in the protection of which all states can be said to have a legal interest. It then provides a list of examples: the prohibition of aggression and genocide, as well as "the principles and rules concerning the basic rights of the human person, including protection from slavery and racial discrimination." This is apparently a nonexhaustive list. So what other international obligations in the field of human rights, if any, may be regarded as having an *erga omnes* character?

Partly as a consequence of the proliferation of international rules, particularly in the field of human rights, the need for a certain hierarchy in these rules has made itself felt.[103] In response to this need, international law has developed, in its characteristically unsystematic manner, a number of different labels for the purpose of distinguishing the more important international rights and obligations from the less important ones.[104] Apart from obligations *erga omnes*, these labels include "*jus cogens*," "nonderogable rights," and "international crimes."[105] The exact scope of each of these categories has not always been clearly defined, and the categories partly overlap, though no two are identical. It may be wondered, first, which human rights obligations are included in each of these categories, and, second, which of these human rights obligations have an *erga omnes* character.

The concept of *jus cogens*, or a peremptory norm of international law,[106] has been defined in Article 53 of the Vienna Convention on the Law of Treaties. Article 53 provides:

A treaty is void if, at the time of its conclusion, it conflicts with a peremptory norm of general international law. For the purposes of the present Convention, a peremptory norm of general international law is a norm accepted and recognized by the international community of States as a whole as a norm from which no derogation is permitted and which can be modified only by a subsequent norm of general international law having the same character.

103. See, generally, Th. C. van Boven, "Distinguishing Criteria of Human Rights," in *The International Dimensions of Human Rights* (1982), K. Vasak (ed.), pp. 43–48; and, especially, Meron, *supra* note 100, pp. 1–23.

104. On the advantages and disadvantages of this approach, see Meron, *supra* note 100, p. 22.

105. See G. Gaja, "Obligations *Erga Omnes*, International Crimes and *Jus Cogens*: A Tentative Analysis of Three Related Concepts," in *International Crimes of States* (1989), J. H. H. Weiler, A. Cassese, and M. Spinedi (eds.), pp. 151–60.

106. For a thorough examination of the concept, with an extensive bibliography, see L. Hannikainen, *Peremptory Norms (Jus Cogens) in International Law* (1988).

It may be deduced from this definition that a peremptory norm of international law must always have an *erga omnes* character. As the International Law Commission has put it, "it would seem contradictory if, in the case of a breach of a rule so important to the entire international community as to be described as a 'peremptory' rule, the relationship of responsibility was established solely between the State which committed the breach and the State directly injured by it."[107] What is less obvious, however, is which international obligations in the field of human rights constitute *jus cogens*. Article 53 itself does not provide any examples. The most plausible view is that all rules of the customary international law of human rights constitute *jus cogens*.[108] Some have argued, however, that all the provisions of the Universal Declaration of Human Rights constitute *jus cogens*.[109] Others have taken a more restrictive view.[110] Examples most commonly cited include the prohibitions of slavery, genocide, and racial discrimination.

The concept of nonderogability has been used in several human rights treaties. The International Covenant on Civil and Political Rights (Article 4), the European Convention on Human Rights (Article 15), and the American Convention on Human Rights (Article 27) each list a number of rights that states parties have undertaken to respect under all circumstances, even in times of emergency. Since the underlying objective here is not the same as that of *jus cogens*, it should cause no surprise that not all nonderogable rights mentioned in each of these instruments have the status of *jus cogens*.[111] In fact, it is even questionable whether all of these nonderogable rights have the status of customary international law. But the four rights that are earmarked concurrently in the three instruments as nonderogable (right to life, freedom from torture, freedom from slavery, and freedom from ex post facto laws), certainly qualify as both customary international law and *jus cogens*. Consequently, the corresponding obligations of these three rights have an *erga omnes* character.

The concept of international crimes (not to be confused with

---

107. *YILC*, 1976, vol. II, Part Two, p. 102.

108. Diss. op. Tanaka, *South West Africa* case, ICJ Reports 1966, p. 298. Schachter, *supra* note 94, p. 340. American Law Institute, *Restatement (Third) of the Foreign Relations Law of the United States* (1987), § 702, Reporters' Note 11.

109. A. Verdross, "Jus Dispositivum and Jus Cogens in International Law," 60 *AJIL* (1966), p. 59. M. S. McDougal, *Human Rights and World Public Order* (1980), p. 274.

110. M. Lachs, "The Law of Treaties," in *Recueil d'études de droit international en hommage à Paul Guggenheim* (1968), p. 399; I. Brownlie, *Principles of Public International Law*, 4th ed. (1990), p. 513; I. Sinclair, *The Vienna Convention on the Law of Treaties*, 2d ed. (1984), pp. 216–17.

111. See Meron, *supra* note 100, pp. 15–16.

"crimes under international law"),[112] is defined in Article 19 of part 1 of the International Law Commission's draft articles on state responsibility, which divides internationally wrongful acts into two rubrics, international crimes and international delicts:

1. An act of a State which constitutes a breach of an international obligation is an internationally wrongful act, regardless of the subject-matter of the obligation breached.

2. *An internationally wrongful act which results from the breach by a State of an international obligation so essential for the protection of fundamental interests of the international community that its breach is recognized as a crime by that community as a whole, constitutes an international crime.*

3. *Subject to paragraph 2, and on the basis of the rules of international law in force, an international crime may result, inter alia, from*:

(a) a serious breach of an international obligation of essential importance for the maintenance of international peace and security, such as that prohibiting aggression;

(b) a serious breach of an international obligation of essential importance for safeguarding the right of self-determination of peoples, such as that prohibiting the establishment or maintenance by force of colonial domination;

(c) *a serious breach on a widespread scale of an international obligation of essential importance for safeguarding the human being, such as those prohibiting slavery, genocide and apartheid*;

(d) a serious breach of an international obligation of essential importance for the safeguarding and preservation of the human environment, such as those prohibiting massive pollution of the atmosphere or of the seas.

4. Any internationally wrongful act which is not an international crime in accordance with paragraph 2, constitutes an international delict.[113] (emphasis added)

The provision thus has a certain similarity with the definition of *jus cogens* contained in Article 53 of the Vienna Convention on the Law of Treaties. Both the designation of a rule of *jus cogens* and the designation of an international crime require recognition as such by the international community "as a whole." Unlike Article 53, however, this provision mercifully provides a nonexhaustive number of sub-categories and within those sub-categories, a nonexhaustive number

112. While the term *international crimes* refers to the responsibility of states, the term *crimes under international law* refers to the responsibility of individuals. See *YILC*, 1976, vol. II, Part Two, pp. 118–19. The International Law Commission has for many years been attempting to define the contents and implications of the concept of crimes under international law in a draft Code of crimes against the peace and security of mankind; since 1983 it has been doing so on the basis of reports by its special rapporteur for this subject, Mr. Doudou Thiam.

113. *YILC*, 1976, vol. II, Part Two, pp. 95–96. Adopted by consensus "to the applause of the members of the Commission." See B. G. Ramcharan, *The Concept and Present Status of the International Protection of Human Rights* (1989), p. 299. On Article 19 see, generally, J. H. H. Weiler et al. (eds.), *International Crimes of State: A Critical Analysis of the ILC's Draft Article 19 on State Responsibility* (1989).

of examples. Of special interest from the point of view of the present study is the subcategory contained in paragraph 3(c): "a serious breach on a widespread scale of an international obligation of essential importance for safeguarding the human being." It follows that for a breach of a human rights obligation to qualify as an international crime within the terms of this provision, both the obligation itself and the breach must reach a certain level of importance. On the one hand, the obligation in question must be of such essential importance for safeguarding the human being that its breach is recognized as a crime by the international community as a whole. On the other hand, its breach must be serious and on a widespread scale. As examples of practices that meet both these criteria, the provision lists slavery,[114] genocide, and *apartheid.*

The distinction, among internationally wrongful acts, between international crimes and international delicts remains somewhat controversial, mainly because the International Law Commission has not yet decided which legal consequences flow from it.[115] But if one accepts the distinction, as most authorities seem to do, it is evident that the obligation not to commit international crimes constitutes an obligation *erga omnes.*[116] What is again less evident, however, is which breaches of human rights obligations, other than slavery, genocide, and *apartheid*, ought to be characterized as international crimes. The International Law Commission's commentary to Article 19(3)(c) offers little further guidance in this regard.[117] Some authors have tried to restrict the number of human rights violations that might qualify as international crimes by introducing further criteria. It has been suggested, for example, that in order to qualify as an international crime a breach of a human rights obligation must in addition represent a threat to international peace and security.[118] Article 19 offers no support for this assertion, however. One breach that should certainly be characterized as an international crime, even though it may not nec-

114. A minor flaw in this reasoning is that "slavery" does not need to be on a widespread scale to qualify as such. Article 1 of the 1926 Slavery Convention defines slavery as "the status or condition of *a person* over whom any or all of the powers attaching to the right of ownership are exercised" (emphasis added).

115. See, for example, S. C. McCaffrey, "The Thirty-seventh Session of the International Law Commission," 80 *AJIL* (1986), pp. 187–88.

116. This is specifically provided in Article 5(3) of part 2 of the ILC's draft Articles on state responsibility. See *YILC*, 1985, vol. II, Part Two, p. 25 (quoted *infra*, section 2.4).

117. *YILC*, 1976, vol. II, Part Two, p. 121.

118. M. Mohr, "The ILC's Distinction Between 'International Crimes' and 'International Delicts' and its Implications," in *United Nations Codification of State Responsibility* (1987), M. Spinedi and B. Simma (eds.), pp. 133–34.

essarily represent a threat to international peace and security, is the systematic practice of torture.[119]

In the absence of much state practice concerning the willingness of states to invoke a state's international responsibility if they have not been directly injured by a breach, the response of states to the Tehran hostage crisis represents an interesting case study. On 4 November 1979, the U.S. embassy in Tehran was overrun by demonstrators and its staff taken hostage with the apparent complicity of the Iranian authorities. On 10 January 1980, the United States introduced in the Security Council a draft resolution that would have provided for mandatory sanctions against Iran in accordance with Articles 39 and 41 of the UN Charter.[120] One of the key issues before the Council was whether such a step was justified on the grounds that all states had suffered an injury as a result of the incident. The Mexican representative, for example, expressed the conviction that not only the United States but also the international community had been harmed and that the United Nations should therefore intervene effectively.[121] The Soviet representative, on the other hand, took the view that this was a bilateral dispute between the United States and Iran and that it did not constitute a threat to international peace and security.[122] The draft resolution was hit by a Soviet veto.

In April and May 1980, the foreign ministers of the nine member states of the European Community adopted several declarations expressing their grave concern at "this serious and prolonged infringement of the ground rules of international law." The declarations emphasized that the attitude of the Iranian authorities was "contrary to the principles . . . on which the international community is founded" and expressed the belief "that this situation should be a

119. Second Report by the UN Special Rapporteur on Torture and Other Cruel, Inhuman or Degrading Treatment or Punishment, Mr. P. Kooijmans, UN Doc. E/CN.4/1987/13, p. 15. N. S. Rodley, *The Treatment of Prisoners Under International Law* (1987), p. 97.

120. UN Doc. S/13735 of 10 January 1980. In its draft resolution, the United States chose not to rely on Charter Article 94(2). On the basis of that provision, the Council conceivably might have decided upon measures to give effect to the interim measures ordered by the International Court of Justice on 15 December 1979 (ICJ Reports 1979, pp. 20–21). This reinforces the view that since an interim order is not equivalent to a judgment within the meaning of Charter Art. 94(2), it cannot give rise to enforcement measures under that Charter provision. See J. P. A. Bernhardt, "The Provisional Measures Procedure of the International Court of Justice through U.S. Staff in Tehran: Fiat Iustitia, Pereat Curia?" 20 *Virginia Journal of International Law* (1980), p. 608.

121. Mr. Muñoz Ledo (Mexico), 13 January 1980. His delegation would abstain, however, on the grounds that the dispute did not constitute a threat to international peace and security. See UN Doc. S/PV.2191 Add.1, para. 57.

122. Mr. Troyanovsky (USSR), 13 January 1980, UN Doc. S/PV.2191 Add.1, para. 48.

matter of concern to the whole international community." By stress-
ing both the importance of the obligations concerned to the international community as a whole and the seriousness of the breaches
themselves, the statements bore a strong and probably not coinci-
dental resemblance to Article 19 of part 1 of the International Law
Commission's draft articles on state responsibility. The apparent underlying intention was to indicate that Iran had incurred legal responsibility toward all states and that accordingly all states were entitled to
respond through the application of sanctions. Accordingly, on 18 May
1980, the EC ministers decided to apply the sanctions provided for in
the (vetoed!) draft Security Council resolution of 10 January 1980, in
particular the suspension of all contracts concluded after 4 November
1979.[123]

On 24 May 1980, following the institution of proceedings by the
United States, the International Court of Justice delivered a judgment according to which Iran had incurred responsibility toward the
United States, entailing an obligation to make reparation for the injury caused.[124] The Court stopped short of finding that Iran had incurred responsibility toward all states or toward the international
community as a whole. It came close to doing so, however, when it
recalled "the extreme importance of the principles of law which it
[was] called upon to apply in the present case" and when it observed
that it "consider[ed] it to be its duty to draw the attention of the entire
international community . . . to the irreparable harm that may be
caused by events of the kind now before the Court."[125]

The question must be faced, therefore, whether the response by
the member states of the European Community to the events in Tehran should be interpreted as evidence of a growing inclination of
states to consider serious breaches of human rights obligations as international crimes to which they are entitled to respond by taking
reprisals, even if they have not been directly affected. Such a conclusion would be somewhat premature, however.[126] First, although
the case had an obvious human rights dimension, both the Court and
the interceding states appear to have regarded it primarily as a breach
of diplomatic immunities. Second, the measures taken largely had
the character of mere retorsion rather than of reprisals. The United
Kingdom explicitly refused to apply sanctions retrospectively to con-

123. 13 *Bull. EC* (1980), No. 4, paras. 1.2.2, 1.2.7, and 1.2.9.
124. ICJ Reports 1980, p. 42.
125. ICJ Reports 1980, p. 43.
126. A. Cassese, "Remarks on the Present Legal Regulation of Crimes of States," in
International Law at the Time of its Codification: Essays in Honour of Roberto Ago (1987),
vol. III, pp. 49–64. See also P. M. Dupuy, "Observations sur la pratique récente des
'sanctions' de l'illicite," 87 *RGDIP* (1983), pp. 505–48.

tracts concluded after 4 November 1979.[127] Even then, only a limited number of states—all belonging to the Western bloc—were prepared to take such measures, so that it would be difficult to cite the case as evidence of general state practice. At a more limited level, however, the case could certainly be cited as evidence of a growing inclination of states to consider themselves injured by serious breaches of international obligations of a humanitarian character and consequently as entitled to take the modest action of requiring the offending state to halt the breach.

From the material presented earlier in this section, it may be concluded that human rights obligations constituting *jus cogens*, as well as obligations the infringement of which amount to international crimes, all represent obligations *erga omnes*. This raises the question whether in fact not all international human rights obligations, arising from either a treaty or customary international law, should be regarded as obligations *erga omnes*. Such is indeed the approach adopted in both the International Law Commission's draft articles on state responsibility[128] and the American Law Institute's *Restatement (Third) of the Foreign Relations Law of the United States*.[129] That there are good reasons for taking such a line will be demonstrated in the following section.

2.4 The Injured State

The issues preoccupying us here may also be approached from the point of view of the subject of international law that suffers the injury. If a state commits an internationally wrongful act consisting of a breach of a human rights obligation, and the victims themselves are nationals of the offending state, which subject or subjects of international law suffer an injury? The international community as a whole? Some states? All states? Other subjects of international law? None at all?

Two propositions may be regarded as axiomatic. The first is that, as the International Law Commission has put it (following in the footsteps of its rapporteur Professor Ago), "[i]n international law there is always a correlation between the obligation of one subject and the subjective right of another."[130] International obligations do not exist *in abstracto*; they must be owed toward one subject or to several or all

127. 13 *Bull. EC* (1980), No. 5, pp. 26–27.

128. Art. 5(2)(e)(3), part 2, draft articles on state responsibility, *YILC*, 1985, vol. II, Part Two, p. 25 (quoted *infra*, section 2.4).

129. American Law Institute, *Restatement (Third) of the Foreign Relations Law of the United States* (1987), § 703 (1) and (2).

130. *YILC*, 1976, vol. II, Part Two, p. 76.

subjects of international law. It follows that if an international obligation is infringed, one or more subjects are injured in their rights. The second axiom is that international responsibility can be invoked only by the subject or subjects that have been injured by the internationally wrongful act.[131] Subjects not injured in their rights cannot bring an international claim. A subject's general interest in the observance of international law is insufficient justification for the presentation of such a claim. A state having such an interest is not to be regarded as an "injured" state since it has not suffered an infringement of a subjective right. This applies also to a state that has been granted the right to intervene in a case before the International Court of Justice on the grounds that it has "an interest of a legal nature" that may be affected by the decision in the case.[132]

In 1979, Professor Felix Ermacora, in his capacity as Expert on the Question of the Fate of Missing and Disappeared Persons in Chile, appointed by the UN Commission on Human Rights, wrote in his report to the General Assembly: "Under general and conventional international law the Government of Chile has an obligation *erga omnes*, in particular to the international community, to respect the basic rights of the human person and the Government is responsible, *inter alia*, to the international community for breaches of its obligations."[133] This raises the question whether, as suggested by *Barcelona Traction*, responsibility can indeed be incurred "to the international community." From an operational point of view, the response to this must be negative, simply because the international community as such has no legal personality. Surely the United Nations, if only because it does not comprise all states, cannot be equated with the international community. It would appear to follow that under general international law, an internationally wrongful act cannot create a new legal relationship between an offending state and the international community as such.[134]

On the other hand, if a state infringes an undertaking toward an international organization, this may mean that it incurs responsibility

---

131. *Supra* note 35.

132. See Article 62, Statute of the International Court of Justice. In a number of recent cases, the Court has narrowly interpreted Articles 62 and 63 and denied states that had requested the right to intervene permission to do so. See, generally, C. M. Chinkin, "Third-Party Intervention Before the International Court of Justice," 80 *AJIL* (1986), pp. 495–531. See also Ph. C. Jessup, "Intervention in the International Court," 75 *AJIL* (1981), pp. 903–9.

133. UN Doc. A/34/583/Add.1 of 21 November 1979, para. 190.

134. Second report on State responsibility, by Roberto Ago, Special Rapporteur, *YILC*, 1970, vol. II, p. 184. But compare this to Professor Ago's subsequent remarks, which seem to be much more sympathetic toward the idea of a role for the international community, in Weiler, *supra* note 113, p. 238.

toward the organization. This is a question that was at stake in the *South West Africa* cases. In the case concerning *Military and Paramilitary Activities in and Against Nicaragua*, the International Court of Justice considered whether the United States was justified in taking counter-measures against Nicaragua on the grounds that the latter had infringed an alleged undertaking to organize free elections. The Court found that the document in question had not been intended as a legal undertaking, but even if it had been, "it could not have justified the United States insisting on the fulfilment of a commitment made not directly towards the United States, but towards the Organization, the latter being alone empowered to monitor its implementation." [135]

What is the position with regard to multilateral treaties? If an infringement occurs, are states parties to such treaties injured individually or collectively or both? According to legal doctrine, the obligations resulting from a multilateral treaty may establish either a network of bilateral obligations between the parties or integral or *erga omnes* obligations. [136] Examples in the first category are the traditional relationship between the receiving and the sending state under the Vienna Convention on Diplomatic Relations and the relationship between the coastal state and the flag state under the UN Convention on the Law of the Sea. If a breach occurs between the states involved in such a relationship, in principle there is only one injured state. In case of a particularly serious breach, for example, a serious infringement of the law on diplomatic immunities [137] or a case of massive marine pollution, [138] however, all parties to the treaty suffer an injury. Examples in the second category are treaties on disarmament, the environment, and human rights. Such treaties establish obligations that run from each party toward all the others. One party's breach of such a treaty in principle equally injures all the others, although one or more may be particularly affected.

Of particular interest for the identification of the injured state under general international law is Article 5 of part 2 of the International Law Commission's draft articles on state responsibility. This elaborate

---

135. ICJ Reports 1986, para. 262.

136. See, generally, D. N. Hutchinson, "Solidarity and Breaches of Multilateral Treaties," 59 *BYIL* (1988), pp. 151–215; K. Sachariew, "State Responsibility for Multilateral Treaty Violations: Identifying the 'Injured State' and its Legal Status," 35 *NILR* (1988), pp. 273–89; and B. Simma, "Bilateralism and Community Interest in the Law of State Responsibility," in *International Law at a Time of Perplexity: Essays in Honour of Shabtai Rosenne* (1989), Y. Dinstein (ed.), pp. 821–44.

137. See the case concerning *US Diplomatic and Consular Staff in Tehran*, ICJ Reports 1979, p. 43.

138. See Art. 19(3)(d), draft articles on state responsibility, *YILC*, 1976, vol. II, Part Two, p. 96.

article—provisionally adopted at the Commission's thirty-seventh session—deserves to be quoted here in full:

1. For the purposes of the present articles, "injured State" means any State a right of which is infringed by the act of another State, if that act constitutes, in accordance with part 1 of the present articles, an internationally wrongful act of that State.

2. *In particular, "injured State" means:*

(a) if the right infringed by the act of a State arises from a bilateral treaty, the other State party to the treaty;

(b) if the right infringed by the act of a State arises from a judgment or other binding dispute-settlement decision of an international court or tribunal, the other State or States parties to the dispute and entitled to the benefit of that right;

(c) if the right infringed by the act of a State arises from a binding decision of an international organ other than an international court or tribunal, the State or States which, in accordance with the constituent instrument of the international organization concerned, are entitled to the benefit of that right;

(d) if the right infringed by the act of a State arises from a treaty provision for a third State, that third State;

(e) *if the right infringed by the act of a State arises from a multilateral treaty or from a rule of customary international law, any other State party to the multilateral treaty or bound by the relevant rule of customary international law, if it is established that:*

(i) the right has been created or is established in its favour,

(ii) the infringement of the right by the act of a State necessarily affects the enjoyment of the rights or the performance of the obligations of the other States parties to the multilateral treaty or bound by the rule of customary international law, or

(iii) *the right has been created or is established for the protection of human rights and fundamental freedoms;*

(f) if the right infringed by the act of a State arises from a multilateral treaty, any other State party to the multilateral treaty, if it is established that the right has been expressly stipulated in that treaty for the protection of the collective interests of the States parties thereto.

3. In addition, "injured State" means, if the internationally wrongful act constitutes an international crime [and in the context of the rights and obligations of States under articles 14 and 15], all other States.[139] (emphasis added)

The article represents an impressive tour de force for the purpose of defining the injured state. Paragraph 1 gives the general rule. Paragraphs 2 and 3 then give more precise indications by using two different criteria: the *source* and the *nature* of the right infringed. Paragraph 2 proceeds from the simplest case (the infringement of a bilateral treaty) to more complicated cases (the infringement of a mul-

---

139. *YILC*, 1985, vol. II, Part Two, p. 25.

tilateral treaty or a rule of customary international law). Special reference is made to infringements of human rights and fundamental freedoms (paragraph 2(e)(iii)) and to international crimes (paragraph 3). The provision does not define the actual remedies to which the injured state is entitled in each of these different cases (these are still to be worked out). It must be assumed, however, that the injured state should at least be entitled to bring a legal claim against the offending state aimed at requiring the offending state to halt the infringement.

In its commentary, the International Law Commission summarily explained its thinking behind paragraph 2(e)(iii). The Commission observed that "[t]he interests protected by [rules of international law concerning the obligation of States to respect human rights and fundamental freedoms] are not allocatable to a particular State. *Hence the necessity* to consider in the first instance every other State party to the multilateral convention, or bound by the relevant rule of customary law, as an injured State" (emphasis added).[140] This is a crucial argument, following directly from the premise that an international obligation cannot exist *in abstracto* and from the circumstance that if the victims of a breach of a human rights obligation are nationals of the offending state, no single state is necessarily more affected by the breach than any other state. It follows that all states bound by the obligation are equally injured by the breach. This reasoning was also adopted in the American Law Institute's *Restatement (Third) of the Foreign Relations Law of the United States*.[141] It applies equally to obligations resulting from treaties and to those resulting from rules of customary international law.

The reference in paragraph 2(e)(iii) is to "human rights and fundamental freedoms." The commentary is not very clear on this point, but it seems to indicate that while the Universal Declaration of Human Rights and other relevant instruments are pertinent for determining the scope of this notion, not every one of the obligations enumerated in these instruments necessarily qualifies as customary international law. Nevertheless, it appears that the notion of "human rights and fundamental freedoms," even if restricted to rights and freedoms having the status of customary international law or to those contained in treaties, is wider than the concept of international obligations "of essential importance for safeguarding the human being," which the Commission used to define international crimes. The notion of human rights and fundamental freedoms must also be wider than the concept of "basic rights of the human person" used in the *Barce-*

140. *YILC*, 1985, vol. II, Part Two, p. 27.
141. American Law Institute, *Restatement (Third) of the Foreign Relations Law of the United States* (1987), § 703, Reporters' Note 3.

lona Traction dictum. The International Law Commission, after initial hesitation, has thus provided a more comprehensive definition of international human rights obligations having an *erga omnes* character than the International Court of Justice in *Barcelona Traction*.

The commentary suggests that not every single infringement "even if an isolated act or mission [*sic*] (which might not even be intentional) must necessarily be qualified as giving rise to the application of the present provision."[142] This comment may have been inspired by the view of some scholars that isolated or minor infringements of international human rights obligations are a matter of domestic jurisdiction and that international responsibility can arise only if there has been a consistent pattern of reliably attested violations of such obligations.[143]

It does not seem that this commentary is an accurate description of the law, however.[144] As has been demonstrated above, although the UN response to violations of human rights was initially restricted to consistent patterns of gross violations, in recent years such action has been extended also to isolated infringements.[145] Much of the contemporary diplomatic action examined above in Chapter 1 relates to individual cases. There is no evidence that states would consider such action permissible only if the individual cases acted upon were representative of a wider pattern of violations (although states sometimes indicate that they will act on such cases *particularly* if they are part of a systematic policy or a wider pattern).[146] In *Ireland v. the United Kingdom*, the European Commission of Human Rights cogently observed: "Although one single act contrary to the Convention is sufficient to establish a violation, it is evidence that the violation can be regarded as being more serious if it is not simply one outstanding event but forms part of a number of similar events which might even form a pattern."[147] In other words, while a pattern of breaches of interna-

142. *YILC*, 1985, vol. II, Part Two, p. 27.

143. F. Ermacora, in his capacity as UN Expert on the Question of the Fate of Missing and Disappeared Persons in Chile, UN Doc. A/34/583/Add.1, 21 November 1979, p. 86. Schachter, *supra* note 94, p. 330. R. A. Mullerson, "Human Rights and the Individual as Subject of International Law: A Soviet View," 1 *European Journal of International Law* (1990), pp. 40–43. Th. van Boven, book review of Th. Meron, *Human Rights and Humanitarian Norms as Customary Law* (1989), 85 *AJIL* (1991), p. 213.

144. Cf. Th. Meron, *Human Rights and Humanitarian Norms as Customary Law* (1989), pp. 103–4.

145. *Supra* Chapter 2, section 2.2.4.

146. *Supra* Chapter 1, note 86. Cf. also the Vienna mechanism established by the Conference on Security and Co-operation in Europe, which clearly applies both to "situations" and individual cases. *Supra* Chapter 1, note 163.

147. *Ireland v. UK*, 25 January 1976. Two elements are necessary for the existence of a "practice": repetition of acts and official tolerance. See 19 *YECHR* (1976), pp. 752–68.

tional human rights obligations may constitute a serious delict, possibly even an international crime, a single breach is sufficient to create an internationally wrongful act. To assume that some internationally wrongful acts may be invoked by states while others may not would be incompatible with the axiom referred to above that infringements of all international obligations must be invokable by one or more subjects of international law.[148]

The *Restatement (Third) of the Foreign Relations Law of the United States* apparently attempts to take a middle position by distinguishing according to the origin of the international obligation that has been infringed. The *Restatement* suggests that while a state may be held responsible for a single, isolated breach of a human rights treaty, it may be held responsible for an infringement of customary human rights law only if the breaches amount to a consistent pattern of violations committed by way of state policy.[149] But this distinction, based on a difference in the legal consequences of an infringement of treaty law on the one hand and of customary law on the other, must be rejected. It is incompatible with the basic principle, emphatically endorsed by the International Law Commission after an exhaustive survey of state practice, international jurisprudence, and legal opinion, that "[t]he origin of the international obligation breached by a State does not affect the international responsibility arising from the internationally wrongful act of that State."[150]

Within the International Law Commission itself, paragraph 2(e)(iii) does not seem to have been very controversial, although some members expressed initial hesitations. Only paragraph 3 appears to have caused serious discussion, but primarily, it seems, because the Commission is still to consider the remedies to which an injured state is entitled. Sir Ian Sinclair reserved his position on these grounds. Nikolai Ushakov remarked that not all states were injured by an international crime such as aggression and that not all states could claim reparation from the aggressor. Stephen McCaffrey said he was opposed to the concept of a crime of a state and moreover that paragraph 3 was superfluous because the acts referred to were already covered by paragraphs 2(e)(i) and 2(e)(iii).[151]

Within the Sixth Committee of the UN General Assembly, Article 5 got a mixed reception. Although some delegations welcomed the

---

148. *Supra* note 130.
149. American Law Institute, *Restatement (Third) of the Foreign Relations Law of the United States* (1987), § 702, Comment m.
150. Art. 17(2), draft articles on state responsibility and accompanying commentary, *YILC*, 1976, vol. II, Part Two, pp. 79–87.
151. *YILC*, 1985, vol. I, pp. 310–11.

new text, several others (belonging to different political groups) expressed reservations. In general, those who were critical stated that Article 5 ought to be simplified and that it should provide only the general rule for identifying the injured state (as contained in paragraph 1).[152] Moreover, several delegates considered that a distinction should be made between states suffering a direct injury and those suffering an indirect injury.[153] Some delegations felt that Article 5 should cover only the former category[154] and that in any case the more "extreme" remedies should only be available to states that had been directly injured.[155] Three delegations expressed the view that paragraph 2(e)(iii) was unacceptable.[156]

In spite of its less than enthusiastic reception at the General Assembly, Article 5 must be regarded as an important touchstone for the purpose of identifying the subject or subjects of international law that are injured by an internationally wrongful act consisting of a breach of a human rights obligation. This is because the criticisms that states directed at the provision appear to have been prompted not so much by disagreement with the suggested solutions to the question addressed in Article 5, that is, which subject or subjects of international law may invoke international responsibility in such a case. Instead, delegations were concerned about the form of responsibility that might apply and in particular the more far-reaching remedies to which states that had been only remotely injured by an infringement might be entitled. Only three delegations (the German Democratic Republic, Hungary, and Kuwait) objected specifically to the principle that all states parties to a multilateral treaty and all states bound by a rule of customary international law are injured if a human rights obligation is infringed by one of them. In the light of subsequent political changes in these states, it may be assumed that they no longer hold these restrictive views.

Actual state practice also offers some support for the view expressed in paragraph 2(e)(iii) that if a state party to a human rights treaty commits an infringement, the other states parties consider that they have suffered an injury as a result of which they are entitled to insist on cessation of the breach. This may be observed, for example, at the annual meetings of states parties to the International Covenant

152. German Democratic Republic, Canada, and Hungary, UN Doc. A/C.6/40/SR.25, 27 and 30.

153. Bulgaria, CSSR, Algeria, Spain, and Tunisia, UN Doc. A/C.6/40/SR.27, 29, 31, 32, and 33.

154. Federal Republic of Germany and France, UN Doc. A/C.6/40/SR.24 and 34.

155. Ireland, UN Doc. A/C.6/40/SR.28.

156. The German Democratic Republic, Hungary, and Kuwait, UN Doc. A/C.6/40/SR.25, 30 and 34.

on Civil and Political Rights. Although these meetings have so far been devoted largely to organizational matters, infringements have also been raised occasionally.

At the 1982 meeting of states parties to the Covenant, under the agenda item "other matters," the representative of the Netherlands appealed to states parties that had declared a public emergency to comply faithfully with the nonderogable provisions of the Covenant.[157] At the same meeting, the Swedish representative argued that states parties to the Covenant were under an obligation vis-à-vis the other parties to honor their commitments. He said that it was unfortunate if a state party which under the Optional Protocol procedure had been found to have violated the Covenant, did not take the measures recommended by the Human Rights Committee (this was a barely veiled reference to Uruguay).[158] There were no objections to these observations.

At the 1983 meeting of states parties to the Covenant, the Soviet representative attempted to prevent a repetition of the events of the previous year by proposing the deletion of the agenda item "other matters." The Netherlands' representative opposed the proposal on the grounds that "the human rights treaties did not establish reciprocal rights and duties among the various contracting parties, but rather a collective pledge. That meant that the states parties collectively had the specific function of monitoring how the implementation of the Covenant was being interpreted."[159] This observation may have overstated the collective element in the supervision process at the expense of the bilateral element. Significantly, however, the Netherlands' representative's statement made it perfectly clear that the states parties themselves remained entitled to partake in the supervision of the fulfillment of the obligations undertaken, in spite of the existence under the Covenant of a specific implementation procedure. The Dutch view was supported by France, Italy, Portugal, Costa Rica, and Australia and contradicted by no one. The item "other matters" was maintained on the agenda.

2.5 Judicial Remedies

An internationally wrongful act resulting from a breach of a human rights obligation gives rise to international responsibility of the offending state vis-à-vis the injured state(s). International remedies may be pursued against it by the injured states. In general, three broad cate-

157. Mr. Walkate (Netherlands), 17 September 1982, UN Doc. CCPR/SP/SR.5, p. 6.
158. Mr. Nordenfelt (Sweden), 17 September 1982, UN Doc. CCPR/SP/SR.5, p. 7.
159. Mr. Hamer (Netherlands), 18 November 1983, UN Doc. CCPR/SP/SR.7, p. 4.

gories of international remedies may be distinguished: a right to claim reparation, a right to take reciprocal measures, and a right to take reprisals.[160] As indicated before, reprisals will not be further considered here.[161]

The remedy of reciprocal measures consisting of the termination or suspension of the operation of a treaty as a consequence of its breach has been carefully defined in Article 60 of the Vienna Convention on the Law of Treaties. Its paragraph 5 clearly indicates, however, that these remedies do not apply to "provisions relating to the protection of the human person contained in treaties of a humanitarian character." According to the Swiss delegate who proposed the inclusion of this paragraph in the Vienna Convention, it was intended to cover inter alia conventions concerning the status of refugees, the prevention of slavery, the prohibition of genocide, and the protection of human rights generally.[162] It follows that the *exceptio non adimpleti contractus* does not apply with regard to human rights treaties. The Vienna Convention entered into force on 27 January 1980, and its Article 4 provides that the Convention has no retroactive effect. Nevertheless, because Article 60(5) codifies customary international law, the principle applies also to human rights treaties concluded before that date.[163]

The purpose of a claim for reparation has been set out in the oft-quoted dictum of the Permanent Court of International Justice in the *Chorzów Factory* case:

The essential principle contained in the actual notion of an illegal act—a principle which seems to be established by international practice and in particular by the decisions of international tribunals—is that reparation must, as far as possible, wipe out all the consequences of the illegal act and re-establish the situation which would, in all probability, have existed if that act had not been committed.[164]

The precise scope of the duty to provide reparation is somewhat uncertain, partly as a result of terminological differences between au-

160. American Law Institute, *Restatement (Third) of the Foreign Relations Law of the United States* (1987), § 703, Comment a.

161. On that subject see, for example, M. Akehurst, "Reprisals by Third States," 44 *BYIL* (1970), pp. 1–18; Dupuy, *supra* note 126, pp. 505–48; and J. I. Charney, "Third State Remedies in International Law," 10 *Michigan Journal of International Law* (1989), pp. 57–101.

162. B. Simma, "Reflections on Article 60 of the Vienna Convention on the Law of Treaties and its Background in International Law," 20 *ÖZöffR* (1970), pp. 74–75. E. Schwelb, "The Law of Treaties and Human Rights," 16 *ArchVR* (1974/75), pp. 14–26.

163. Second Report on the Law of Treaties, by the Special Rapporteur, G. G. Fitzmaurice, *YILC*, 1957, vol. II, p. 54.

164. *Chorzów Factory* case (Merits), PCIJ, Series A, No. 17 (1928), p. 47.

thorities.[165] The International Law Commission has not yet reached agreement on the provisions regarding this matter that should be included in its draft articles on state responsibility.[166] Professor Graefrath, a former member of both the International Law Commission and the Human Rights Committee set up under the International Covenant on Civil and Political Rights, has distinguished the following elements: cessation, restitution, compensation, and a guarantee against continuation or repetition of the breach (satisfaction).[167] Each of these elements may be relevant in the case of an internationally wrongful act resulting from a breach of a human rights obligation. Cessation of the breach is of obvious importance and will often be the first element of a claim for reparation. Restitution may consist of the release of persons detained contrary to international law. Compensation may consist of pecuniary compensation to be awarded to individual victims of the breach. A guarantee against continuation or repetition may consist of the introduction of new policies and regulations or the prosecution of officials responsible for the breach.

The possible contents of an inter-state claim for reparation do not differ significantly from the contents of claims that may be submitted by individuals under international recourse procedures. In one of the first "views" adopted under the Optional Protocol procedure of the International Covenant on Civil and Political Rights, the Human Rights Committee concluded "that the State party is under an obligation to provide the victim with effective remedies, including his immediate release and compensation for the violations which he has suffered and to take steps to ensure that similar violations do not occur in the future."[168] A similar formula has been employed in numerous other views adopted by the Committee under the Optional Protocol. In some cases, the Committee has taken the view that a state party was obliged to provide medical care to a detainee or to provide a passport for travel abroad. In other cases, the Committee has taken the view that a state party was under an obligation to inves-

---

165. See I. Brownlie, *Principles of Public International Law*, 4th ed. (1990), pp. 457–63 and literature cited there, in particular C. D. Gray, *Judicial Remedies in International Law* (1987).

166. The ILC's new special rapporteur on state responsibility, Professor G. Arangio-Ruiz, has suggested an approach somewhat different from that of his predecessor, Professor W. Riphagen. See the report of the ILC on its 41st session, UN Doc. A/44/10, pp. 190–91. For a critical analysis, see B. Simma, "International Crimes: Injury and Countermeasures. Comments on Part 2 of the ILC Work on State Responsibility," in Weiler, *supra* note 113, pp. 283–315.

167. B. Graefrath, "Responsibility and Damages Caused: Relationship Between Responsibility and Damages," 185 *RCADI* (1984), p. 73.

168. *Weinberger v. Uruguay*, 29 October 1980, 36 GAOR, Supp. No. 40, p. 119.

tigate a death in detention or to bring to justice persons found to be responsible.[169]

Unlike the Human Rights Committee, the European Court of Human Rights has consistently refused to indicate which specific measures should be taken by a state that has infringed its obligations under the European Convention on Human Rights. The Court has restricted itself to declaring whether a breach of the Convention has occurred, leaving it to the state party to decide how the breach should be remedied. Under Article 50 of the Convention, however, the Court may afford "just satisfaction" to the injured party if the internal law of a state party does not allow full reparation to be made. Under this provision, the Court has in numerous cases awarded damages for immaterial and material loss, including costs and expenses.[170]

As we have seen, consistent case law under the ILO Constitution and the European Convention on Human Rights indicates that the state filing a complaint on the grounds that another state party has failed to comply with its obligations under these instruments does not need to demonstrate any special interest beyond being a party to the instrument in question.[171] Could it be said that, following the *erga omnes* dictum in the *Barcelona Traction* case, the same applies if an application alleging a breach of a human rights obligation were filed under some general title of jurisdiction, such as Article 36 of the Statute of the International Court of Justice or under some general arbitration clause? In other words, would a state whose direct interests or whose nationals had not been affected have *locus standi* in such circumstances?

So far this question has not arisen in practice, and initial legal opinion has been cautious. Judge F. de Castro, in his dissenting opinion in the *Nuclear Tests* case, took the view that the *Barcelona Traction* dictum should be taken, as he put it, *cum grano salis*. He said he was "unable to believe that by virtue of this dictum the Court would regard as admissible, for example, a claim by State A against State B that B was not applying 'principles and rules concerning the basic rights of the human person' . . . with regard to the subjects of State B or even State C."[172] Professor Pieter van Dijk, who in his doctoral dissertation examined at length the question of the requirement of an interest to

169. See the UN publications *Human Rights Committee: Selected Decisions under the Optional Protocol*, vol. 1 (1985), UN Doc. CCPR/C/OP/1, and vol. 2 (1990), CCPR/C/OP/2.

170. P. van Dijk and G. J. H. van Hoof, *Theory and Practice of the European Convention on Human Rights*, 2d ed. (1990), pp. 171–85.

171. *Supra* section 2.2.

172. *Nuclear Tests* case, diss. op. de Castro, ICJ Reports 1974, p. 387. Judge de Castro was not a judge in the *Barcelona Traction* case.

sue, also reached a negative conclusion. He based his view in particular on the circumstance that many states have resisted the inclusion of a jurisdictional clause in multilateral human rights treaties or have made reservations to such clauses. While he admitted that disputes on human rights questions have not been excluded in declarations accepting the compulsory jurisdiction of the International Court under Article 36 of its Statute, he argued that declaring such disputes admissible would be "contrary to the evident intention" of states when accepting the Court's compulsory jurisdiction.[173] Frowein and Sinclair have also been skeptical of the possibility that disputes concerning *erga omnes* obligations might be declared admissible by the Court.[174]

The correctness of these assessments is open to question, however, especially in view of more recent developments in both state practice and legal opinion. While it is certainly true that there has been a long-standing reluctance of states to submit to the settlement of disputes through international tribunals, it should not be assumed that this reluctance applies more in the field of human rights than in other areas considered sensitive by governments. The recent acceptance by the Soviet Union—long the leading opponent of such arrangements—of the compulsory jurisdiction of the International Court of Justice with regard to the interpretation and application of six human rights treaties[175] demonstrates that a deep-seated and widespread *opinio juris* against the judicial settlement of international disputes on human rights questions should not be presumed too easily.

There is no hard and fast rule of international law prohibiting international tribunals from pronouncing—on the basis of some general title of jurisdiction—on disputes concerning the infringement of human rights obligations affecting in dividuals who are not nationals of the state bringing the claim. States accepting the compulsory jurisdiction of the International Court under Article 36 of its Statute do so voluntarily and they tend to formulate their reservations quite carefully (which often results in unnecessary reservations, such as on matters within domestic jurisdiction). It could therefore be expected that states wishing to exclude the possibility of a human rights case being brought against them would have formulated similarly careful reservations to prevent this from happening. The reason why states have not made reservations with regard to disputes on human rights may be simply that in the past this eventuality was not considered. But

173. P. van Dijk, *Judicial Review of Governmental Action and the Requirement of an Interest to Sue* (1980), pp. 473–74 and 520.

174. Frowein, *supra* note 97, pp. 259–60. Remarks by Sir Ian Sinclair, in Weiler, *supra* note 113, p. 225.

175. Reproduced in 83 *AJIL* (1989), p. 457.

it could be said with equal justification that states may be embarrassed to exclude such disputes from their general acceptances of the Court's jurisdiction.

Indeed, persuasive legal authority indicates that, in the absence of relevant reservations, such an application would in principle be admissible.[176] Although the International Law Commission has not addressed this question specifically, it follows from its definition of a state injured by a breach of a human rights obligation that such a state has a legal claim for reparation against the offending state. It is difficult to see which other, more limited, legal consequences would flow from the designation of a state as "injured."[177] A refusal by the offending state to provide reparation would give rise to a legal dispute within the terms of Article 36(2) of the Statute of the International Court. The Court could consider such a dispute, unless it had been explicitly excluded by either the offending or the injured state in their declarations accepting the Court's compulsory jurisdiction. It would make no difference whether the human rights obligation that was allegedly breached derived from a treaty or from customary international law, as long as both states were bound by it.

It should perhaps be emphasized that the approach outlined here does not assume that states may rely on an *actio popularis* in response to breaches of international human rights obligations (that is to say, if *actio popularis* is defined as a remedy under which an applicant may bring a claim without having been injured and without having to demonstrate any special status or special interest).[178] Bringing a claim in response to an alleged infringement of an international human rights obligation and submitting it for adjudication to an international tribunal may well be in the general interest. However, such action cannot be taken just by any state, but only by states bound by the same obligation as the one infringed by the offending state. The applicant

176. Sep. op. Petrén, *Nuclear Tests* case, ICJ Reports 1974, p. 303. Chr. Dominicé, "Die Internationale Verbrechen und deren rechtliches Regime," in *Völkerrecht und Rechtsphilosophie: Festschrift Verosta* (1980), P. Fischer et al. (eds.), p. 247. O. Schachter, "International Law in Theory and Practice," 178 *RCADI* (1982), pp. 198–99. American Law Institute, *Restatement (Third) of the Foreign Relations Law of the United States* (1987), § 703, Comment a, Reporters' Note 3. M. Sassòli, "Mise en oeuvre du droit international humanitaire et du droit des droits de l'homme: une comparaison," 68 *Annuaire suisse de droit international* (1987), pp. 40–41. K. Mbaye, "L'intérêt pour agir devant la CIJ," 209 *RCADI* (1988), p. 307. Th. Meron, *Human Rights and Humanitarian Norms as Customary Law* (1989), p. 199.

177. The International Law Commission's commentary to Article 5 of part 2 of its draft articles on state responsibility indicates that in any case an injured state would be entitled to require a state committing an international crime to stop the breach, but it seems unlikely that this entitlement would not apply also to breaches of international human rights obligations generally. See *YILC*, 1985, vol. II, Part Two, p. 27.

178. See *supra* text accompanying note 37.

state derives its *locus standi* not from an *actio popularis*, but simply from having suffered an injury to its own rights.

2.6 Further Preliminary Objections

Having considered the question of *locus standi*, what remain to be examined are two further preliminary objections that might be raised against an inter-state human rights claim: the requirement of prior exhaustion of local remedies and the alleged self-contained character of human rights treaties.

The requirement of prior exhaustion of local remedies is a well-established rule of customary international law.[179] There can only be a breach of an international obligation concerning the treatment of aliens after local remedies have been exhausted by the individuals concerned.[180] The purpose of the rule is to provide the state with an opportunity to redress the wrong done to individual victims and thus to prevent the occurrence of a wrong to the state of which they are nationals. The principle has traditionally been applied in the context of the exercise of diplomatic protection, in other words, with regard to individuals who are nationals of the interceding state. But could it be said that in the field of human rights the principle applies more generally, that is, irrespective as to whether the victims of the breach are nationals of the interceding state?

Two opposing arguments may be distinguished. On the one hand, it could be argued that since states are already disinclined to accept international claims regarding nationals of the interceding state, the requirement of exhaustion of local remedies would apply *a fortiori* if the individuals concerned are foreign nationals. On the other hand, it could be maintained that if a human rights obligation has been breached, and especially if an international crime has been committed, the interceding state suffers a direct injury to itself that is not dependent on the exhaustion of local remedies by the individual victims. The importance of the subject matter involved would justify such immediate consequences.[181] The International Law Commission, in its work on state responsibility, has considered it "premature" to address the issue and has limited the scope of its draft article on exhaustion of domestic remedies to "aliens," the traditional category of

179. *Interhandel* case, ICJ Reports 1959, p. 27. See, generally, C. F. Amerasinghe, *Local Remedies in International Law* (1990).

180. See Article 22 of the International Law Commission's draft articles on state responsibility and accompanying commentary, in *YILC*, 1977, vol. II, Part Two, p. 30.

181. Cf. Art. 5(2)(e)(iii) and 5(3) of part 2 of the ILC's draft articles on state responsibility, see *supra* section 2.4.

nationals of the interceding state.[182] It seems reasonable to assume, however, that the requirement does apply to international claims on behalf of victims of human rights violations generally, irrespective of their nationality.[183] It would indeed be remarkable if a state were required to await the exhaustion of local remedies before being able to exercise diplomatic protection on behalf of its own nationals, but not when making a claim based on violations of the human rights of foreign nationals.

The International Covenant on Civil and Political Rights (Article 48(1)(c)), the European Convention on Human Rights (Article 26), the American Convention on Human Rights (Article 46(1)(a)) and the African Charter on Human and Peoples' Rights (Article 50) all provide, more or less clearly, that inter-state applications can only be considered by their respective supervisory bodies after local remedies in the offending state have been exhausted by the individual victims. The first three instruments all provide that whether local remedies have been exhausted must be determined in accordance with the generally recognized principles of international law. In order to determine what the position is under general international law, it is therefore of interest to examine what case law has been produced under these instruments. In fact, of these four instruments, inter-state complaints have only been filed under the European Convention. This also happens to be the most interesting instrument in this respect, because from the text of the Convention itself it is not immediately obvious whether the local remedies rule applies merely to applications by individuals or also to applications by states.

In the *Pfunders* case, Austria therefore contended that the local remedies rule did not apply to inter-state applications because the system of the European Convention was based on the concepts of collective guarantee and the public interest. However, the European Commission of Human Rights rejected the contention, inter alia on the grounds that the considerations, which under general international law had inspired the introduction of the local remedies rule, applied *a fortiori* to applications concerning persons who were not nationals of the interceding state.[184] This finding was confirmed in subsequent cases.[185] But in practice the requirement of exhaustion of local remedies has not played a very important role in inter-state applications under the European Convention, because standing case law also provides that the rule does not apply to inter-state applications

---

182. *YILC*, 1977, vol. II, Part Two, p. 46.
183. Meron, *supra* note 176, p. 182.
184. *Austria v. Italy*, 4 YECHR (1961), pp. 148–50.
185. E.g., *Cyprus v. Turkey*, 18 YECHR (1975), p. 82.

alleging legislative measures or administrative practices incompatible with the Convention.[186] The underlying thought may have been that in such cases other states parties suffer a direct injury, since there may not be any individual victims who could exhaust local remedies. It may also have been assumed that any individual victims would not be able to successfully challenge legislative measures and administrative practices anyway.[187]

Any inter-state applications to international tribunals alleging breaches of human rights obligations are likely to focus on general practices rather than on individual cases. This, combined with the principle, recognized also under general international law, that the local remedies rule applies only if the remedies are "effective"[188] and not "obviously futile,"[189] means that in practice in inter-state claims in human rights cases the local remedies rule is unlikely to be a major restricting factor.

The second preliminary objection that might be raised against an inter-state claim alleging a breach of a human rights obligation contained in a treaty is that the only remedies which may be employed in response to a breach are the ones provided for in the treaty itself. According to this argument, human rights treaties establish self-contained regimes that exclude the employment of remedies available to an injured party under general international law. Thus, an international claim to the effect that a state had breached an obligation under the International Covenant on Civil and Political Rights should be declared inadmissible on the grounds that only the procedures provided for in the Covenant could be resorted to in order to redress the alleged breach. If the offending state had accepted neither the right of inter-state complaint under Article 41 nor the right of individual complaint under the Optional Protocol, this would then be the end of the matter. The only supervisory procedure that is an integral part of the Covenant is the reporting procedure, which does not provide for formal input by other states parties.

Do human rights treaties themselves indicate whether or not they are intended to be self-containing? Article 44 of the International Covenant on Civil and Political Rights provides that the implementation provisions of the Covenant "shall not prevent the States Parties to the present Covenant from having recourse to other procedures

186. *Greece v. UK*, 2 *YECHR* (1958–59), p. 184. *Second Greek case*, 13 *YECHR* (1970), p. 134. *Ireland v. UK*, 15 *YECHR* (1972), p. 242.
187. See E. McGovern, "The Local Remedies Rule and Administrative Practices in the European Convention on Human Rights," 24 *ICLQ* (1975), pp. 125–27.
188. Article 22 of the ILC's draft articles on state responsibility and accompanying commentary, *YILC*, 1977, vol. II, Part Two, pp. 30 and 47–48.
189. *Amabatielos* case, *RIAA*, vol. 12, p. 119.

for settling a dispute in accordance with general or special international agreements in force between them." In other words, disputes concerning the interpretation or application of the Covenant could be dealt with, for example, under the range of dispute settlement procedures enumerated in Article 33(1) of the UN Charter or subjected to judicial settlement under Article 36(2) of the Statute of the International Court of Justice. This fairly uncomplicated interpretation is confirmed by the Covenant's *travaux préparatoires*. The aim of the drafters of the Covenant was to prevent a conflict of competence with the dispute settlement procedures provided for in other international instruments, and the solution for this problem envisaged by the majority of delegations was the *juxtaposition* of the respective machineries.[190] Article 16 of the International Convention on the Elimination of All Forms of Racial Discrimination contains a similar provision.

The significance of Article 44 becomes apparent when it is compared to Article 62 of the European Convention on Human Rights. Under the latter provision, states parties "agree that, except by special agreement, they will *not* avail themselves of treaties, conventions or declarations in force between them for the purpose of submitting, by way of petition, a dispute arising out of the interpretation or application of this Convention to a means of settlement other than those provided for in this Convention" (emphasis added). In other words, unlike the Covenant, the European Convention on Human Rights does establish a self-contained regime for settling inter-state disputes.[191] No such clauses are contained in the American Convention on Human Rights or the African Charter on Human and Peoples' Rights.

State practice on this matter is relatively straightforward, at least as far as the practice of the United Nations is concerned in holding states accountable for infringements of human rights standards. States parties to the International Covenant on Civil and Political Rights have occasionally argued that the supervisory procedures of the Covenant prevailed over the general supervisory procedures

190. UN Doc. A/6546, para. 509. In the same sense, M. Nowak, *CCPR-Kommentar zum UNO-Pakt über bürgerliche und Politische Rechte und zum Fakultativprotokoll* (1989), p. 665.

191. In order to emphasize the point, the Council of Europe's Committee of Ministers has declared that parties to the European Convention should "normally" utilize only that Convention's inter-state procedure against states that have also made the declaration under Article 41 of the International Covenant on Civil and Political Rights. See Resolution (70) 17 of 15 May 1970, in Council of Europe, *European Convention on Human Rights: Collected Texts* (1987), pp. 208–9.

of the United Nations and that therefore the latter could not be used against them.[192] This argument has never been accepted by the political bodies of the United Nations, however, and it has not prevented UN initiatives to investigate human rights violations in the states in question. The same applies to the thematic procedures established by the UN Commission on Human Rights. The Special Rapporteur on Torture, who clearly acts under the aegis of "accountability" rather than "responsibility," has not hesitated to intercede with the governments of states that are parties to the UN Convention against Torture and Other Cruel, Inhuman or Degrading Treatment or Punishment.[193] Inter-state practice is more difficult to find, but the one clear instance militates against the self-containment theory. In 1982, the Government of the Federal Republic of Germany declared, in response to a parliamentary question, that in case of noncompliance with the International Covenant on Civil and Political Rights, the other states parties could employ the remedies available under general international law, in addition to those provided for under the Covenant.[194]

Case law of the International Court of Justice, however, is somewhat ambiguous. It may be recalled how the Court observed in the *Barcelona Traction* case that "on the universal level, the instruments which embody human rights do not confer on States the capacity to protect the victims of infringements of such rights irrespective of their nationality."[195] This might mean that, in the Court's view, states parties are not entitled to resort to any remedies under general international law to respond to breaches of these instruments.[196]

In the case concerning *Military and Paramilitary Activities in and Against Nicaragua*, the Court observed, also rather equivocally, that "where human rights are protected by international conventions, that protection takes the form of such arrangements for monitoring or ensuring respect for human rights as are provided for in the conventions themselves."[197] The implication—which is not clearly expressed—of this observation may have been that Nicaragua's violations of human rights could only have been responded to by the competent organs of the Organization of American States and not by

192. Mr. Diez (Chile), 15 November 1976, UN Doc. A/C.3/31/SR.46, para. 19. Mr. Lopatka (Poland), 5 March 1982, E/CN.4/1982/SR.51/Add.1, pp. 18–21.
193. See the Special Rapporteur's explanations on this issue in UN Doc. E/CN.4/1988/17, pp. 2–4.
194. Under-Secretary Hamm-Brücher, 9 September 1982, 44 *ZaöRV* (1984), p. 526.
195. ICJ Reports 1970, p. 47.
196. For a more likely interpretation, see *supra* text accompanying note 101.
197. ICJ Reports 1986, p. 134.

its individual members, such as the United States.[198] The Court thus came dangerously close to suggesting that human rights conventions constitute self-contained regimes, without actually saying so. A more "optimistic" interpretation would be that, as in its ambiguous observation in *Barcelona Traction*, the Court was simply making a factual comment: most human rights treaties indeed have their own mechanisms to promote compliance. The Court may not have intended to say that such mechanisms are exclusive.[199]

The opinion of jurists on this question is also far from unanimous. Followers of the restrictive school of thought[200] rely, first, on the argument that states have only been prepared to enter into human rights agreements on the understanding that these could not be enforced one way or the other, except through the remedies specifically provided for in the agreements; and second, on the above-mentioned pronouncements of the International Court of Justice. Some adherents of this view are motivated by the fear of abuse if states parties were permitted to enforce human rights agreements through unilateral measures, although this fear appears to extend primarily to the use of coercive measures. According to some scholars, "chaos and violence"[201] or "vigilantism"[202] might come to reign among states if this were permitted. The altogether more convincing followers of the opposite school of thought[203] hold that human rights treaties contain reciprocal obligations and that they are subject to the ordinary remedies available under general international law. Unless the agreement specifically provides otherwise, the parties may resort to such remedies against a state party breaching the agreement, in addition to any remedies provided for by the agreement itself. The defenders of the self-contained character of human rights treaties have the burden of

---

198. For a critique of this implication, see F. R. Tesón, "Le Peuple, c'est Moi! The World Court and Human Rights," 81 *AJIL* (1987), pp. 174–77.

199. See N. S. Rodley, "Human Rights and Humanitarian Intervention: The Case Law of the World Court," 38 *ICLQ* (1989), p. 330. For a very restrictive interpretation, see H. Thirlway, "The Law and Procedure of the International Court of Justice 1960–1989," 60 *BYIL* (1989), pp. 92–102.

200. E.g., Frowein, *supra* note 98, pp. 79–80; *id.*, *supra* note 97, pp. 255–56; Schachter, *supra* note 94, p. 334; Sachariew, *supra* note 136, pp. 285–86.

201. P. Weil, "Towards Relative Normativity in International Law?" 77 *AJIL* (1983), pp. 432–33. Similarly, Dupuy, *supra* note 126, pp. 544–48.

202. Remarks by S.C. McCaffrey, in Weiler, *supra* note 113, p. 244.

203. E.g., L. Henkin, "Human Rights and Domestic Jurisdiction," in *Human Rights, International Law and the Helsinki Accord* (1977), Th. Buergenthal (ed.), pp. 29–33; Chr. Tomuschat, "Die Bundesrepublik Deutschland und die Menschenrechtspakte der Vereinten Nationen," 26 *Vereinte Nationen* (1978), p. 8; B. Simma, *supra* note 97, pp. 641–44; *id.*, "Self-contained Regimes," 16 *NYIL* (1985), pp. 111–36; American Law Institute, *Restatement (Third) of the Foreign Relations Law of the United States* (1987), § 703(1), Comment a, Reporters' Note 2; Sassòli, *supra* note 176, p. 39; Mullerson, *supra* note 143, p. 41.

proof of demonstrating that the intention of parties to treaties with an implementation mechanism was to exclude ordinary inter-state remedies. Such proof has so far not been furnished.

In the absence of any specific inter-state remedies contained in a human rights agreement or if such remedies are merely optional and have not been accepted by the offending state, the followers of the restrictive school of thought hold that the use of any remedies can only be decided upon by the states parties collectively. Presumably, decisions would then have to be unanimous. The proponents of this view base their argument on the integral character of the obligations concerned and on the fact that a breach injures the collective interests of the parties rather than those of the parties individually.[204] Obviously, general acceptance of this view would paralyze any effort to ensure effective compliance with human rights agreements through inter-state remedies. State practice provides no support for it, however. In 1972, the International Committee of the Red Cross invited states to indicate through a questionnaire how, in view of common Article 1 of the Geneva Conventions for the Protection of War Victims, states should respond to gross infringements of the Conventions.[205] The majority of states took the view that states parties to the Conventions could respond both collectively and individually to such infringements.[206]

2.7 A Duty to Invoke State Responsibility?

In 1986, the ministers of foreign affairs of the member states of the European Community solemnly declared that "[t]he protection of human rights is the legitimate and continuous duty of the world community and of nations individually."[207] We have so far examined the *right* of states to invoke the international responsibility of a state that infringes an international human rights obligation affecting persons within its jurisdiction. Could it be said that states are indeed under a *duty* to invoke this responsibility?

Under common Article 1 of the Geneva Conventions of 1949, "[t]he High Contracting Parties undertake to respect *and to ensure respect* for the present Convention in all circumstances" (emphasis added). The same wording may be found in Article 1 of Protocol I to the Conventions. According to the official commentary to the Conventions by

---

204. Sachariew, *supra* note 136, pp. 282–85.
205. Common Article 1 provides: "The High Contracting Parties undertake to respect and to ensure respect for the present Convention in all circumstances."
206. See Cassese, *supra* note 136, pp. 58–60.
207. *Supra* Chapter 1, note 78.

the International Committee of the Red Cross, these words mean what they say: if a state does not fulfill its obligations, the other parties to the Conventions (whether they are neutral, allied, or enemy) can—and must—seek to bring it around to respect its obligations.[208] Article 89 of Protocol I, moreover, provides that "[i]n situations of serious violations of the Conventions or of this Protocol, the High Contracting Parties undertake to act, jointly or individually, in co-operation with the United Nations and in conformity with the United Nations Charter."

Apart from occasional public appeals by Red Cross Conferences and by the ICRC itself,[209] not much state practice with regard to implementation of these provisions is known. Démarches by individual states insisting on fulfillment of the Geneva Conventions and their Protocols tend to be made privately, if they are made at all. No objections are known to have been made by offending states to the effect that such démarches are inadmissible. But neither is there much evidence that interceding states consider that they are under an actual duty to intercede.[210] In 1968, the Tehran Conference on Human Rights noted in one of its resolutions "that States parties to the Red Cross Geneva Conventions sometimes fail to appreciate their responsibility to take steps to ensure the respect of these humanitarian rules in all circumstances by other States, even if they are not themselves directly involved in an armed conflict."[211] In 1972, the ICRC submitted to a Conference of Government Experts the following proposal, entitled "Cooperation of the High Contracting Parties":

The High Contracting Parties, being bound, by the terms of Article 1 common to the Conventions, to respect and to ensure respect for these Conventions in all circumstances, are invited to co-operate in the application of these Conventions and of the present Protocol, in particular by making an approach of a humanitarian nature to the Parties to the conflict and by relief actions. Such an approach shall not be deemed to be interference in the conflict.

208. J. S. Pictet (ed.), *Les Conventions de Genève: Commentaire*, vol. I (1952), p. 27.

209. In 1983 and in 1984, for example, the ICRC repeatedly addressed public appeals to the states parties to the Geneva Conventions to help it ensure the application of international humanitarian law in the Iran-Iraq conflict, because it was unable to do so on its own. See ICRC, *Annual Report 1984*, pp. 60–61.

210. See L. Condorelli and L. Boisson de Chazournes, "Quelques remarques à propos de l'obligation des Etats de 'respecter et faire respecter' le droit humanitaire en toutes circonstances," in *Studies and Essays on International Humanitarian Law and Red Cross Principles in Honour of Jean Pictet* (1984), Chr. Swinarski (ed.), pp. 17–35. See also N. Levrat, "Les conséquences de l'engagement pris par les Hautes Parties contractantes de 'faire respecter' les Conventions humanitaires," in *Implementation of International Humanitarian Law* (1989), F. Kalshoven and Y. Sandoz (eds.), pp. 263–96.

211. Resolution XXIII, Tehran Conference on Human Rights, 12 May 1968, UN Doc. A/CONF.32/41.

Although the proposal met with the approval of the majority of experts, the ICRC, for unexplained reasons, did not submit it to the subsequent Diplomatic Conference.[212]

Probably the clearest example that parties to the Geneva Conventions consider themselves under a duty to actively ensure respect for the Conventions by other states may be found in recent Security Council activities in response to Israel's breaches in the Occupied Territories of its obligations under the Fourth Geneva Convention. In April 1991, in a report to the Security Council, the UN Secretary-General explicitly stated that "[i]n the absence of a decision by Israel to apply in full the provisions of the Fourth Geneva Convention, *the high contracting parties have an obligation under its article 1 to ensure that it is respected*" (emphasis added).[213] The Security Council itself has repeatedly called upon the parties to the Fourth Convention to ensure respect by Israel for its obligations in accordance with Article 1 of the Convention. It has also requested the Secretary-General to further develop his idea to call for a meeting of the parties to the Fourth Convention to discuss possible measures that might be taken by them under the Convention.[214]

The obligations states parties have undertaken under the general human rights treaties tend to be more clearly limited to persons within their respective jurisdictions. These treaties offer fewer clues in support of the argument that states parties are under an obligation to invoke the international responsibility of states breaching the treaty. The strongest case can probably be made with respect to the European Convention on Human Rights, since states parties to this Convention are *ipso facto* parties to its inter-state complaints procedure. In 1967, the Consultative Assembly of the Council of Europe (a body consisting of members of parliament from the Council's member states), in a resolution on violations of human rights in Greece, expressed the view that "in an important and serious case of this kind, the Contracting Parties to the Convention have a duty to act under Article 24 of the Convention."[215] The inter-state application under Article 24 filed three months later by Denmark, Norway, Sweden, and the Netherlands referred specifically to the Assembly's resolution.[216] In 1982, however, in response to similarly serious violations of human

212. ICRC, Conference of Government Experts, second session, Geneva, 1972, *Report on the Work of the Conference*, Vol. I, p. 184. Quoted in G. Abi-Saab, "The Implementation of Humanitarian Law," in *The New Humanitarian Law of Armed Conflict* (1979), A. Cassese (ed.), pp. 341–42.

213. UN Doc. S/22472, p. 14.

214. Security Council Resolution 681 (1990) of 20 December 1990.

215. Resolution 346 (1967) of 23 June 1967, 10 *YECHR* (1967), pp. 94–96.

216. 10 *YECHR* (1967), p. 586.

rights in Turkey, the Assembly merely expressed the opinion that the Article 24 procedure "ought to be utilised in the case of Turkey."[217]

If there is a duty to act, it is more likely to exist in response to international crimes than in response to international delicts. The Convention on the Prevention and the Punishment of the Crime of Genocide provides in its Article 1, "The Contracting Parties confirm that genocide, whether committed in time of peace or in time of war, is a crime under international law which they undertake to prevent and to punish." The UN Convention against Torture and Other, Cruel, Inhuman or Degrading Treatment or Punishment provides that parties are obliged either to try or to extradite alleged torturers, in accordance with the principle of universality of jurisdiction. But this refers to action to be taken vis-à-vis individuals (even though these individuals may have committed their offences as officials or with official complicity). The Convention does not provide that states are obliged to bring inter-state claims in response to infringements. The procedure whereby the Committee against Torture may consider inter-state applications is indeed optional. It would be difficult to maintain that states were under a duty to invoke a state party's responsibility as long as the inter-state remedy provided for by the relevant agreement remained merely optional.

It can therefore be concluded that, under general international law, no international obligation exists to invoke the responsibility of states breaching their international human rights obligations. Nevertheless, the first traces of an obligation to act at an inter-state level against gross infringements of human rights obligations can already be detected. Perhaps the precise contours of such an obligation will become more clearly visible in the future.

3. Conclusions

The question posed at the beginning of this chapter was whether under general international law a state is entitled to bring a valid international claim against another on the grounds that the latter had committed an internationally wrongful act consisting of a breach of its international obligations in the field of human rights, even though the interceding state's own material interests or those of its nationals had not been affected. We can now conclude that this is indeed possible. None of the objections that might be raised against such a claim are persuasive. This conclusion can be based on eminent recent au-

---

217. 25 *YECHR* (1982), Chap. IV, p. 7.

thority, including the International Law Commission's draft articles on state responsibility, the American Law Institute's *Restatement (Third) of the Foreign Relations Law of the United States*, and—to a lesser extent—the case law of the International Court of Justice. It is true that in practice such formal inter-state claims have only rarely been made. But it may be stated with confidence that this has been due to a lack of political will rather than to purely legal impediments.

The first objection that might be raised against such a claim is that the subject matter complained of belongs to the area of domestic jurisdiction. This means that it must be considered whether or not the alleged breach is indeed contrary to an international obligation incumbent on the offending state. If this is the case, the defense of domestic jurisdiction must fail. The extent of the offending state's international obligations in the field of human rights will be found in the treaties to which it is a party and in the relevant rules of customary international law. There is of course no fundamental distinction here between civil and political rights on the one hand and economic, social, and cultural rights on the other. The scope of customary law is by definition somewhat uncertain, but a good starting point is, for example, Section 702 of the *Restatement*.[218]

The second, and more fundamental, objection that might be raised is that the interceding state lacks *locus standi*. Standing case law resulting from inter-state applications under the ILO Constitution and the European Convention on Human Rights indicates that the applicant state does not need to demonstrate any special interest in the application, apart from being a party to the treaty in question. The same would no doubt apply to inter-state applications to an international tribunal under the provisions of any of the other human rights treaties. But what has long remained in doubt is whether an inter-state application might also be declared admissible if it were submitted to some general international tribunal such as the International Court of Justice, based not on a jurisdiction clause in a human rights treaty, but on some general title of jurisdiction, such as Article 36 of the Statute of the Court.

The first major step toward solving this difficulty was made by the International Court of Justice when it observed, in the *Barcelona Traction* case, that there are certain international obligations in the fulfillment of which all states have a legal interest. If one such obligation is breached, all states may invoke the responsibility of the offending state. The Court listed as examples of such *erga omnes* obli-

---

218. *Supra* text accompanying note 21.

gations, genocide and "the principles and rules concerning the basic rights of the human person, including protection from slavery and racial discrimination."

Subsequent consideration of this subject by the International Law Commission has made clear that *erga omnes* obligations in the field of human rights are not limited to rules of *jus cogens* and to international crimes. They include in effect all international obligations established for the protection of human rights and fundamental freedoms, whether they are based on treaty or custom. This is because the interests protected by these obligations are not "allocatable" to a particular state. Since in international law obligations cannot exist *in abstracto*, it becomes necessary to consider every state bound by the same obligation as injured by an infringement. The result of this inescapable logic is that the number of *erga omnes* obligations is probably larger than "the basic rights of the human person" referred to by the International Court of Justice in the *Barcelona Traction* case.

If one such obligation is breached, any other state bound by the same obligation is infringed in its rights. Any such state has the required *locus standi* to bring an international claim against the offending state and, where this can be based on some title of jurisdiction, the right to file an inter-state application with an international tribunal. The contents of such a claim may consist of one or more of the traditional elements of reparation, including cessation of the breach, restitution, compensation provided to the victims, and a guarantee against repetition. If presented to an international tribunal, a declaratory judgment might suffice. Whether one wishes to call this remedy an *actio popularis* is a semantic question that depends on one's definition of *actio popularis*. What is clear is that the interceding state does not need to demonstrate a special interest in the matter, apart from being bound by the same obligation.

Paradoxically, therefore, victims of human rights violations who are nationals of the offending state may benefit from wider protection—that is, from more than 170 states—than may be enjoyed by victims who are nationals of the interceding state under the old system of diplomatic protection. One might expect, therefore, that states who fear to find themselves on the receiving end of such claims would object to such a rule. But this has not been the case. When Article 5(2)(e)(iii) of part 1 of the International Law Commission's draft articles on state responsibility was discussed in the Sixth Committee of the UN General Assembly, only three states (the German Democratic Republic, Hungary, and Kuwait) raised objections of principle. Most states and authors who have objected to the rule have done so on the grounds that they were concerned about the reprisals to which injured states might be entitled, in response to an internationally wrongful act resulting from a breach of a human rights obligation. Abuse of this facility might even result in "chaos and violence," or "vigilantism" according to some scholars. With few exceptions, however, no objections have been raised against the principle that states bound by the same obligation as has been breached are entitled to exercise noncoercive remedies. This is understandable because, as history clearly shows, abuses are much more likely to occur when a state is exercising protection on behalf of its own nationals than when it is acting on behalf of foreign nationals.

The only serious objection to the entitlement to judicial remedies is that multilateral human rights treaties constitute self-contained systems. According to this objection, if a breach of a human rights treaty occurs, the states parties may use only the remedies provided for in the treaty itself (and if these are optional, only the ones specifically accepted by the offending state). In a pinch, additional remedies may be agreed upon unanimously by the parties, but what is essential is that the normal remedies available under general international law are not available. This argument is based on the assumption that states have only been willing to become parties to such treaties on the understanding that the remedies which could be exercised against them are limited to the ones they have specifically accepted in the context of the treaty. The argument is closely connected with the theory that states have only a collective and not an individual interest in the fulfillment of human rights obligations by other states. According to this theory, human rights obligations do not have a reciprocal character, and responsibility of the offending state can only ensue toward the collectivity of states parties and not toward individual states.

Because there is no self-contained system for the enforcement of customary international law, this objection applies solely to claims alleging a breach of a treaty obligation, not to claims based on customary international law. This already demonstrates the weakness of the argument, since acceptance of the argument would lead to the remarkable result that an inter-state claim against a state infringing its obligations under the Genocide Convention could be based on customary law but not on the Convention. In fact, although the case law of the International Court of Justice is somewhat ambivalent on this question, of the multilateral human rights treaties, only the European Convention on Human Rights specifically excludes the employment of remedies other than the ones provided for in the Convention. Political organs of the United Nations have not hesitated to hold states accountable for infringements of human rights treaties, even though these treaties have their own systems of supervision. In the absence of clear and convincing evidence to the contrary, the theory of the self-contained character of human rights treaties must therefore be rejected as unconvincing and unproven.

A final preliminary objection that might be raised is the familiar requirement of prior exhaustion of local remedies. This rule has traditionally applied in the context of the exercise of diplomatic protection on behalf of the interceding state's own nationals. The International Law Commission has considered it "premature" to extend the rule's field of application to claims concerning the treatment of other individuals. It seems fair to assume, however, that the rule applies in this wider context as well. Formal state responsibility for a breach of a human rights obligation can arise only after the victims have exhausted local remedies, although this is subject to the important proviso that the remedies must be "effective" and not "obviously futile." Moreover, the requirement does not apply if the alleged breaches consist of legislative measures and administrative practices.

Having established the *right* of states to bring an international claim against a state committing an internationally wrongful act consisting of a breach of a human rights obligation, one may wonder whether states are under an *obligation* to bring such a claim. Although traces of such an obligation may be found under the Geneva Conventions and the European Convention on Human Rights, it would be premature to conclude that there already exists a general duty of states to invoke an offending state's international responsibility in the field of human rights. There is actually little reason to anticipate a dramatic increase in the number of inter-state claims or of inter-state applications to international tribunals. State practice indicates that governments are likely to remain reluctant to approach other governments on human rights issues affecting foreign nationals. What is important, however, is that there is indeed an entitlement to act as a matter of right. This means that démarches in the field of human rights may be presented as formal legal claims, as is customary in other areas of international relations. It follows that diplomatic protection may indeed be exercised on behalf of victims of human rights violations, irrespective of their nationality. It also follows that governments can no longer evade domestic pressures to act on behalf of foreign victims of human rights violations with the argument that they have no legal right to do so.

Concluding Thoughts

Detailed conclusions have already been drawn at the end of each of the preceding three chapters. It may be useful, however, to pull things together with some brief concluding thoughts.

The central thesis of this study is that, under general international law, a state bound by certain international obligations in the field of human rights is entitled to require another state bound by those obligations to perform them. Since human rights obligations generally apply without distinction as to nationality, it follows that states are entitled to exercise diplomatic protection on behalf of victims of breaches of international human rights obligations, irrespective of their nationality. Accordingly, the area of human rights offers an exception to the general rule that nationality is the essential condition for the exercise of diplomatic protection. In the past, it has already been recognized that diplomatic protection could be exercised on behalf of foreign missionaries, foreign seamen, and foreign staff members of embassies and consulates.[1] The time has now come to recognize that diplomatic protection may also be granted to the much wider group of foreign victims of human rights violations.

Failure to appreciate the true nature of international human rights obligations appears to be one of the main reasons why this is not yet generally accepted. It is often pointed out that under international obligations in the field of human rights, states are required to guarantee certain rights to persons within their jurisdiction. But, so the theory goes, if such persons are infringed in their rights, they cannot themselves enforce these obligations on the international plane, unless the offending state has explicitly consented to this. Moreover, other states cannot enforce these obligations without, again, the offending state's specific consent. This theory does, however, overlook

1. See R. Dolzer, "Diplomatic Protection of Foreign Nationals," in *Encyclopedia of Public International Law*, R. Bernhardt (ed.), vol. 10 (1987), pp. 121–24.

the fact that human rights obligations run toward all states bound by the same obligations. All these states are therefore entitled to require performance of these obligations under the rules of general international law, unless this has been specifically excluded. It would of course be preferable if individual victims could always enforce their own rights at the international level. In the absence of this possibility, the second best option is enforcement by states collectively. But this requires the existence of appropriate international institutions. In the absence of both types of remedies, direct enforcement between individual states is a mechanism that remains necessary at the present stage of development of the international legal order.

In practice, offending states occasionally still attempt to oppose diplomatic action on behalf of victims of human rights violations by invoking the amorphous concept of "interference in internal affairs." The reason why it is not always easy to counter this argument is that it lacks proper legal definition. An interceding state confronted with the catchall charge of interference in internal affairs should therefore ascertain exactly which preliminary objections are being raised, so that these can be appropriately addressed. In practice, it appears that the general argument of interference in internal affairs in response to attempts to protect the human rights of foreign nationals usually includes one or more of the following objections:

1. The alleged breaches are not subject to an international obligation (the matter is within domestic jurisdiction).
2. The alleged breaches do not amount to a threat to international peace and security or a consistent pattern of gross violations (the matter is within domestic jurisdiction).
3. The obligations allegedly breached are not owed to the interceding state (the interceding state lacks *locus standi*).
4. The alleged breaches can only be raised within the context of a self-contained treaty regime (the interceding state lacks *locus standi*).
5. The alleged victims have failed to exhaust local remedies.

The precise merits of each of these objections have been discussed in the preceding chapters. What remains to be emphasized here is that in order to determine whether any of these objections apply, it must first be clarified whether they are made in the context of inter-state responsibility or in the context of inter-state accountability. In practice, the distinction between these two regimes is often insufficiently appreciated.

The notion of state responsibility is comparatively well defined. A breach of an international human rights obligation that may be attributed to the offending state raises that state's international responsibility. The offending state is under a duty to provide reparation, and any other state bound by the same obligation is entitled to insist on its fulfillment. In the large majority of cases, however, states tend to prefer to influence the behavior of other states through measures stopping short of formally invoking their international responsibility. The favored course of action is instead to call on offending states to *account* for their behavior. This may be done on a direct inter-state level (as discussed in Chapter 1) or through intergovernmental organizations (as discussed in Chapter 2). Obviously, a state that is entitled to invoke another state's responsibility is also entitled to the lesser remedy of making it account for its alleged wrongdoings.

The notion of inter-state accountability for violations of human rights has nowhere been formally enshrined as a concept of general international law. In the *Corfu Channel* case, however, the International Court of Justice observed that, whether or not a state had incurred international responsibility, if on its territory an act contrary to international law had occurred, it could be called upon to give an explanation.[2] Examples of collective mechanisms providing for such accountability are the various procedures developed by the UN Commission on Human Rights to investigate human rights abuses and to make recommendations to offending states. Under Charter Articles 55 and 56, member states are under a duty to cooperate with these procedures. Other typical examples are the ILO's freedom of association procedure and the mechanism established by the CSCE at its Vienna meeting in 1989. Under all these procedures, the duty to provide an explanation is not limited to acts contrary to international standards that are specifically binding on the offending state. This is not surprising, since what all these arrangements have in common is that they are designed to protect human rights without attempting to formally determine whether an internationally wrongful act has occurred. The preliminary objections listed above are designed to prevent such a determination and are therefore not applicable in the context of inter-state accountability.

Generally worded resolutions attempting to clarify these matters have already been adopted by some groups of states and by some nongovernmental organizations. The states participating in the CSCE have "categorically and irrevocably" declared that human rights questions are matters of direct and legitimate concern to all partici-

2. *Corfu Channel* case, ICJ Reports 1949, p. 18.

pating states and do not belong to the internal affairs of the state concerned.[3] The International Law Association has similarly expressed the conviction "that the protection of human rights is a matter of international concern; that the claim that violations of human rights within a country are matters of exclusive domestic concern and hence may not be subject to international appraisal, is unfounded in international law; and further that actions (including the making of allegations), consistent with the principles of the U.N. Charter, taken in respect of internationally recognized rights, are not violations of state sovereignty."[4] According to a slightly more sophisticated resolution adopted by the Institut de Droit international, "every State has a legal interest in the protection of human rights"; "[a] State acting in breach of its obligations in the sphere of human rights cannot evade its international responsibility by claiming that such matters are essentially within domestic jurisdiction"; and "[d]iplomatic representations as well as purely verbal expressions of concern or disapproval regarding any violations of human rights are lawful in all circumstances."[5]

It would obviously be helpful if a resolution along similar lines could now be adopted by the UN General Assembly. This might help to lay to rest at last the controversy about the perceived contradiction between the international protection of human rights and the prohibition of interference in internal affairs. As has been demonstrated in this study, the general trends are clear and irreversible. When everything is said and done, the growing international acceptance of the notion of inter-state accountability for violations of human rights is nothing but a crystallization in international law of an increasing sense of transnational solidarity. Under steady pressure from their own citizens, governments no longer consider themselves responsible exclusively for the fate of their own nationals or for members of their own ethnic groups. Inter-state accountability for violations of human rights is a manifestation of the growing awareness that just as peace is indivisible, so too is the welfare of humankind.[6]

3. See *supra* Chapter 1, note 165.

4. Resolution on human rights, *Report of the Fifty-Eighth Conference of the International Law Association*, Manilla, 27 August-2 September 1978, p. 1.

5. Resolution on the protection of human rights and the principle of non-intervention in internal affairs of states, 13 September 1989, *Annuaire de l'Institut de Droit international*, vol. 63-II (1990), pp. 339–45. This resolution was based on a report by Professor G. Sperduti, "La sauvegarde des droits de l'homme et le principe de non-intervention dans les affaires intérieures des Etats," *Annuaire de l'Institut de Droit international*, vol. 63-I (1989), pp. 309–436.

6. See sep. op. Jessup, *South West Africa* case, ICJ Reports 1962, p. 431.

Select Bibliography

There are not many monographs on inter-state accountability for violations of human rights. The only ones encountered in the course of the preparation of this study are all in German: H. Rumpf, *Der internationale Schutz der Menschenrechte und das Interventionsverbot* (1981); Ch. E. Ritterband, *Universeller Menschenrechtsschutz und völkerrechtliches Interventionsverbot* (1982); and M. Hanz, *Zur Völkerrechtlichen Aktivlegitimation zum Schutze der Menschenrechte* (1985). Of these works, the latter is the most interesting.

The best general articles on the subject are L. Henkin, "Human Rights and Domestic Jurisdiction," in *Human Rights, International Law and the Helsinki Accord* (1977), Th. Buergenthal (ed.), pp. 21–40; and Th. Buergenthal, "Domestic Jurisdiction, Intervention and Human Rights: The International Law Perspective," in *Human Rights and Foreign Policy* (1979), P. G. Brown and D. Maclean (eds.), pp. 111–21. The most sophisticated and up-to-date discussion of the subject in a general handbook of international law (with further references to relevant literature) may be found in O. Schachter, "International Law in Theory and Practice," 178 *RCADI* (1982); and in Verdross/Simma, *Universelles Völkerrecht*, 3d ed. (1984). It is the views of Schachter and Simma that were most often relied upon in the preparation of the present study. An excellent general sourcebook, reproducing much of the relevant diplomatic correspondence and UN documentation, is L. B. Sohn and Th. Buergenthal, *International Protection of Human Rights* (1973).

The only comprehensive study of state practice concerning diplomatic action on behalf of foreign victims of human rights violations is E. C. Stowell, *Intervention in International Law* (1921). Although this is a stimulating and pioneering work, one of its drawbacks is that it does not clearly distinguish between peaceful diplomatic action and coercive humanitarian intervention. No analysis appears to have been published of subsequent state practice in this area. Relevant diplomatic correspondence may be found in the usual digests of international law, although in recent decades the compilers of such digests have not generally considered the practice worthy of much coverage (perhaps because they no longer regard it as controversial!). Also helpful are some specialized compilations of diplomatic correspondence, such as J. Lepsius, *Deutschland und Armenien 1914–1918: Sammlung Diplomatischer Aktenstücke* (1919); L. Wolf, *Notes on the Diplomatic History of the Jewish Question* (1919); and C. Adler and A. M. Margalith, *With Firmness in the Right: American Diplomatic Action Affecting Jews, 1840–1945* (1946).

Much more has been written on human rights and non-intervention in the context of the Conference on Security and Co-operation in Europe. Most useful are three collections of essays: Th. Buergenthal (ed.), *Human Rights, International Law and the Helsinki Accord* (1977) (published after the adoption of the Helsinki Final Act in 1975); A. Bloed and P. van Dijk (eds.), *Essays on Human Rights in the Helsinki Process* (1985) (published after the end of the Madrid follow-up conference in 1983); and A. Bloed and P. van Dijk (eds.), *The Human Dimension of the Helsinki Process* (1991) (published after the end of the the Vienna follow-up conference in 1989).

Representative of the defensive East European views, as they existed before the end of the Cold War, on inter-state accountability for violations of human rights are the writings by B. Graefrath and V. Kartashkin, listed below. Their opinions often seem to coincide with the restrictive views of certain Western authors, such as J. S. Watson, "The Limited Utility of International Law in the Protection of Human Rights," 74 *Proceedings of the ASIL* (1980), pp. 1–6. Compare this to the foresights expressed in O. Schachter, "Les aspects juridiques de la politique américaine en matière de droits de l'homme," 23 *AFDI* (1977), pp. 53–74; this article also appeared in English as "International Law Implications of U.S. Human Rights Policies," 24 *New York Law School Review* (1978–79), pp. 63–87.

Little has been published on human rights and non-intervention in the context of the Lomé Conventions. The most comprehensive treatment may be found in G. Oestreich, *Menschenrechte als Elemente der dritten AKP-EWG-Konvention von Lomé* (1990). See also the inaugural lecture by J. A. Winter, "De Europese Gemeenschap, Ontwikkelingssamenwerking en de Rechten van de Mens" [The European Community, Development Cooperation, and Human Rights], Free University of Amsterdam, 20 September 1985.

On the protection of minority rights under the League of Nations, the classic works are J. Stone, *International Guarantees of Minority Rights*

(1932); C. A. Macartney, *National States and National Minorities* (1934); and I. L. Claude, Jr., *National Minorities: An International Problem* (1955).

On the United Nations, the most authoritative analysis of the genesis of Charter Article 2(7) is L. Preuss, "Article 2, Paragraph 7 of the Charter of the United Nations and Matters of Domestic Jurisdiction," 74 *RCADI* (1949), pp. 553–650. Also solid is D. R. Gilmour, "The Meaning of 'Intervene' within Article 2(7) of the United Nations Charter—an Historical Perspective," 16 *ICLQ* (1967), pp. 330–51. On the Charter's human rights provisions, see E. Schwelb, "The International Court of Justice and the Human Rights Clauses of the Charter," 66 *AJIL* (1972), pp. 337–51. The best examination of the first years of General Assembly practice with regard to the protection of human rights is R. Higgins, *The Development of International Law Through the Political Organs of the United Nations* (1963), pp. 58–130. References to relevant UN documents may be found in the UN publication *Repertory of Practice of the UN General Assembly*, vol. 1 and supplements. Unfortunately, this publication tends to be years behind, and it does not cover practice by ECOSOC and the Commission on Human Rights. Many of the relevant documents have been reproduced in L. B. Sohn and Th. Buergenthal, *International Protection of Human Rights* (1973), pp. 556–739. Some interesting notes and documents on more recent developments at the United Nations are contained in B. G. Ramcharan, *The Concept and Present Status of the International Protection of Human Rights* (1989).

Not much has been published specifically on state responsibility for violations of human rights. The highly erudite reports by R. Ago, the International Law Commission's former special rapporteur on state responsibility, contain a mine of information, but, curiously enough, they rarely refer to human rights. An essential starting point for studying this topic are the two individual opinions by Ph. Jessup in the *South West Africa* cases: ICJ Reports 1962, especially pp. 425–33 and ICJ Reports 1966, pp. 325–442. A useful theoretical framework is provided in B. Simma, *Das Reziprozitätselement im Zustandekommen Völkerrechtlicher Verträge* (1972). See also, by the same author, "Fragen der zwischenstaatlichen Durchsetzung vertraglich vereinbarter Menschenrechte," in *Festschrift für Hans-Jürgen Schlochauer* (1981), I. von Münch (ed.), pp. 635–48. On the question of *locus standi*, see P. van Dijk, *Judicial Review of Governmental Action and the Requirement of an Interest to Sue* (1980). On the concept of international crimes, an excellent work is J. H. H. Weiler et al. (eds.), *International Crimes of State: A Critical Analysis of the ILC's Draft Article 19 on State Responsibility* (1989). Authoritative and highly articulate views, reflecting the opinion of their main author, L. Henkin, are contained in §§ 702 and 703 of the American Law Institute's *Restatement (Third) of the Foreign Relations Law of the United States* (1987). A good recent analysis may be found in Th. Meron, *Human Rights and Humanitarian Norms as Customary Law* (1989), pp. 136–245.

*   *   *

Addo, M. K., "Some Issues in European Community Aid Policy and Human Rights," *Legal Issues in European Integration*, 1988/1, pp. 55–85.

Adler, C., and Margalith, A. M., *With Firmness in the Right: American Diplomatic Action Affecting Jews, 1840–1945* (New York: American Jewish Committee, 1946).

Akehurst, M., "Reprisals by Third States," 44 *BYIL* (1970), pp. 1–18.

Akinyemi, A. B., "The OAU and the Concept of Non-Interference in Internal Affairs," 46 *BYIL* (1972–73), pp. 393–400.

Alston, Ph., "Linking Trade and Human Rights," 23 *GYIL* (1980), pp. 126–58.

———. "International Trade as an Instrument of Positive Human Rights Policy," 4 *HRQ* (1982), pp. 155–83.

American Law Institute, *Restatement (Third) of the Foreign Relations Law of the United States* (St. Paul, Minn.: American Law Institute, 1987).

Andrews, S. C., "The Legitimacy of the United States Embargo of Uganda," 13 *Journal of International Law and Politics* (1979), pp. 651–73.

Arangio-Ruiz, G., "Human Rights and Non-Intervention in the Helsinki Final Act," 157 *RCADI* (1977), pp. 199–331.

Ball, M. M., "Issue for the Americas: Non-Intervention v. Human Rights and the Preservation of Democratic Institutions," 15 *International Organization* (1961), pp. 21–37.

Bastid, S., "Remarques sur l'interdiction d'intervention," in *Mélanges offerts à Juraj Andrassy* (La Haye: M. Nijhoff, 1968), V. Ibler (ed.), pp. 13–30.

Bernhardt, R., "Domestic Jurisdiction of States and International Human Rights Organs," 7 *HRLJ* (1986), pp. 205–16.

Berthoud, P., "La compétence nationale des Etats et l'Organisation des Nations Unies," 4 *Annuaire Suisse de Droit International* (1947), pp. 17–104.

Beyerlin, U., "Menschenrechte und Intervention," in *Zwischen Intervention und Zusammenarbeit* (Berlin: Duncker and Humblot, 1979), B. Simma and E. Blenk-Knocke (eds.), pp. 157–99.

Bilder, R. R., "Rethinking International Human Rights: Some Basic Questions," 44 *Wisconsin Law Review* (1969), pp. 171–217.

Bindschedler, R. L., "Der Schutz der Menschenrechte und das Verbot der Einmischung," in *Festschrift für Hans-Jürgen Schlochauer* (New York: De Gruyter, 1981), I. von Münch (ed.), pp. 179–191.

Bloed, A., "Institutional Aspects of the Helsinki Process After the Follow-up Meeting of Vienna," 36 *NILR* (1989), pp. 342–63.

Bloed, A., and van Dijk, P., "Human Rights and Non-intervention," in *Essays on Human Rights in the Helsinki Process* (Boston: M. Nijhoff, 1985), A. Bloed and P. van Dijk (eds.), pp. 57–78.

———. "Supervisory Mechanism for the Human Dimension of the CSCE: Its Setting-up in Vienna, its Present Functioning and its Possible Development towards a General Procedure for the Settlement of CSCE Disputes," in *The Human Dimension of the Helsinki Process* (Boston: Martinus Nijhoff, 1991), A. Bloed and P. van Dijk (eds.), pp. 74–108.

Bloed, A., and van Hoof, F., "Some Aspects of the Socialist View of Human Rights," in *Essays on Human Rights in the Helsinki Process* (Boston: M. Nijhoff, 1985), A. Bloed and P. van Dijk (eds.), pp. 29–55.

Bollecker-Stern, B., *Le préjudice dans la théorie de la responsabilité internationale* (Paris: Pedone, 1973).

Bossuyt, M., "The United Nations and Civil and Political Rights in Chile," 27 *ICLQ* (1978), pp. 462–71.

———. "The Development of Special Procedures of the United Nations Commission on Human Rights," 6 *HRLJ* (1985), pp. 179–210.

———. "Human Rights and Non-Intervention in Domestic Matters," *Review of the International Commission of Jurists*, No. 35, 1985, pp. 45–52.

Boven, Th. C. van, "Distinguishing Criteria of Human Rights," in *The International Dimensions of Human Rights* (Westport, Conn.: Greenwood Press, 1982), K. Vasak (ed.), pp. 43–59.

Brierly, J. L., "Matters of Domestic Jurisdiction," 6 *BYIL* (1925), pp. 8–19.

Buergenthal, Th., "Domestic Jurisdiction, Intervention and Human Rights: The International Law Perspective," in *Human Rights and Foreign Policy* (Lexington, Mass: Heath, 1979), P. G. Brown and D. Maclean (eds.), pp. 111–21.

Buirette-Maurau, P., "Les difficultés de l'internationalisation des droits de l'homme à propos de la Convention de Lomé," 21 *Revue Trimestrielle de Droit Européen* (1985), pp. 463–86.

Bull, H. (ed.), *Intervention in World Politics* (New York: Oxford University Press, 1984).

Cabranes, J. A., "Human Rights and Non-Intervention in the Inter-American System," 65 *Michigan Law Review* (1967), pp. 1147–82.

———. "The Protection of Human Rights by the Organization of American States," 62 *AJIL* (1968), pp. 889–908.

Cançado Trindade, A. A., "The Domestic Jurisdiction of States in the Practice of the United Nations and Regional Organisations," 25 *ICLQ* (1976), pp. 715–65.

Carbonneau, Th. E., "The Convergence of the Law of State Responsibility for Injury to Aliens and International Human Rights Norms in the Revised Restatement," 25 *Virginia Journal of International Law* (1985), pp. 99–123.

Carillo Salcedo, J. A., "Souveraineté des Etats et droits de l'homme en droit international contemporain," in *Protecting Human Rights: The European Dimension*, Studies in Honour of Gérard J. Wiarda (Cologne: Carl Heymanns, 1988), F. Matscher and H. Petzold (eds.), pp. 91–95.

Cassese, A., "Remarks on the Present Legal Regulation of Crimes of States," in *International Law at the Time of its Codification: Essays in Honour of Roberto Ago* (Milan: Giuffre, 1987), vol. III, pp. 49–64.

Cerna, Chr., "Human Rights in Conflict with the Principle of Non-Intervention: The Case of Nicaragua before the Seventeenth Meeting of Consultation of Ministers of Foreign Affairs," in Inter-American Commission on Human Rights, *Human Rights in the Americas: Homage to the Memory of Carlos A. Dunshee de Abranches* (1984), pp. 93–107.

Charney, J. I., "Third State Remedies in International Law," 10 *Michigan Journal of International Law* (1989), pp. 57–101.

Chernichenko, S. V., "Human Rights and Principles of Non-Intervention in the

U.N. Charter," *Soviet Yearbook of International Law* (1964–65), pp. 176–81.

Chkhikvadze, V., "Human Rights and Non-Interference in the Internal Affairs of States," *International Affairs* (Moscow), 1978, No. 12, pp. 22–30.

———. "Interstate Cooperation on Human Rights," *International Affairs* (Moscow), 1985, No. 11, pp. 29–36.

Christenson, G. A., "Attributing Acts of Omission to the State," 12 *Michigan Journal of International Law* (1991), pp. 312–70.

Clark, R. S., *A United Nations High Commissioner for Human Rights* (The Hague: M. Nijhoff, 1972).

Claude, I. L., Jr., *National Minorities: An International Problem* (Cambridge, Mass.: Harvard University Press, 1955).

Cleveland, H., "The Internationalization of Internal Affairs," in *Human Dignity: The Internationalization of Human Rights* (1979), A. Henkin (ed.), pp. 43–46.

Cohen, S. B., "Conditioning U.S. Security Assistance on Human Rights Practices," 76 *AJIL* (1982), pp. 246–79.

Condorelli, L., and Boisson de Chazournes, L., "Quelques remarques à propos de l'obligation des Etats de 'respecter et faire respecter' le droit international humanitaire en toutes circonstances," in *Studies and Essays on International Humanitarian Law and Red Cross Principles in Honour of Jean Pictet* (Boston: M. Nijhoff, 1984), Chr. Swinarski (ed.), pp. 17–35.

Dean, R. N., "Beyond Helsinki: the Soviet View of Human Rights in International Law," 21 *Virginia Journal of International Law* (1981), pp. 55–95.

Delbrück, J., "Menschenrechte im Schnittpunkt zwischen universalem Schutzanspruch und staatlicher Souveränität," 22 *GYIL* (1979), pp. 384–402.

Delbrueck, J., "International Protection of Human Rights and State Sovereignty," in *Third World Attitudes Toward International Law* (Boston: M. Nijhoff, 1987), F. E. Snyder and S. Sathirathai (eds.), pp. 263–74.

Dijk, P. van, *Judicial Review of Governmental Action and the Requirement of an Interest to Sue* (Alphen aan den Rijn: Sijthoff and Noordhoff, 1980).

———. "The Final Act of Helsinki—Basis for a Pan-European System?" 11 *NYIL* (1980), pp. 97–124.

Dijk, P. van, and Bloed, A., "The CSCE, Human Rights and Non-Intervention," 5 *Liverpool Law Review* (1983), pp. 117–142.

Dimitrijevic, V., "The Place of Helsinki on the Long Road to Human Rights," 13 *Vanderbilt Journal of Transnational Law* (1980), pp. 253–73.

Dolzer, R., "Diplomatic Protection of Foreign Nationals," in *Encyclopedia of Public International Law*, R. Bernhardt (ed.), vol. 10 (New York: North-Holland Publishing Co., 1987), pp. 121–24.

Dupuy, P. M., "Observations sur la pratique récente des 'sanctions' de l'illicite," 87 *RGDIP* (1983), pp. 505–48.

Dyke, J. van, "The Role of State Sovereignty and 'Domestic Jurisdiction' in Limiting the Topics Examined by the Asean," 23 *Indian Journal of International Law* (1983), pp. 567–74.

Eide, A., "Human Rights and Non-Intervention in the All-European System," *Bulletin of Peace Proposals*, 1977, pp. 209–15.

Ermacora, F., "Human Rights and Domestic Jurisdiction (Article 2, par. 7, of the Charter)," 124 *RCADI* (1968), pp. 375–451.

———. "Über die Völkerrechtliche Verantwortlichkeit für Menschenrechtsverletzungen," in *Ius Humanitatis: Festschrift für Alfred Verdross* (Berlin:

Duncker and Humblot, 1980), H. Miehsler, E. Mock, B. Simma, and I. Tammelo (eds.), pp. 357–78.

Falk, R., *Human Rights and State Sovereignty* (New York: Holmes and Meier, 1981).

Farer, T. J., "Intervention and Human Rights: The Latin American Context," 12 *California Western International Law Journal* (1982), pp. 503–7.

Fawcett, J. E. S., "Human Rights and Domestic Jurisdiction," in *The International Protection of Human Rights* (London: Thames and Hudson, 1967), E. Luard (ed.), pp. 286–303.

Feinberg, N., "The International Protection of Human Rights and the Jewish Question (an Historical Survey)," 3 *Israel Law Review* (1968), pp. 487–500.

Fisler Damrosch, L., "Politics Across Borders: Nonintervention and Nonforcible Influence over Domestic Affairs," 83 *AJIL* (1989), pp. 1–50.

Fox, D. T., "Doctrinal Development in the Americas: From Non-intervention to Collective Support for Human Rights," 1 *New York University Journal of International Law and Politics* (1968), pp. 44–64.

Franck, T. M., and Rodley, N. S., "After Bangladesh: The Law of Humanitarian Intervention by Military Force," 67 *AJIL* (1973), pp. 275–305.

Frowein, J. A., "The Interrelationship between the Helsinki Final Act, the International Covenants on Human Rights, and the European Convention on Human Rights," in *Human Rights, International Law and the Helsinki Accord* (Montclair, N.J.: Allanheld, Osmun, 1977), Th. Buergenthal (ed.), pp. 71–82.

———. "Die Verpflichtungen erga omnes im Völkerrecht und ihre Durchsetzung," in *Festschrift für Hermann Mosler* (Berlin, New York: Springer, 1983), R. Bernhardt, W. K. Geck, G. Jaenicke, and H. Steinberger (eds.), pp. 241–62.

Gaja, G., "Obligations *Erga Omnes*, International Crimes and *Jus Cogens*: A Tentative Analysis of Three Related Concepts," in *International Crimes of States* (New York: De Gruyter, 1989), J. H. H. Weiler, A. Cassese, and M. Spinedi (eds.), pp. 151–60.

Ganji, M., *International Protection of Human Rights* (Geneva: Librairie E. Droz, 1962).

Garcia Amador, F. V., "State Responsibility: Some New Problems," 94 *RCADI* (1958), pp. 369–489.

Geck, W. K., "Internationaler Schutz von Freiheitsrechten und nationale Souveränität," 35 *Juristenzeitung* (1980), pp. 73–77.

Gilmour, D. R., "The Meaning of 'Intervene' within Article 2(7) of the United Nations Charter—an Historical Perspective," 16 *ICLQ* (1967), pp. 330–51.

Graefrath, B., *Die Vereinte Nationen und die Menschenrechte* (Berlin: VEB Deutscher Zentralverlag, 1956).

———. "International Cooperation and Human Rights," *Law and Legislation in the German Democratic Republic*, 1973, No. 2, pp. 5–17.

———. "Internationale Zusammenarbeit der Staaten zur Förderung und Wahrung der Menschenrechte," *Neue Justiz*, 1977, No. 1, pp. 1–7.

———. "Responsibility and Damages Caused: Relationship Between Responsibility and Damages," 185 *RCADI* (1984), pp. 19–143.

Gray, C. D., *Judicial Remedies in International Law* (New York: Oxford University Press, 1987).

Gross, L., "The Charter of the United Nations and the Lodge Reservations," 41 *AJIL* (1947), pp. 531–54.

Guillaume, G., "Article 2: Paragraphe 7," in *La Charte des Nations Unies* (Brussels: Braylant, 1985), J.-P. Cot and A. Pellet (eds.), pp. 141–60.

Guo Shan, "China's Role in Human Rights Field," *Beijing Review*, 1987, Nos. 5 and 6, pp. 25–26.

Gütermann, Chr., *Das Minderheitenschutzverfahren des Völkerbundes* (1979).

Hannikainen, L., "Human Rights and Non-Intervention in the Final Act of the CSCE," 48 *Nordisk Tidsskrift for International Ret* (1979), pp. 27–37.

———. *Peremptory Norms (Jus Cogens) in International Law* (Helsinki: Lakimiesliiton kustannus, 1988).

Hannum, H., "International Law and Cambodian Genocide: The Sounds of Silence," 11 *HRQ* (1989), pp. 82–138.

Hanz, M., *Zur Völkerrechtlichen Aktivlegitimation zum Schutze der Menschenrechte* (Munich: Florentz, 1985).

Henkin, L., "Human Rights and Domestic Jurisdiction," in *Human Rights, International Law and the Helsinki Accord* (Montclair, N.J., Allanheld, Osmun, 1977), Th. Buergenthal (ed.), pp. 21–40.

———. *The Age of Rights* (New York: Columbia University Press, 1990).

Higgins, R., *The Development of International Law Through the Political Organs of the United Nations* (New York: Oxford University Press, 1963).

———. "Aspects of the Case Concerning the Barcelona Traction, Light and Power Company, Ltd.," 11 *Virginia Journal of International Law* (1971), pp. 327–43.

———. "Reality and Hope in International Human Rights: A Critique," 9 *Hofstra Law Review* (1981), pp. 1485–99.

———. "Intervention and International Law," in *Intervention in World Politics* (New York: Oxford University Press, 1984), H. Bull (ed.), pp. 29–44.

Hutchinson, D. N., "Solidarity and Breaches of Multilateral Treaties," 59 *BYIL* (1988), pp. 151–215.

Jessup, Ph. C., "The Defense of Oppressed Peoples," 32 *AJIL* (1938), pp. 116–19.

———. Responsibility of States for Injuries to Individuals," 46 *Columbia Law Review* (1946), pp. 903–28.

Jhabvala, F., "The Soviet-Bloc's View of the Implementation of Human Rights Accords," 7 *HRQ* (1985), pp. 461–91.

Jones, G. J., "The Principle of Non-Intervention in the Internal Affairs of States, with Special Reference to the Implementation of Human Rights," 5 *International Relations* (1977), pp. 154–61.

———. *The United Nations and the Domestic Jurisdiction of States* (Cardiff: University of Wales Press, 1979).

Kalshoven, F., "International Concern with Human Rights: Can It Be Effective," 21 *GYIL* (1978), pp. 119–49.

Kamminga, M. T., "The Thematic Procedures of the UN Commission on Human Rights," 34 *NILR* (1987), pp. 299–323.

———. "Human Rights and the Lomé Conventions," 7 *Netherlands Quarterly of Human Rights* (1989), pp. 28–35.

Kartashkin, V., "Human Rights and Peaceful Coexistence," 9 *HRJ* (1976), pp. 5–20.

———. "International Relations and Human Rights," *International Affairs* (Moscow), 1977, No. 8, pp. 29–38.

———. "The Socialist Countries and Human Rights," in *The International Di-*

mensions of Human Rights (Westport, Conn.: Greenwood Press, 1982), K. Vasak (ed.), pp. 631–44.

Kelsen, H., *The Law of the United Nations* (London: Stevens, 1950).

Kimminich, O., "Konferenz über Sicherheit und Zusammenarbeit in Europa und Menschenrechte," 17 *ArchVR* (1977/78), pp. 274–94.

Köck, H. F., "Ist Art. 2 Zif. 7 der Vereinten Nationen tot?" 22 *ÖZöffR* (1971), pp. 562–71.

Kohnstamm, M., and Sanders, C., "Kan Suriname Nederlandse Ontwikkelingshulp Afdwingen?" [Can Suriname Enforce Dutch Development Aid?] 63 *NJB* (1988), pp. 54–55.

Kooijmans, P. H., *The Doctrine of the Legal Equality of States* (Leiden: A. W. Sythoff, 1964).

———. "Inter-State Dispute Settlement in the Field of Human Rights," 3 *Leiden Journal of International Law* (1990), pp. 87–98.

Kranz, J., "Lomé, le dialogue et l'homme," 24 *Revue Trimestrielle de Droit Européen* (1988), pp. 451–79.

Kunig, Ph., *Das völkerrechtliche Nichteinmischungsprinzip: Zur Praxis der Organisation der afrikanischen Einheit (OAU) und des afrikanischen Staatenverkehrs* (Baden-Baden: Nomos Verlagsgesellschaft, 1981).

Lauterpacht, H., "The International Protection of Human Rights," 70 *RCADI* (1947), pp. 5–105.

———. *International Law and Human Rights* (London: Stevens and Sons, 1950).

Leary, V., "When Does the Implementation of International Human Rights Constitute Interference into the Essentially Domestic Affairs of a State?— the Interactions of Articles 2 (7), 55 and 56 of the UN Charter," in *International Human Rights Law and Practice* (Chicago: American Bar Association, 1978), J. C. Tuttle (ed.), pp. 15–21.

Leckie, S., "The Inter-State Complaints Procedure in International Human Rights Law: Hopeful Prospects or Wishful Thinking?" 10 *HRQ* (1988), pp. 249–303.

Levrat, N., "Les conséquences de l'engagement pris par les Hautes Parties contractantes de 'faire respecter' les Conventions humanitaires," in *Implementation of International Humanitarian Law* (Boston: M. Nijhoff, 1989), F. Kalshoven and Y. Sandoz (eds.), pp. 263–96.

Lillich, R. B. (ed.), *Humanitarian Intervention and the United Nations* (Charlottesville: University Press of Virginia, 1973).

———. "Duties of States Regarding the Civil Rights of Aliens," 161 *RCADI* (1978), pp. 329–442.

———. "A United States Policy of Humanitarian Intervention and Intercession," in *Human Rights and American Foreign Policy* (Notre Dame, Ind.: University of Notre Dame Press, 1979), D. P. Kommers and G. D. Loescher (eds.), pp. 278–98.

———. "The Current Status of the Law of State Responsibility for Injuries to Aliens," in *International Law of State Responsibility for Injuries to Aliens* (Charlottesville: University Press of Virginia, 1983), R. B. Lillich (ed.), pp. 1–35.

Lillich, R. B., and Neff, S. C., "The Treatment of Aliens and International Human Rights Norms: Overlooked Developments at the UN," 21 *GYIL* (1978), pp. 97–118.

Lindemann, H. H., "Die Auswirkungen der Menschenrechtsverletzungen in

Surinam auf die Vertragsbeziehungen zwischen den Niederlanden und Surinam," 44 *ZaöRV* (1984), pp. 64–91.

Loeber, D. A., "The Soviet Concept of 'Domestic Jurisdiction,'" *Internationales Recht und Diplomatie*, 1961, pp. 165–90.

Macartney, C. A., *National States and National Minorities* (London: Oxford University Press, 1934).

McGovern, E., "The Local Remedies Rule and Administrative Practices in the European Convention on Human Rights," 24 *ICLQ* (1975), pp. 119–27.

Manin, A., "The Helsinki Final Act and Human Rights," 4 *Chinese Yearbook of International Law and Affairs* (1984), pp. 175–83.

Marie, J.-B., "La situation des droits de l'homme au Chili: enquête de la Commission des droits de l'homme des Nations Unies," 22 *AFDI* (1976), pp. 305–35.

———. "La pratique de la Commission des Droits de l'Homme de l'ONU en matière de violation des droits de l'homme," 15 *Revue Belge de Droit International* (1980), pp. 355–80.

Marie, J.-B., and Questiaux, N., "Article 55: alinéa c," in *La Charte des Nations Unies* (Brussels: Braylant, 1985), J.-P. Cot and A. Pellet (eds.), pp. 863–84.

Markovic, M., "Implementation of Human Rights and the Domestic Jurisdiction of States," in *International Protection of Human Rights* (New York: Interscience Publishers, 1968), A. Eide and A. Schou (eds.), pp. 47–68.

Mbaye, K., "L'intérêt pour agir devant la CIJ," 209 *RCADI* (1988), pp. 227–341.

Medina Quiroga, C., *The Battle of Human Rights: Gross, Systematic Violations and the Inter-American System* (Boston: M. Nijhoff, 1988).

Meron, Th., "On a Hierarchy of International Human Rights," 80 *AJIL* (1986), pp. 1–23.

———. "State Responsibility for Violations of Human Rights," 83 *Proceedings of the ASIL* (1989), pp. 372–385.

———. *Human Rights and Humanitarian Norms as Customary Law* (New York: Oxford University Press, 1989).

Milojevic, M., "Les droits de l'homme et la compétence nationale des états," in Institut International des Droits de l'Homme, *René Cassin Amicorum Discipulorumque Liber*, vol. IV (1972), pp. 331–72.

Mitrovic, T., "Non-Intervention in the Internal Affairs of States," in *Principles of International Law Concerning Friendly Relations and Cooperation* (Dobbs Ferry, N.Y.: Oceana Publications, 1972), M. Sahovic (ed.), pp. 219–77.

Mohr, M., "The ILC's Distinction Between 'International Crimes' and 'International Delicts' and its Implications," in *United Nations Codification of State Responsibility* (New York: Oceana Publishers, 1987), M. Spinedi and B. Simma (eds.), pp. 115–41.

Movchan, A. P., "The Human Rights Problem in Present-Day International Law," in *Contemporary International Law* (Moscow: Progress Publishers, 1969), G. Tunkin (ed.), pp. 233–50.

Mullerson, R. A., "Human Rights and the Individual as Subject of International Law: A Soviet View," 1 *European Journal of International Law* (1990), pp. 33–43.

Neuhold, H., "Die Prinzipien des KSZE-Dekalogs und der 'Friendly-Relations-Declaration' der UNO-Generalversammlung," in *Zwischen Intervention und Zusammenarbeit* (Berlin: Duncker and Humblot, 1979), B. Simma and E. Blenk-Knocke (eds.), pp. 441–502.

Newman, F. C., "Interpreting the Human Rights Clauses of the UN Charter," 5 *HRJ* (1972), pp. 283–291.

Newsom, D. D. (ed.), *The Diplomacy of Human Rights* (Lanham, Md.: University Press of America, 1986).

Nowak, M., *CCPR-Kommentar zum UNO-Pakt über bürgerliche und politische Rechte und zum Fakultativprotokoll* (Arlington, Va.: N. P. Engel, 1989).

O'Donnel, T. A., "The Margin of Appreciation Doctrine: Standards in the Jurisprudence of the European Court of Human Rights," 4 *HRQ* (1982), pp. 474–96.

Oestreich, G., *Menschenrechte als Elemente der dritten AKP-EWG-Konvention von Lomé: Sanktionsinstrument oder Zielvorgabe einer Entwicklungszusammenarbeit im Dienste des Menschen?* (Berlin: Duncker and Humblot, 1990).

Oppenheim, L., and Lauterpacht, H., *International Law*, vol. I, 8th ed. (New York: Longmans, 1955).

Ostroumov, G., and Belenkov, S., "Socialist Foreign Policy and Human Rights," *International Affairs* (Moscow), 1982, No. 5, pp. 30–38.

Penkower, M. N., *The Jews Were Expendable: Free World Diplomacy and the Holocaust* (Urbana: University of Illinois Press, 1983).

Preuss, L., "Article 2, Paragraph 7 of the Charter of the United Nations and Matters of Domestic Jurisdiction," 74 *RCADI* (1949), pp. 553–650.

Rabinowicz, A. M. K., "Classical International Law and the Jewish Question," 24 *NILR* (1977), pp. 205–231.

Rajan, M. S., *United Nations and Domestic Jurisdiction*, 2d ed. (London: Asia Publishing House, 1961).

———. *The Expanding Jurisdiction of the United Nations* (Dobbs Ferry, N.Y.: Oceana Publishers, 1982).

Ramcharan, B. G., "State Responsibility for Violations of Human Rights Treaties," in *Contemporary Problems of International Law: Essays in Honour of Georg Schwarzenberger* (London: Stevens, 1988), Bin Cheng and E. D. Brown (eds.), pp. 242–61.

———. *The Concept and Present Status of the International Protection of Human Rights* (Boston: Nijhoff, 1989).

Rechetov, Y., "International Responsibility for Violations of Human Rights," in *UN Law/Fundamental Rights* (Alphen aan den Rijn: Sijthoff and Noordhoff, 1979), A. Cassese (ed.), pp. 237–48.

Reuter, P., "Le dommage comme condition de la responsabilité internationale," in *Estudios de Derecho Internacional: Homenaje al Professor Miaja de la Muela*, vol. II (Madrid: Editorial Tecnos, 1979), pp. 837–46.

Ritterband, Ch. E., *Universeller Menschenrechtsschutz und völkerrechtliches Interventionsverbot* (Bern, Haupt, 1982).

Rodley, N. S., *The Treatment of Prisoners Under International Law* (Oxford: Clarendon Press, 1987).

———. "Human Rights and Humanitarian Intervention: The Case Law of the World Court," 38 *ICLQ* (1989), pp. 321–33.

Rolin-Jaequemyns, G., "Note sur la théorie du droit d'intervention," 8 *Revue de Droit International et de Legislation Comparée* (1876), pp. 673–82.

Rosenstock, R., "The Declaration of Principles of International Law Concerning Friendly Relations: A Survey," 65 *AJIL* (1971), pp. 713–35.

Ross, A., "The Proviso Concerning 'Domestic Jurisdiction' in Article 2(7) of the Charter of the United Nations," 2 *ÖZöffR* (1950), pp. 562–71.

Rougier, A., "Maroc: la question de l'abolition des supplices et l'intervention européenne," 17 *RGDIP* (1910), pp. 98–102.

———. "La théorie de l'intervention de l'humanité," 17 *RGDIP* (1910), pp. 468–526.

Rumpf, H., *Der internationale Schutz der Menschenrechte und das Interventionsverbot* (Baden-Baden: Nomos, 1981).

Russell, H. S., "The Helsinki Declaration: Brobdingnag or Lilliput?" 70 *AJIL* (1976), pp. 242–72.

Sachariew, K., "State Responsibility for Multilateral Treaty Violations: Identifying the 'Injured State' and its Legal Status," 35 *NILR* (1988), pp. 273–89.

Sassòli, M., "Mise en oeuvre du droit international humanitaire et du droit des droits de l'homme: une comparaison," 68 *Annuaire suisse de droit international* (1987), pp. 24–61.

Schachter, O., "The Twilight Existence of Nonbinding International Agreements," 71 *AJIL* (1977), pp. 296–304.

———. "Les aspects juridiques de la politique américaine en matière de droits de l'homme," 23 *AFDI* (1977), pp. 53–74.

———. "International Law Implications of U.S. Human Rights Policies," 24 *New York Law School Review* (1978–79), pp. 63–87.

———. "International Law in Theory and Practice," 178 *RCADI* (1982).

Schwelb, E., "The International Court of Justice and the Human Rights Clauses of the Charter," 66 *AJIL* (1972), pp. 337–51.

———. "The 'Actio Popularis' in International Law," 2 *Israel Yearbook on Human Rights* (1972), pp. 46–56.

———. "The Law of Treaties and Human Rights," 16 *ArchVR* (1974/75), pp. 1–27.

Seidl-Hohenveldern, I., "Actio Popularis im Völkerrecht?" 14 *Communicazioni e Studi Milano* (1975), pp. 803–13.

Shelton, D., "State Responsibility for Aiding and Abetting Flagrant Violations of Human Rights," in *Essays on the Concept of a 'Right to Live'* (Brussels: Braylant, 1988), D. Prémont (ed.), pp. 222–32.

———. "Private Violence, Public Wrongs and the Responsibility of States," 13 *Fordham International Law Journal* (1989–90), pp. 1–34.

Shen Baoxiang, Wang Chenquan, and Li Zerui, "On the Question of Human Rights in the International Realm," *Beijing Review*, 1982, No. 30, pp. 13–22.

Shestack, J. J., and Cohen, R., "International Human Rights: A Role for the United States," 14 *Virginia Journal of International Law* (1973), pp. 673–701.

Simma, B., *Das Reziprozitätselement im Zustandekommen Völkerrechtlicher Verträge* (Berlin: Duncker and Humblot, 1972).

———. "Souveränität und Menschenrechtsschutz nach westlichem Völkerrechtsverständnis," 4 *EuGRZ* (1977), pp. 235–40.

———. "Fragen der zwischenstaatlichen Durchsetzung vertraglich vereinbarter Menschenrechte," in *Festschrift für Hans-Jürgen Schlochauer* (New York: De Gruyter, 1981), I. von Münch (ed.), pp. 635–648.

———. "Self-contained Regimes," 16 *NYIL* (1985), pp. 111–36.

———. "International Crimes: Injury and Countermeasures. Comments on Part 2 of the ILC Work on State Responsibility," in *International Crimes of State* (New York: De Gruyter, 1989), J. H. H. Weiler, A. Cassese, and M. Spinedi (eds.), pp. 283–315.

————. "Bilateralism and Community Interest in the Law of State Responsibility," in *International Law at a Time of Perplexity: Essays in Honour of Shabtai Rosenne* (Boston: M. Nijhoff, 1989), Y. Dinstein (ed.), pp. 821–44.

Smits, R. J. H., "The Second Lomé Convention: An Assessment with Special Reference to Human Rights," *Legal Issues of European Integration* (1980/2), pp. 47–74.

Sohn, L. B., and Buergenthal, Th., *International Protection of Human Rights* (Indianapolis, Ind.: Bobbs-Merrill, 1973).

Sperduti, G., "La sauvegarde des droits de l'homme et le principe de non-intervention dans les affaires intérieures des Etats," *Annuaire de l'Institut de Droit International*, vol. 63-I (1989), pp. 309–436.

Spinedi, M., and Simma, B. (eds.), *United Nations Codification of State Responsibility* (New York: Oceana Publishers, 1987).

Starace, V., "La responsabilité résultant de la violation des obligations à l'égard de la communauté internationale," 153 *RCADI* (1976), pp. 271–317.

Stone, J., *International Guarantees of Minority Rights* (London: Oxford University Press, 1932).

Stowell, E. C., *Intervention in International Law* (Washington, D.C.: Byrne, 1921).

Straus, O. S., "Humanitarian Diplomacy of the United States," *Proceedings of the ASIL* (1912), pp. 45–54.

Suzuki, E., "A State's Provisional Competence to Protect Human Rights in a Foreign State," 15 *Texas International Law Journal* (1980), pp. 231–60.

Szasz, P. C., "The International Legal Aspects of the Human Rights Program of the United States," 12 *Cornell International Law Journal* (1979), pp. 161–74.

Szawlowski, R., "The International Protection of Human Rights—a Soviet and Polish View," 28 *ICLQ* (1979), pp. 775–81.

Tammes, A. J. P., "Means of Redress in the General International Law of Peace," in *Essays on the Development of the International Legal Order: In Memory of Haro F. van Panhuys* (Rockville, Md.: Sijhoff and Nordhoff, 1980), F. Kalshoven, P. J. Kuyper and J. G. Lammers (eds.), pp. 1–20.

Tanzi, A., "Is Damage a Distinct Condition for the Existence of an Internationally Wrongful Act?" in *United Nations Codification of State Responsibility* (New York: Oceana Publishers, 1987), M. Spinedi and B. Simma (eds.), pp. 1–33.

Tesón, F. R., "Le Peuple, c'est Moi! The World Court and Human Rights," 81 *AJIL* (1987), pp. 173–83.

————. *Humanitarian Intervention: An Inquiry into Law and Morality* (Dobbs Ferry, N.Y.: Transnational Publishers, 1988).

Tomuschat, Chr., "Die Bundesrepublik Deutschland und die Menschenrechtspakte der Vereinten Nationen," 26 *Vereinte Nationen* (1978), pp. 1–10.

————. "Neuformulierung der Grundregeln des Völkerrechts durch die Vereinte Nationen, Bewegung, Stillstand oder Rückschritt?" 38 *Europa-Archiv* (1983), pp. 729–38.

Tumanov, V. A., "International Protection of Human Rights: Soviet Report," in *International Enforcement of Human Rights* (Berlin: Springer Verlag, 1987), R. Bernhardt and J. A. Jolowicz (eds.), pp. 21–24.

Tunkin, G. I., *Theory of International Law* (Cambridge, Mass.: Harvard University Press, 1974).

Umozurike, O., "The Domestic Jurisdiction Clause in the OAU Charter," 78 *African Affairs* (1979), pp. 197–209.

United States Secretary of State, *Charter of the United Nations: Report to the President on the Results of the San Francisco Conference* (1945), Department of State Publication 2349.

Valticos, N., *International Labour Law* (Deventer: Kluwer, 1979).

———. "Droit international du travail et souverainités étatiques," in *Mélanges Fernand Dehousse* (Paris: Fernand Nathan, 1979), vol. 1, pp. 123–32.

———. *Droit International du Travail*, 2d ed. (Paris: Dalloz, 1983).

———. "Les commissions d'enquête de l'Organisation internationale du Travail," 91 *RGDIP* (1987), pp. 847–79.

Verdross, A., "The Plea of Domestic Jurisdiction before an International Tribunal and a Political Organ of the United Nations," 28 *ZaöRV* (1968), pp. 33–40.

———. "Le principe de la non-intervention dans les affaires relevant de la compétence nationale d'un état et l'article 2(7) de la Charte des Nations Unies," in *Mélanges offerts à Charles Rousseau* (Paris: A. Pedone, 1974), pp. 267–76.

Verdross, A., and Simma, B., *Universelles Völkerrecht*, 3d ed. (Berlin: Duncker and Humblot, 1984).

Vincent, R. J., *Nonintervention and International Order* (Princeton, N.J.: Princeton University Press, 1974).

Vincineau, M., "Quelques commentaires à propos de la 'Déclaration sur l'inadmissibilité de l'intervention et de l'ingérence dans les affaires intérieures des états,'" in *Mélanges offerts à Charles Chaumont* (Paris: A. Pedone, 1984), pp. 555–77.

Waldock, C. H. M., "The Plea of Domestic Jurisdiction Before International Legal Tribunals," 31 *BYIL* (1954), pp. 96–142.

Watson, J. S., "Autointerpretation, Competence, and the Continuing Validity of Article 2(7) of the UN Charter," 71 *AJIL* (1977), pp. 60–83.

———. "The Limited Utility of International Law in the Protection of Human Rights," 74 *Proceedings of the ASIL* (1980), pp. 1–6.

Weil, P., "Vers une normativité relative en droit international?" 86 *RGDIP* (1982), pp. 6–47.

———. "Towards Relative Normativity in International Law?" 77 *AJIL* (1983), pp. 413–42.

Weiler, J. H. H., Cassese, A., and Spinedi, M. (eds.), *International Crimes of State: A Critical Analysis of the ILC's Draft Article 19 on State Responsibility* (New York: De Gruyter, 1989).

Weis, P., "Diplomatic Protection of Nationals and International Protection of Human Rights," 4 *HRJ* (1971), pp. 643–78.

Weissbrodt, D., "Human Rights Legislation and United States Foreign Policy," 7 *Georgia Journal of International and Comparative Law* (1977), pp. 231–87.

Winter, J. A., "De Europese Gemeenschap, Ontwikkelingssamenwerking en de Rechten van de Mens" [The European Community, Development Cooperation, and Human Rights], Inaugural Lecture, Free University of Amsterdam, 20 September 1985.

Wolf, L., *Notes on the Diplomatic History of the Jewish Question* (London: Spottiswoode, Ballantyne, 1919).

Wright, Q., "Is Discussion Intervention?" 50 *AJIL* (1956), pp. 102–10.

Young-Anawaty, A., "Human Rights and the ACP-EEC Lomé II Convention: Business as Usual at the EEC," 13 *New York University Journal of International Law and Politics* (1980), pp. 63–98.

Zoller, E., *Enforcing International Law through U.S. Legislation* (Dobbs Ferry, N.Y.: Transnational Publishers, 1985).

Zourek, J., "Le respect des droits de l'homme et des libertés fondamentales constitue-t-il une affaire interne de l'Etat?" in *Estudios de Derecho Internacional: Homenaje al Professor Miaja de la Muela*, vol. I (Madrid: Editorial Tecnos, 1979), pp. 603–25.

Table of Cases

Permanent Court of International Justice

International Court of Justice

ILO Commissions of Inquiry

Human Rights Committee

European Commission and Court of Human Rights

Inter-American Court of Human Rights

Index

This book was set in Baskerville and Eras typefaces. Baskerville was designed by John Baskerville at his private press in Birmingham, England, in the eighteenth century. The first typeface to depart from oldstyle typeface design, Baskerville has more variation between thick and thin strokes. In an effort to insure that the thick and thin strokes of his typeface reproduced well on paper, John Baskerville developed the first wove paper, the surface of which was much smoother than the laid paper of the time. The development of wove paper was partly responsible for the introduction of typefaces classified as modern, which have even more contrast between thick and thin strokes.

Eras was designed in 1969 by Studio Hollenstein in Paris for the Wagner Typefoundry. A contemporary script-like version of a sans-serif typeface, the letters of Eras have a monotone stroke and are slightly inclined.

Printed on acid-free paper.